THE FUTURE OF EXECUTIVE DEVELOPMENT

THE FUTURE

OF EXECUTIVE

DEVELOPMENT

Mihnea C. Moldoveanu and Das Narayandas

STANFORD BUSINESS BOOKS
STANFORD UNIVERSITY PRESS
STANFORD, CALIFORNIA

Stanford University Press
Stanford, California

Special discounts for bulk quantities of Stanford Business Books are available to corporations, professional associations, and other organizations. For details and discount information, contact the special sales department of Stanford University Press. Tel: (650) 725–0820, Fax: (650) 725–3457

Printed in the United States of America on acid-free, archival-quality paper

Library of Congress Cataloging-in-Publication Data

Names: Moldoveanu, Mihnea C., author. | Narayandas, Das, author.
Title: The future of executive development / Mihnea C. Moldoveanu and Das Narayandas.
Description: Stanford, California : Stanford Business Books, an imprint of Stanford University Press, 2022. | Includes bibliographical references and index.
Identifiers: LCCN 2021013029 (print) | LCCN 2021013030 (ebook) | ISBN 9781503628724 (cloth) | ISBN 9781503629813 (ebook)
Subjects: LCSH: Executives—Training of. | Management—Study and teaching.
Classification: LCC HD30.4 .M65 2022 (print) | LCC HD30.4 (ebook) | DDC 658.4/07124—dc23
LC record available at https://lccn.loc.gov/2021013029
LC ebook record available at https://lccn.loc.gov/2021013030

Cover design: Andrew Brozyna

I dedicate this book to Calin Moldoveanu, from whom I learned to watch, sense, and take note of what my mind is doing when it is "learning."

—Mihnea Moldoveanu

Thank you Sunitha, my soulmate and partner, for your unstinting love, encouragement, and support.

—Das Narayandas

CONTENTS

PREFACE

You are about to read a study of the field of executive development written by two people who have both led executive development organizations and studied the industry in detail, using broad empirical evidence drawn from interviews with clients and their organizations' CLOs and CEOs. The study is both descriptive and prescriptive in nature: it aims to give guidance on what organizations employing executives and managers should seek and do, and what executive development providers should heed and think of doing.

Prediction is hard—especially about the future, as Yogi Berra quipped. But no study of "The Future of X" can escape making predictions about X—and that is no less true of the executive development field than it is of any other X. Accordingly, we do make predictions—even in a year that has seen most industries—including this one—disrupted by governments' responses to a global pandemic that have rendered most of the models of interaction between suppliers and providers disrupted and restructured, with consequences that seem hard to predict. This study is based on a five-year-long research project in which both of us have observed, measured, integrated, thought, and done many things in the space of this industry. We have surveyed executives coming to executive development programs, interviewed them, spoken to the CEOs and CLOs of the organizations for which they work, spoken to the key decision makers in suppliers and aggregators of executive development programs and experiences, restructured and redesigned our own executive development programs to heed the insights we gleaned, observed and measured the outcomes of our interventions, and mapped out the skill base of executives at various organizational levels, the skill development vehicles most suppliers offer, and the outcomes of these programs for the organizations we interacted with. Most of the trends we speak about have been borne out and even amplified by the global COVID-19 episode. The future is coming more quickly than we anticipated when we started our journey. But it is not a different future from the one we contemplated when we set off on our journey five years ago.

We are writing as both observers and researchers of the field—and actors and decision makers within the field. That is—unfortunately—rare in the realm of monographs and scholarly works, which deploy research to give answers to questions asked from an observer's perspective alone. But the first-person perspective contributes an in-the-moment feel of reality, and an understanding of the predicament of the decision maker who must act now, with limited information that is critical to making the prescriptions, predictions, and suggestions imminently useful and valuable to other doers and executives. Each one of us was the Senior Dean in charge of executive education at our respective schools (the Rotman School of Management at the University of Toronto and the Harvard Business School at Harvard University) during the time this book was written. Our positions enabled us to both observe the phenomenon up close and tailor our understanding and our research to the first-person vantage point: knowledge is for action, understanding is for intervening, and prediction is for planning moves and responses. We have accordingly written a book that aims to speak directly to academics and students of executive development as a field on one hand and, on the other, to executives (CEOs and CLOs) of organizations that are clients of executive development suppliers, decision makers in business schools, consultancies, and coaching and other executive development organizations that want to understand for the purpose of doing—and not just for that of writing, publishing, contemplating, or talking about doing.

Our approach rests on a few foundational assumptions—roughly, the kinds of beliefs that people working in this field need to believe to be true in order to get up in the morning and look in the mirror without experiencing a personal crisis:

- First, that executive development matters to organizations: that it is a useful way for organizations to acquire new capabilities that enable them to do better at what they seek to do. That is by no means obvious. CEOs and their top management teams have at least two levers for changing their organizations: selection and development. They can simply fire and rehire, hire into brand new organizational structures, or simply acquire organizations that have always had the capabilities they seek—instead of investing in the development of their executives. Restructuration is not costless, but given the increasing precision with which the market for talent is working and the increasing granularity with which it is allowing talent managers to hire for "bundles of skills"—verified by LinkedIn or other platforms—the cost-benefit picture of this option has been improving and will continue to improve steadily. The development option is facing a steadily rising bar of efficacy and quality for its success. This is the assumption that motivates many of our suggestions and exhortations for immediate change in the industry.

- Second, that executive development is causally efficacious in helping executives acquire skills which they then successfully apply in their organizations in ways that allow the latter to build capabilities that are valuable and distinctive. This is also by no means an obviously valid assumption. In fact, as we will show, there are scenarios in which the industry can run—and perhaps has been running—on vapor ware: on executives pretending to learn, taught by providers who pretend to teach, paid for by organizations that pretend to care and to benefit, even though each party derives personal benefits that have little to do with skill acquisition and transfer and capability development. But this would not be—and is not—a survivable or robust equilibrium: the "gig would have been up"—or will be up—pretty quickly if the interactive beliefs of organizational leaders, executive learners, and executive program providers do not cohere. This is the assumption that underlies our focus on skill acquisition, skill application, and the conversion of skill into capability as the core source of value of executive development activity sets.

- Third, that the causal links between what we try to do and what we aim for in executive development are intelligible and analyzable. Writers about executive learning and teaching are apt to talk about ineffable, hard-to-describe-and-measure abilities such as intuition, judgment, wisdom, and so forth. They are, perhaps, right in suggesting these are characteristics that are *difficult* to identify, measure, and even precisely name. But, we will argue, they are not right in arguing that they are *impossible* to identify, articulate, and measure, and in most settings, "hard" is used as a euphemism for "impossible," which is misleading. One of the roles of the type of thinking called "scientific" is to turn quality into quantity—to make distinctions and create concepts that allow humans to identify, measure, and manipulate variables that matter to their lives. And even as we write as doers and executives in the field, we are also scientists and students of human and organizational behavior, and we are seeking to apply ourselves as scientists to the identification and measurement of executive skills. We believe that without a new way to talk about skills that enables us to intervene in ways that help humans acquire net new abilities, any talk of executive development—of improving, changing, and restructuring it—is moot and irrelevant. This is the assumption on which our analysis of the executive's skill set and the new taxonomy of executive skills and abilities that we introduce is based.

We would like to acknowledge the help of many who have made this study possible: our dedicated and highly competent Harvard Business School Division of Research team—Kerry Herman, Amram Migdal, and Christine Snively—who enabled us to reach far and deep into the wealth of data and feedback from Executive Development Program participants; our Rotman School of Management research, editorial, and production team—Jasmina Djikic, Yeni Choi, and Raluca Cojocariu—who enabled us to update our context and design the best possible graphical interface for our thoughts; and, of course, the many participants in executive development programs at Harvard and the University of Toronto, without whose astute and attuned collaboration this study would not have been possible.

THE FUTURE OF EXECUTIVE DEVELOPMENT

1

THE SKILLS GAP AND THE SKILLS TRANSFER GAP

Executive development programs have entered a period of rapid transformation, driven on one side by the proliferation of a new technological, cultural, and economic landscape commonly referred to as "digital disruption" and on the other by a widening gap between the skills and capabilities participants and their organizations demand and those provided by their executive program providers. We document—on the basis of some one hundred interviews with Fortune 500 executives—a current and growing awareness of a mismatch between executive development offerings and the skill sets executives need in a VUCA, Web 2.0–enabled economy. On the basis of a comprehensive study of the executive development industry, we posit that a trio of forces of digital disruption—specifically the disintermediation of the services of instructors and facilitators, the disaggregation of the previously bundled experiences that constitute an executive program, and the decoupling of the sources of value participants derive from any one experience—together open up the executive education industry to a radical restructuration. We argue that any consequential strategic action on the part of providers must address two major current gaps: the gap between the skills required by participants and those provided by suppliers ("the skills gap"), and the gap that separates skill acquisition from skill application ("the skills transfer gap"). We canvass the literature on skill measurement, acquisition, and transfer to establish the enduring power of these distinctions in explaining the success of various training and education programs and use these distinctions to structure the strategic decisions that both organizations committed to organizational development and providers of executive development programs must in short order make.

Executive Development in Disequilibrium

Organizations today urgently require new managerial and executive capabilities to handle an array of challenges, from coping with narrowing profitability gaps to enabling continuous innovation, increasing customer responsiveness to meeting regulatory requirements, and contending with demand-side volatility and uncertainty to managing increasingly complex new services and value chains. To meet these objectives, organizations must develop predictive prowess, agility, innovativeness, resilience, creativity, and other capabilities they are finding difficult to cultivate in their executive and managerial teams. These resulting tensions are fueling a growing feeling among business leaders that business schools and organizations providing executive development are not adequately preparing the individuals who will be recruited to populate these teams (Canals 2011). An "executive skills gap" between the skills needed to cope with a volatile, uncertain, complex, and ambiguous (VUCA) business landscape and the skills being imparted by executive development programs is increasingly obvious—and costly.

Business executives attending executive programs are seeking not information or knowledge, but skills (Schrage 2014) of a kind and quality not being delivered by executive development programs. An IBM survey of fifteen hundred chief executives (Palmisano 2013) provides an example of not developing the right skills in individuals capable of applying them at the right time and in the right context: a majority of those surveyed worry about their own as well as their executive team members' ability to manage complex predicaments in the competitive, regulatory, operational, and organizational environments in which they work. CEOs also report a scarcity of the trust, creativity, resiliency, fault-tolerance, and experimental zest and intensity that characterize high-performing organizations.

Concomitantly, a pattern is emerging of next-in-line executives being bypassed for promotions to top leadership positions (Ringel, Taylor, and Zablit 2015) in favor of individuals untested in executive predicaments but who are up-to-date on technical, interpersonal, and functional skills, albeit likely to require ongoing support and continuous investment in the requisite management and leadership abilities. Executive learning and development providers—business schools, professional consultancies, and corporate universities, among others—face a pivotal time of challenges posed by technology-driven disruption of business activities characterized by VUCA conditions—as well as unprecedented opportunities to develop new programs and services that address the growing "executive skills gap."

VUCA Worlds Reward the Adaptive: The Pressing Demand for New Skill Sets

Demand for executive and managerial talent is growing. It is driven in part by shortages of skills and capabilities in established economies and in part by the growth of emerging economies. Witness the premiums and increasingly frequent bidding wars for managerial and executive talent. In the wake of the financial crisis of 2007–2008, many organizations greatly expanded their leadership development activities, and professional services firms such as Morgan Stanley, Deloitte, and others appointed chief talent officers (CTOs) to attract, retain, and develop top performers (Canals 2011). Discontinuous changes in organizational scale, scope, and culture confound efforts to navigate disruption and complexity, ever more intense competition, and demand volatility. Consider just the latter. A snapshot of volatility across industries (Boston Consulting Group 2015) over the period 2002–2010 reveals heightened unpredictability in the form of greater average error in earnings forecasts and increasing costs of getting the prediction wrong—as signaled by the gross difference in revenue margins between leaders and laggards in any one industry.

This picture brings into sharp focus the stress VUCA environments exert on organizational capability and executive skill. Predictability proxies for the capacity of organizations and executive teams to manage across periods of uncertainty and disruption; the cost of "getting it wrong" highlights the irreversible and unforgiving nature of the resource allocation process across industries. Observed an executive of the Singapore Workforce Development Agency: "The pace at which skills become obsolete has increased, which makes it harder to plan for changing needs. As new needs emerge, skills are acquired in an ad hoc way on based on need rather than any developmental template." The value of high-velocity, adaptive, insightful leadership should rise with the accelerating pace of change and increasing likelihood and cost of making errors, and that is precisely what we are seeing.

The race for organizational capability and competition for attracting and retaining the skill base on which it rests is intensified in VUCA environments. Mature market leaders are dropping out of the top-three industry positions. More recent arrivals outside of the top five market leaders are within five or fewer years of attaining market leadership. These effects propagate across industries, and "disrupted industries" (for example, banks in the 2000s, specialty retail in the 1990s) constitute the leading edges of "waves of organizational failure." The effect is more pronounced over longer periods. A Boston Consulting Group snapshot of the media industry compares the effects of the VUCA landscape (greater volatility in the position of market leaders) with those of environments of unbridled expansion (1970s–1980s) and increased competition (1980s–1990s) and finds that starting as early as 1985, market leaders are up to fifty times more likely to drop out of their top positions, and the rate at which they do so increased by a factor of five in the years 2005–2010, relative to the decade from 1990–2000 (Reeves and Moldoveanu 2011).

Many executives have acknowledged the extreme compression of the time scale on which dramatic change occurs at the technological, industry, customer demographics and preferences, organizational, operational, and interpersonal levels. Observed a pharmaceutical executive: "Ten years ago we had a decade to adjust and prepare for what was coming, but today the adjustment cycles are much shorter. How do you prepare for that? For instance, digital transformation is something we are not prepared for because our leaders came from a different school of thought. We are not moving as fast as we would like." "We need a strong pool of internal candidates for the CEO role," remarked an executive in Newcastle Permanent Bank Building Society Ltd. "If I decide to leave or the board tells me it's time to go, we need executives capable of stepping into the CEO role on an interim basis and also, ideally, as potential candidates for the role on a permanent basis."

A 2011 study revealed that only 15 percent of North American companies believed they had enough qualified successors (Fernández-Aráoz, Groysberg, and Nohria 2011). Tailoring efforts to the development of particular skills and needs is critical considering the leadership talent shortage that will only grow as baby boomers retire (Silvestri 2013). These findings suggest a crossroads in the preparation—selection, training, development, and nurturing—of the elites of leading organizations, an intersection of crisis and opportunity that manifests in the domains of talent officers and executive program developers as extreme ambiguity. Remarked an executive at a large cable provider: "We have to create a pipeline for jobs that don't exist. Yes, certain roles we know to develop for, but also there are new areas to develop for. We don't even know what they are yet."

A simple, compelling—but troubling—explanation for the shortcomings of executive development as presently constituted is that skills learned in seminars, case discussions, classrooms, and laboratories are rarely applied in the contexts in which they would be most useful. The considerable literature on applicable skill development, and what we know about the effectiveness of teaching with respect to developing skills that will be applied (Baldwin and Ford 1988), suggest that only about 10 percent of the $100 billion (in 1988 dollars) outlay on corporate training and development—which currently sits at $180 billion—can be expected to produce any results. "Employees often take a class and say, 'Gee, this is great,' and go back to their jobs and do the same old thing"—a director of one university's executive program in leadership told us.

Breakthrough learning environments like Google's internal training programs recognize and tackle the applicable skills challenge head on by tailoring in-house programs to participants' specific circumstances and social, technical, and physical environments. Learning on the job co-locates skill acquisition and skill application—making the successful transfer of applicable skill more likely. Remarked the head of global learning and development at a professional service firm: "One of my boss's pillars is to revolutionize the way we learn by focusing on informal learning, collaborative learning that is dynamic, social, and personal. When we talk about leadership development, those are the terms we use. Not just 'can you go to a program at Harvard?'" The challenges posed by VUCA markets and the organizational capability gaps they precipitate demand a fundamental rethinking of the approach to developing the executives and who will lead the organizations of the future.

The Trust Economy and Digital Disruption in Higher Education

Executive learning—and indeed all of higher education—is being disrupted by technological, cultural, and demographic shifts that, in combination, pose a special set of VUCA-type challenges. In any industry, "digital disruption" is seeded by (1) mass-distributed access to information; (2) ubiquitous and secure private communication in point-to-point, point-to-multipoint, and multipoint-to-multipoint configurations; and (3) distributed, inexpensive access to low-cost computational power ("the cloud").

These conditions factored in the reconstitution—and continue to be observed in the constant churn—of the media, publishing, retail, travel, enterprise software, and music industries. The knowledge economy industries of the 1990s and early twenty-first century—financial services, health care, and education—have persisted thus far in the wake of the digital disruption wave in largely unchanged form. But inexpensive, instantly accessible, ubiquitous information, computational power, and connectivity have laid the foundation for a successor to the knowledge economy: the trust economy. Two more waves are coming quickly, and we will closely examine the dynamics of their propagation.

Positional advantages in networks of trust are important new sources of market power, supplanting the information and knowledge ("what can be done with information") asymmetries that were the respective sources of advantage in the pre-Google era (Moldoveanu and Baum 2014). Disruptors like Uber and Airbnb understood that knowing and being known by the right people for the right thing at the right time can morph into the foundation for new kinds of relationships with clients and customers based on being tested, transparent, and thereby trusted—and that Web 2.0 platforms could be stretched to support an information-sharing environment sufficiently rich to sustain trust networks that proved capable of unraveling the age-old industries of travel lodging and personal transportation. In rapid succession, the "trust me, I know best" sellers' economy of the 1980s and 1990s gave way to the "tell me, so I'll know" buyers' economy of the 2000s, and that is giving way to today's "show me, so I can trust you" economy. Uber was able to "Uberize" its market thanks to novel platforms designed to build trust through maximum responsiveness, transparency and predictability, precisely what is required to disrupt the largest, most conservative industries.

Onto the growing web of online platforms that make lecture- and seminar-based teaching transparent and replicable at low cost—currently a $50 billion market—has been grafted the platform model, a newly customized executive learning model being used by some of the world's largest organizations (Anderson and van Wijk 2010). The monopoly on legitimacy that academic institutions have commanded for the past two hundred years is being eroded by such platforms, with a preponderance of executives expressing a preference for learning from seasoned practitioners and academics rather than academics alone (edX 2015–2020). That many—perhaps even most—research findings published in leading social science journals are not replicable or are likely to be invalid as stated (Ioannidis 2005) is further eroding the claims to validity and reliability upon which academics have traditionally relied to establish cognitive jurisdiction over areas of practice. Legitimacy—rather than measurable, replicable, superior learning outcomes—has been the basis on which the executive development market has built trust. That will likely change.

Sudden increases in the value of responsiveness, transparency, and predictability disrupt an established industry via several mechanisms, all of which are currently in play in the executive development space: (1) fragmentation and reintegration of products and services consequent to the disaggregation of services and value chains; (2) disintermediation of service chains and multiparty services; and (3) decoupling of products' and services' sources of utility.

Let us consider each in turn.

Disaggregation and Unbundling of Services and Value Chains

Massively distributed online learning systems (Kroner 2014) promise to deliver, as needed, context- and setting-specific "skills on demand" to managers and executives. Such offerings can be found in free as well as fee-based configurations and standalone and "certificate bundle" formats. They exhibit increasing levels of intimacy with—and understanding of—learners' needs. State-of-the-art platforms such as edX, Coursera, Udacity, LinkedIn Learning , Udemy, Emeritus, and 2U have amassed large repositories of leading-edge content contributed by both traditional suppliers of learning experiences like colleges and universities and leading practitioners and learning organizations including Google, Apple, Goldman Sachs, and McKinsey. Thinkific has just launched a very low-cost, white-label learning management system that allows every academic or executive with a calling for teaching to launch a course, and every organization to develop its own curriculum. Companies availing themselves of this new "Digital Learnopolis" are realizing that it enables a revolutionary change in the way skill development happens—and are actively bringing that change about, through their practices. Explained one pharmaceutical executive: "We are creating 'learning labs' that will serve as rapid response teams to bring training and development solutions to immediate needs and pressing business problems. We were criticized for being like business schools in being too slow in response to the immediate needs of the business. Business schools need time to ramp up for any program if it is going to be at all reflective of our business needs rather than a standard offering, and we have been criticized for being like that when issues have come up over the course of our restructuring and integration. We are responding by creating a pool of moderator-facilitators that can react within weeks or even days to immediate business needs with training and development programs." With *trust* and *legitimacy* increasingly distributed across many platforms and providers of learning experience, the traditional "bundle" of skill development signaled by a degree or certificate is being broken up.

Technological disruption at its most powerful breeds and encourages cultural shifts. Enhanced access and communication technologies that enable learning on demand are challenging the notion and nature of courses, classes, assignments, quizzes, exams, questions, dialogues, forums, and "grades." The unbundling of the learning experience is transforming learning and certification processes, and changing habits and expectations, orienting learners toward the learning vehicles that offer the fastest and cheapest upskilling relevant to the problems and predicaments they face. Owing to the short feedback loop that links investment to outcome in executive development, these shifts are manifesting more quickly in that market than in any other segment of the higher education space. The current and near-term dynamics of the executive education and leadership development industries may therefore be good predictors of what is coming to the higher education space worldwide.

Disintermediation of Service Chains and Multiparty Service Bundles

Faculty members, prominent leaders, executives in residence, professors of practice, guest lecturers, and other agents of learning have long been the basis of business organizations' trust in the competence and excellence of prominent executive development programs. Digital disruption disintermediates existing value chains and often gives rise to new ones, as in the case of distributed database technologies that assumed the role of trusted third-party, fee-collecting middlemen in the global payments system traditionally filled by the commercial and retail banking sector (World Economic Forum 2013). Integrators, aggregators, and content providers like edX and Coursera, as they become more prominent and capable, are challenging business schools, universities, consultancies, and talent development organizations for the role of intermediator between learner and content, learner and method, learner and teacher, and learner and context. Udacity, to use one example, has found that the key to profitable growth and a very large valuation is cutting out the "middleman" universities from the learning production function, and aggregators and intermediators of business skill development vehicles—such as ExecuLearn and

Coursera Enterprise are following suit, by taking their platform offerings directly to faculty members and smaller programs, as opposed to the university organizations that house them. And white-label learning management engines like Thinkific, complete with billing and payment systems, are allowing every faculty member to teach her course to any organization or learner worldwide.

Decoupling of Sources of Products' and Services' Utility

Executive development programs like those run by business schools have long viewed the value they provide to extend beyond content, and even participants' learning experiences and skill enhancement, to the advantages afforded by networking and expansion of social capital, the prestige that attends being selected into and graduated from a leading program, and association with others whose mindsets reflect different countries and businesses. In Chapter 2, we will unpack these sources of value, and show how each can be replicated independently, or "decoupled" from one another in the new technological and cultural landscape of learning.

Decoupling is not unbundling. The latter refers to separating the constituent components of an executive program—lectures, case discussions, and project-based learning sessions, among others—which, when offered in conjunction, constitute the basis for a credential such as a certificate or degree. Decoupling involves separating out, and offering alternative means of appropriating, the different sources of value in each component. A case discussion, for instance, has value in fostering connections and ties on the basis of shared preparation, disseminating knowledge about a particular industry or company, and developing dialogical and argumentation skill through participation in a discussion that emulates what happens in the boardroom. Having identified and articulated these sources, it is possible to design and deploy alternatives or substitutes that perform better along each dimension at lower cost.

The Economics of Executive Development Are Being Disrupted

E-learning technologies and platforms already complement business schools' classroom teaching and learning formats and significantly lower the cost curve for delivery or provide a radically unbundled and potentially disintermediated set of alternatives to the MBA degree. Terwiesch and Ulrich (2014) compared the economics and "production functions" of traditional MBA programs with expert-delivered chunks of video content that can be consumed at a student's own pace (asynchronously), combined with mediated and unmediated discussion forums and instruments for testing and quizzing skill acquisition. Given the current requirement to subsidize tenured and tenure-stream academics' research from the revenue streams generated by tuition and fees—to the extent of an estimated $400,000 for each research article produced, according to Terwiesch and Ulrich—business schools face a stark choice between staying their current course and thereby risking an unmanageable cost structure or embracing the asynchronous interaction opportunities afforded by online platforms to bring their cost structures in line with revenue while serving learning needs vastly different from anything higher education has experienced.

Executive programs are even more sensitive than MBA programs to return-on-investment (ROI) considerations. Organizations view payment for participant attendance at executive programs as an investment. "Every dollar we put into our people," asserted an executive at McCann Health, "that's not a cost, it's an investment." But organizations are also under quarterly pressure to minimize or justify a large set of consolidated costs as well as to measure and reap the benefits of skill transfer and capability enhancement. Consider that a typical executive education program offered by a high-end provider

- Costs organizations or participants between $1,500 and $5,000 per participant per day

- Averages five days per year

- Has an "optimal" scale of twenty to thirty participants

- Must be run five to ten times per year to accommodate the executive echelons of organizations with ten-thousand-plus employees

Organizations thus face a typical annualized executive development cost of between $750,000 and $7,500,000—net of the costs of

- Selecting participants

- Measuring the degree to which participants' newly acquired skill sets are advantageously applied within the organization

- Measuring the degree to which individual skill sets coalesce into sets of organizational capabilities

- Losing the investment, as well as the executives themselves, for those who parlay the credentials and social capital gained from participation in development programs into employment elsewhere

Assuming, conservatively, these pre- and post-training costs to amount to around 30 percent of the cost of the programs, externally provided executive development costs an organization between $1 million and $10 million per year, depending on industry, organizational culture and structure, and the nature of the programs in which the organization invests. Observed an executive in Ernst & Young's assurance business: "To invest a large amount of money in eleven thousand partners is extremely expensive. Plus, we need to do things for all eleven thousand. So imagine in September last year we assembled three thousand partners from around the world in Orlando for three days to do training. Not cheap. So we're constantly under pressure to prove that what we're doing is adding value to justify the time and expense."

Now consider that the aggregation of currently available cloud services (such as Amazon Web Services, Google Cloud, Digital Ocean) has evolved to the point that on-demand skills and training can be provisioned to *any* executive at any time for less than $20 per user, per year. These cloud services make computation and storage-on-demand possible in increments that accommodate per-user matching of cost to value, offer client relation management tools that can include pre- and post-tracking of managerial workforce performance (for example, Salesforce.com), and are capable of delivering content related to specific functional skills available from high-profile providers (including executives, consultants, and business school academics) on-demand, via dedicated, high-visibility, high-reliability platforms. They can further include authentication plus user management plus content provisioning systems that support customization of internal learning management systems (using kernels and modules from, for example, Instructure, Moodle, Blackboard, or D2L).

At $20 per user per year, *half of all employees* of a ten-thousand-employee organization could benefit from an intensive, year-round program of skill development provisioned through an internally created and maintained cloud-based learning fabric for around $100,000 per year, less than one-fiftieth of the $5 million to $10 million per year the same organization would spend on equivalent executive and managerial development programs run by dedicated incumbent providers. The ten-fold growth in the number of corporate universities (from three hundred in 2004 to some two thousand in 2016) (Meister 2001) plausibly reflects the massive decrease in the cost base of learning infrastructures that can be deployed on demand in response to specific organizational needs, and the impact of which can be amplified by coaches, knowledge experts, and learning gurus who will curate content, map and measure skill acquisition and capability development, and guide participants to the most valuable outcomes.

Executive Skill Development Under Scrutiny

Providers of executive development face an unprecedented set of opportunities for responding to the organizational capability and executive skills gaps posed by the VUCA economy. If we imagine an executive's core competencies and skills as a LEGO set, each piece of which represents a key skill or competence, executive development critically depends on identifying these pieces and their ideal configuration. Schools' packaging of knowledge and skills is currently not guided by a map of these skills or a blueprint of how these pieces fit together (Canals 2011). Moreover, as we will show shortly, this LEGO set is about to undergo a major upgrade informed by two decades of research in learning science and executive skill development that has shown each piece to be composed of smaller pieces that reflect a much larger palette of skills and competencies with which to describe managerial and executive ability. These constituents can now be recombined in ways that respond to what we know about the nature of the gap between desired and developed skill sets and about the factors on which executive programs can and should be measured.

Developing Useful Skills That Are Applied to What Matters:
The Mission of Executive Development Programs and Interventions

Signaling participants' qualifications to their employers and the labor market, signaling costly personal investment in skill and self-development, and entry into an elite group of "graduates" or "alumnae" are among several functions served by executive development programs. Value also accrues to opportunities such programs present for networking with and learning from participants at varying levels within and across organizations and industries, and to the purely personal objective of self-development - independent of job requirements.

But it is important to be precise about the pivotal role that skill development—understood as the acquisition and refinement of applicable, relevant, useful skills—plays in the design and deployment of executive development programs. This can be illustrated by a thought experiment. Suppose that leading providers of executive learning programs discovered that the skills and capabilities they teach, develop, nurture, or otherwise impart to participants lack the value they are widely perceived to possess, whether because the content is outdated, the means by which the skills are developed are no longer suited to participants' modes of learning, or the skills are not applied on the job. Suppose that, upon discovering this, these premier providers modified their marketing message to convey *only* the networking and signaling value of their programs. The message would go something like this:

> Come spend time with us. You will build great new connections and get to signal the market that you have invested three weeks of your time and $40,000 to attend our program, in which you will get to know at least thirty other people who have made the same investment.

Then the fine print might say:

> We know our content to be dated and methods of teaching and learning facilitation to be ineffective, but networking and certification are the most important deliverables of programs like ours. It is time to be realistic about what education is all about so do not ask for more and be grateful that we are being truthful.

Would you consider attending? Should you attend if admitted? The obvious answer is "no" to both questions. You might exploit the signaling value of the program by posting your admission letter on LinkedIn or Instagram, and if other admitted would-be participants were to do the same thing, also capture the networking value of the program, all for the time it takes to complete the application and the price of the application fee. But you should not and likely would not attend because of the absence of a credible promise of developing new and useful skills. Skill development, after all, is the basis of the selection and signaling value of such programs.

A credible promise of skill development is also the basis of meaningful ties formed with like-minded others who are serious about self-development and improving their skills. Confidence in the shared objective of learning new skills is what makes such relationships valuable in the first place. Skill development—whether through teaching; facilitated, mutual, or blended learning; guided experimentation; or coaching—is the *raison d'être* of executive programs. It supplies their substance and justification for assembly. Therefore, to achieve the requisite insight into the present and future of executive learning programs, we must unpack the black box of the skill set of the executive.

What Is the Executive's Skill Set?
Unpacking the Black Box

"What skills are to be developed?" is a question asked and answered surreptitiously throughout primary, secondary, and higher education, at various levels of rigor. Skill sets such as reading, writing, and programming sit at one end of a spectrum. Communicating to, collaborating with, and relating to other humans sit at the other. Curriculum revisions are pursued on the basis of learning outcome measures and students' relative and absolute performance on standardized tests.

Executive education being the segment of the education market most sensitive to return on investment, human resources and talent development executives legitimately feel the need and often struggle to assess programs' impacts on their people and organizations (Gentry et al. 2013). Managers "routinely judge executive classes [on] relevance, and whether they help them address immediate challenges," observed David Garvin (2007), who adds that custom and company-specific programs place the "greatest premium on immediate relevance and practical applications." Even as they find themselves at an impasse regarding the training and development of the next generation of managers and leaders, providers of executive education have been slow, and perhaps even reluctant, to try to articulate specific families of executive and managerial skills associated with superior individual and organizational performance. Given the centrality of executive skill development, and the value of learned skills in the workplace, no overarching vision of the landscape of executive education can escape the challenge of attempting at least a broad outline of skills that constitute the executive's toolbox.

How a skills gap in executive development is addressed will be guided by which perspective on its origin prevails. It might be argued that the *right* skills and capabilities are not being taught or developed, either because academic pedagogical practice has drifted, with the independently evolving interests of academics, too far from real business practice, or that the skill sets needed to succeed in the new economy are changing too quickly. Or, it might be argued, the right skills *are* being cultivated but *not applied*, that is, participants are not *transferring what is learned in the classroom, lab, and online to the workplace*. These are vastly different diagnoses, and each would take program designers in a different direction. Heeding the former leads them to try to *get the right content* into existing programs, heeding the latter to try to *get the right pedagogy and learning technology*.

Organizations and academics alike are challenged to articulate a core "executive skill set" that contributes to organizational capability and success. No well-established taxonomy is at hand, even though many recognize how much value one would bring: "Our organization struggles with general agreement on what top talent and top capabilities look like and what is required," noted an executive at a large insurance provider. "People have very different perspectives. The challenge is getting your arms around what those capabilities are."

Established research and databases on skills do not offer much help. Working mostly in the 1950s and 1960s, learning scientists, psychometricians, and labor market econometricians prepackaged skill mapping and skill measurement. Their questionnaires, measurements, and tabulation methods were designed primarily for large-scale educational programs (for example, K–12 or college) and a manufacturing and resource-intensive economy that decidedly predates today's information, knowledge, and trust economy, in which computational prowess and factual and general information are free and distributed and access to information and communication are ubiquitous, distributed, and inexpensive. The U.S. Department of Labor's ONET database of academic papers and policy recommendations references dozens of skills related to manual dexterity, visual acuity, and motor coordination valuable in a manufacturing economy but scant higher-level cognitive and noncognitive skills needed by organizations today. Skills essential to solving complicated, complex, ill-defined, ill-structured problems that arise in socially embedded, multi-user, multistakeholder environments are subsumed under "complex problem-solving skill," which—we are assured by those who crafted the database—is prevalent in magistrates and CEOs, and far less so among academics or high school administrators (among many others).

We want to build a map of the executive's skill set that is sufficiently precise and complete to allow us to claim that *every executive must possess at least a subset thereof.* Although it may never be the case that any one executive will possess all of these skills, their mapping should serve to focus inquiry into what distinguishes an executive's skill set from the distinctive skill sets of, for example,

- A recently graduated, BS-level-certified mechanical engineer

- A certified car mechanic who has graduated from a vocational school

- A marketing specialist who has worked for five years in the ad-words department of a magazine

- A neurosurgeon with ten years of practice removing growths from the temporal lobes of people's brains

- A CIA field operative based in Tehran

- A flight attendant who has just received specialized training in in-flight security operations

- A PhD-trained artificial intelligence researcher or developer

- A playwright and director of successful Indie films

- An Olympic-medal-level decathlete

Each of these individuals possesses a set of skills. In these cases—of specialized talent performing specialized tasks using combinations of know-how and know-what for which detailed training programs have been designed—it seems straightforward to answer questions such as the following:

- What is the specific skill any one of these people possesses?

- How do we distinguish among the different skills that one person possesses?

- How do we measure them?

A skill is a demonstrated ability to complete particular tasks at a certain level of accuracy, reliability, and speed. It may be cognitive or noncognitive in its nature, more or less "mental" in the way it is exercised, and more or less relational and social in the way it is instantiated. The skill sets associated with the individuals listed earlier vary broadly in terms of their measurability and even observability. We routinely take them to be teachable—or at least learnable—as opposed to "innate," and associate their development with structured programs of study, learning, training, apprenticeship, and development.

The challenge we set for ourselves here is to articulate an *executive* skill set that is just as compelling as the skill sets we would naturally assume to be required by master practitioners. Just as the skill sets of a playwright, neurosurgeon, and AI researcher are clearly identifiable and distinguishable from one another—even if not always easy to articulate and measure—so the skill sets of the executive and high-potential manager should be discernible, if perhaps more difficult to articulate and measure. Categories rest on the distinctions that create them, and the right distinctions should cut the phenomenon at the joints. So let us make a few key distinctions.

Cognitive Skills: Functional

The skills associated with the standard models, methods, and languages of business that are operative in different functions of a company are both a set of *representations* (for example, a model of an industry as a set of profit-maximizing agents; of behavior as a set of choices guided by a value-maximization principle; of an organization as a nexus of formal and informal contracts among self-interested principals and agents; of an investment as a set of potentially stochastic inflows and outflows, and so on); and a set of *methods* (such as for valuing European call options and other derivatives; mapping a set of cash flows onto an income statement and balance sheet; inferring from a multivariate data set the effects of a new organizational effectiveness program relative to such programs in other companies and industries; developing a bottom-up demand analysis for a new product based on an understanding of demographics, demand characteristics, and the competitive-cooperative landscape of buyers and sellers offering complements and substitutes). They are often part of the "technical skills" imparted by an MBA curriculum or one of the increasingly popular "MBA alternatives"—one-year masters programs in financial risk management, management of technology, and so on—seeking to tool up high achievers with backgrounds across the spectrum of disciplines and vocations with a repertoire of "business" skills. Professional education courses, certificates, diplomas, and nano-, pico-, and femto-degrees proffered by distributed, online, and blended alternative business education that come with names like "Digital Marketing," "Project Management," "Financial Risk Management," and "Big Data Techniques for Database Design" read like an extension of precisely this set of "applied cognitive skills." They all entail the sort of simple combination of know-what (models) and know-how (methods) characteristic of our "basic cognitive skills" category.

Meta-Cognitive Skills

Chester Barnard's *Functions of the Executive* (1938) was among the first signs of growing awareness that leadership, high-level management, and the exercise of an executive's functions rely on a set of skills that lie beyond mere functional expertise. Progress in articulating these skills had to await the development of distinctions and models of generalized problem definition and awareness of the specific difficulties of problem solving in unstructured, ambiguous, complicated domains involving multiple stakeholders with different, sometimes conflicting interests and commitments (see, for example, Simon (1973) on ill-structured problems; Churchman (1967) on wicked problems; Moldoveanu and Leclerc (2015) on ill-defined problems and problems in different complexity classes).

Not all business problems are created equal, and the difference between them is not merely one of degree of difficulty. There is a difference of kind and quality between solving a classifier algorithm design problem in an artificial intelligence lab and leading a large group of heterogeneous AI researchers with different theoretical and cultural backgrounds who are charged with developing a beta-ready release of an app that translates spoken Mandarin to written English in real time to success in three quarters, or between conducting a market analysis for the launch of a new enhanced-reality headset and getting a group of marketers, engineers, and financiers to agree on the right set of assumptions underlying the analysis so it can go forward in the first place. It is through such distinctions that we can tease out the set of "higher level" cognitive skills executives exercise to build new models that optimally integrate across multiple functions and disciplines, and define and structure problems in ways that are intelligible and ultimately agreeable to multiple stakeholders who previously could not previously speak to one another because they lacked a common dialect.

The VUCA-specific significance of these skills receives support from studies like IBM's Global Chief Executive Officer survey, which concluded from the input of the fifteen hundred CEOs who participated that "rapid escalation of complexity is the biggest challenge confronting [the world's public and private sector leaders]" (Palmisano 2013). The study further found that more than half of those surveyed doubted their ability to manage the anticipated rise in the complexity of the chief executive's predicament. On the positive side, managing the complexity of business predicaments emerges as a core characteristic of more successful executives and organizations.

Affective and Perceptual Skills

Peter Salovey and J. D. Mayer's (1990) articulation of "affective skill" was popularized by Daniel Goleman (1995) using the term "emotional intelligence." We are now accustomed to speak of emotional intelligence as of a skill or set of skills as well defined, measurable, and observable as IQ or analytical reasoning, though the real challenge of measurement and observation lies not in the past, but in the future. The term has nevertheless come to stand for a set of previously more nebulous "people skills" that are an essential part of the executive skill set.

Exploiting advances in affective and cognitive neuroscience to further elaborate these skills, we can characterize the emotionally *intelligent* executive as possessing a comparative advantage in the exercise of such skills as making reliably valid inferences about others' intentions from observations of their verbal and nonverbal behavior (empathic accuracy, enhanced "theory of mind" functions); changing affective states and moods in response to the context, content, and constraints of a situation (for example, "being angry at the right person at the right time for the right reason in the right way," a venerable Aristotelian ideal); and exhibiting openness to understanding and validating alternative and often opposing emotional commitments and attitudes. Solving "wicked problems" is not a merely cognitive function; heart and mind must work together to make progress in solving problems that involve the hearts and minds of others, whose perspectives can lead to a better solution even if they are in tension with one another and with our own. Observed an executive at Farmers Insurance: "We think about how we can train people in empathy. Understanding that customers call an insurance company when they have a loss gives us the opportunity to prepare our people, beforehand, to be more responsive and sympathetic." It matters less that the language of business persons is not currently precise enough to make all the right distinctions—that, for instance, it is empathic accuracy rather than "sympathy" that we should seek, or that sympathy and responsiveness are often in tension—than it does that the affective dimension of an executive's skill set clearly recognized by organizations as paramount to the development of their executives.

Self-Command, Self-Control, Self-Regulation: The X-Skills

Heckman's (Cunha, Heckman, Lochner, and Masterov 2006; Heckman 2006) investigations of the relative lifetime value of various skills brought econometric rigor to a set of findings related to the value of self-control, self-command, and self-regulation, a nexus of skills appropriately, if somewhat confusingly, labeled "executive functions of the mind-brain," which have been percolating and gathering steam and empirical heft since Mischel's finding (1974; Mischel, Shoda, and Rodriguez 1989) that three-to-four-year-old children's ability to suppress temptation is highly predictive of their success in high school and college, after controlling for IQ or general intelligence. Perhaps surprisingly, the tightest formulation of the "executive functions of the brain," the one most relevant to executives, is provided by Stuss (2011), whose work on the clinical management of neurodegenerative conditions (Alzheimer's, dementia) distinguishes among functions of the frontal lobes of the brain that have to do with the energization of different tasks and subtasks (do-THIS-now), partitioning of large problems into manageable tasks and objectives, allocation of tasks and objectives to different subproblems (do-THIS-first), and suppression of temptation and unconstructive impulses when engaging in a wide array of tasks (do-THAT-not-THIS).

Self-awareness can also be considered a relevant executive skill rather than attribute or characteristic, particularly in view of recent discoveries of its relationship to an *interoceptive* function of the mind-brain that enables an individual to accurately answer questions such as "How am I feeling now?" To avoid the confusion that arises when we speak of these skills as "executive functions of the executive's mind-brain," we henceforward term the self-awareness-self-command-self-control-self-regulation nexus *X-skills*, in part as a nod to Leibenstein's model of X-inefficiency within a firm (1976)—the inefficiency that arises from an imperfection at the firm level with respect to optimally allocating resources to tasks in the face of competing goals, under time constraints.

However self-evident to executives and their coaches and advisors, the X-skill nexus has, to date, not been explicitly included in the executive skill set that is explicitly selected for and developed in most consecrated programs. In part, this reflects an education fieldwide bias regarding the link between self-discipline and factors outside the control of the higher education system (such as genetics, "personality," early childhood development), and in part, possibly, scarcity of this very skill among researcher-educators. Executive developers must come to grips with the importance of this skill set and its relevance to the executive function as well as the possibility that it may be learned, developed, and, at the very least, rigorously selected for.

No task calls upon the exercise of the X-nexus skill base more strenuously, regularly, and explicitly than one very familiar to most and perhaps all executives—that of conducting an effective meeting, one that leads to actionable outcomes, and in which all participants feel heard, understood, empowered, and validated, such that each shall support the decision at which the group arrives, regardless of whether or not it is her or his preferred option.

Individual Skills Versus Relational Skills

Some cognitive skills are exercised privately, in the confines of office or cubicle, others publicly, in the context of high stakes board, client, or management team meetings. The same holds for affective skills, some (such as affective flexibility, X-factor skills) exercisable in an individual or relational setting, others (for example, empathic accuracy) only in an interpersonal setting. The value of the relational skills needed to solve ill-defined, ill-structured problems in socially and culturally embedded, multistakeholder situations has for some time been recognized in the labor market (Johnson, Manyika, and Lee 2005). In developmental and educational systems, we think of people who are more or less inclined to social interactions, more or less extroverted, to the left or to the right on the Asperger spectrum, more or less conscientious, industrious and open—and so forth. We think of relational *dispositions, inclinations, traits,* and *abilities* as opposed to skills—in spite of the fact that in general business parlance, "people skills" are highly valued—which limits the degree to which executive programs seek to *develop* these skills. To get clear about relational skills—or "people skills"—we interviewed several high-ranking executives and participants in executive programs, reflected on our experiences as executives, and conducted some group discussions aiming to get clear about the *skills* involved in that most paradigmatic of executive activities—*running a meeting. Running* a meeting is, of course, a mere reference to a complicated process: setting it up; introducing it; having everyone around the table or the Zoom or Google Hangout screen feel empowered to speak his or her mind, in ways that are undiminished by ritual and free from coercion; having everyone at the same time feel and think that progress has been made, that words matter and commitments count, and that reasons as well as feelings will be heeded and addressed in a timely and forthright and authentic fashion. There is a hard-to-quantify quantity of fluidity and interpersonal "co-presence" in highly collaborative and empowering interactions that are recognizable once they are experienced but difficult to describe or prescribe *ex ante.* Given that a skill is an observed propensity to complete a task in a certain amount of time at a certain level of quality and a certain reliability, we asked ourselves and our interlocutors to try hard to articulate the tasks which, if successfully completed, often jointly lead to the kind of high-integrity, effective, open, and responsive interpersonal experience that most teams wish for and very few if any achieve in their get-togethers. And here they are:

- Tuning in to someone in a way that makes it clear to them they are being listened to and heard

- Sensing the emotionality, mood, and expression of another person and giving clear signs to her that the fullness of her presence is heeded and felt

- Paraphrasing accurately the statements of others around the table, in ways that get them to feel their points of view, claims, sentiments, reasons, arguments, questions, challenges, and concerns have been understood

- Reacting in ways that are clearly visible to others around the table (or the Microsoft Teams screen) to demagogical, needlessly aggressive, deceitful, or subversive moves and maneuvers made by others

- Responding to questions, challenges, and concerns—as well as to perceived sentiments and moods—of participants, in ways that make it clear to them their contributions and actions count, and that they are understood

- Energizing (deenergizing) discussions—by changing tone, loudness, body language, choice of words—in order to accelerate (decelerate) or amplify (attenuate) particular moments in a meeting

- Articulating claims, reasons, and the arguments for them in ways that create agreement among participants regarding the facts, principles that are necessary for the discussion to proceed

- Deconstructing claims, arguments, and reasons put forth by others to make explicit those assumptions that would benefit from public questioning and deliberation

Once we state matters in this form—as tasks whose successful completion obviously contributes to the enactment of an important organizational function—the fact that there are relational *skills* that enable executives to carry out these tasks more reliably, more efficiently, and at a higher level seems clear. These skills may supervene on natural abilities—like a more acute sense of perception or interoception—but it seems plausible that they can also be *learned*. Thinking of them as learnable would, of course, change both current human resources practices and executive development practices, and such change seems difficult, but is not impossible, as we will argue in Chapters 4 and 5.

From "Which Skills?" to
"How Will You Develop Them?"

Executive program designers need to understand not only the skills maps and the skills gaps that characterize and beset an organization, but also how and when and how well skills acquired are *applied*. To yield a return on investment, new skills must not only be acquired but also applied in the context of the organization that invests in their development. Skill development needs to satisfy the following simple equation:

SKILL DEVELOPMENT = SKILL ACQUISITION + SKILL TRANSFER

To be effective, executive programs must address both elements of the right-hand side of this equation: participants should acquire new and useful skills that should transfer to the work they do within their organizations. However, at this point we may take neither acquisition nor transfer of skills for granted.

Skill Acquisition: The Differences That Make a Difference

Just as we employed key distinctions to illuminate the landscape of useful executive skills, we make sense of how skills are acquired by way of another pair of distinctions.

ALGORITHMIC SKILLS VERSUS NONALGORITHMIC SKILLS

The first distinction is that between algorithmic and nonalgorithmic skills first articulated in Moldoveanu and Martin (2008). The nature of a skill that relates to the ability to perform a task will reflect the nature of that task. If its execution can be written as an algorithm, that is, a step-by-step procedure like a recipe or computer program, a task is algorithmic. To perform an algorithmic task that solves a specific problem requires an algorithmic skill. Examples include basic calculations of ROI and NPV in finance and accounting; equilibrium calculations in the microeconomics of consumer behavior; the computation of Nash Equilibria in a noncooperative game; or figuring out the optimal configuration for a COVID vaccine supply chain in countries that lack vaccine manufacturing capacity, such as Canada. Other processes do not admit of an algorithmic description—such as "creating a welcoming, open communication environment," "conceptualizing a predicament that is acceptable to multiple parties initially at odds," and "credibly and publicly taking responsibility for an error" or "authentically and truthfully validating your strongest critic in a board meeting."

The algorithmic-nonalgorithmic distinction does not map trivially into the cognitive-noncognitive distinction. Most algorithmic skills are cognitive, but not all cognitive skills are algorithmic. And while many perceptual and affective skills (such as empathic accuracy) seem difficult to characterize in algorithmic terms, some affective skills (for example, altering breathing patterns in predictable ways in order to quiet the mind to the point at which severe perceptual field ambiguity can be contemplated without a rise of more than 10 percent in heart rate) are algorithmic in nature.

This distinction is critical to how skills are construed and learned. Algorithmic skills are more readily "digitalized" and made amenable to online, distributed instruction that follows the basic schema see-try-do-repeat:

- See it done in detailed step-by-step sequence

- Try to do it (with step-by-step feedback)

- Do it yourself (with feedback on outcome and output)

- Repeat the attempt and measure improvement from one iteration to the next

As evidenced by the success of Lynda.com (now LinkedIn Learning, part of Microsoft) as a learning vehicle for basic tools and techniques ranging from video editing to cooking and low-level programming to Web design, a large class of task-related skills—cognitive, motor or perceptual—can be remotely specified and tested for, and in many cases taught and learned without direct contact between instructor and learner.

Development of nonalgorithmic skills typically proceeds with rich, textured, and subtle feedback and constant dialogue between learner and learning facilitator that can change the nature of the learner's objective function "on the fly." "Presence" in interpersonal communications and "attunement" to the emotional states of others are usually viewed as leadership skills best developed in the context of a coaching relationship that features frequent, accurate feedback. Coaches routinely employ, or believe or state that they employ—a "method," but no coach can specify an *algorithm* for getting to presence or attunement, because their methods are not algorithms but rather subtly worded heuristics, prompts, nudges, and principles whose application is sensitively dependent on the who, the what, and the how of context.

Their acquisition being highly dependent on close contact and interaction, such skills are unlikely to be absorbed into the digital world of online learning as we know it now. Resonant with the foregoing discussion, one executive at a mobile technology company characterized algorithmic skills the development of which can be deployed on a broad, global scale as "low-touch" and nonalgorithmic skills peculiar to senior leaders that require greater focus on developing plans, individual and group coaching, and customized approaches as "high-touch."

Finally, even if executives increasingly rely in their work on interacting with large data sets that live in structured databases and with the algorithmic processes that work upon them, it need not be that the executive skill sets are themselves purely algorithmic. A componential analysis of the skills required in large-scale business optimization and prospecting projects that employ big data analytics (Moldoveanu 2015) finds that algorithmic skills like model testing, calibration, selection, and coding, and a select set of database design and optimization skills, need to be complemented by nonalgorithmic skills such as relating, persuading, sensing, structuring, and presenting (Figure 1.1).

Always-Teachable Skills Versus Only-Learnable Skills

Not all skills are teachable, and, while it may be that not all skills are learnable, there are important skills that are learnable but not teachable. It is important to distinguish between skills that can be taught and learned and skills that can only be learned, sometimes with facilitation and feedback, but never via specific codified instruction. Riding a bicycle is a classic example of an important and valuable skill that cannot be taught by having the uninitiated owner read a manual or set of instructions or pursue a degree in classical mechanics. Competence at this skill is built through a delicate interplay of perception (gaze control, feedback and feed-forward balance signals), movement (arms, legs, torso, hips), and predictive processes ("slope coming") that produce synchrony and synergy among several sensory and motor functions. Not surprisingly, the skill is best and most successfully taught to eager children by loving, attentive, patient parents and siblings or friends who rely on frequent demonstration and intense, frequent feedback.

"Giving effective face-to-face negative *feedback*" is a similar kind of skill highly relevant to executive learners. Like riding a bike, it cannot be "taught" using a set of methods composed of the usual suspects. But it can be learned under the patient guidance of a savvy coach or guru able to guide the learner to a "better approach," "better" being defined in terms not only of "more soothing" or "less offensive" or "more informative" but also of fit with the learner's style and "way of being." Of course, some skills currently only learnable can become teachable, and that is the role of pedagogical innovation.

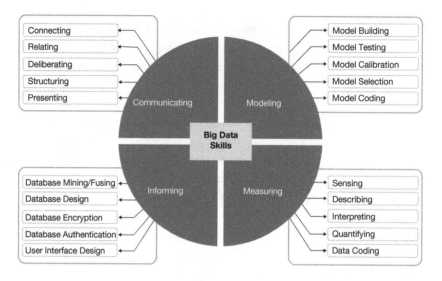

Figure 1.1. The "Managing with Big Data" Skill Set

The difference this distinction makes to the design of executive programs is simple: teachable skills can be imparted via offerings that incorporate teacher and student roles; skills that can only be learned but not taught entail the development of a learning environment that affords participants an appropriate combination of guidance, autonomy, and support conveyed by a process that tends to be amorphous and difficult to specify or choreograph.

The algorithmic/non-algorithmic and always teachable/only learnable distinctions not only illuminate the process of skill acquisition but also explain to a considerable extent the dynamics of the executive program industry. Diverting acquisition of algorithmic skills, especially of the sort that are always teachable, to the digital cloud frees the face-to-face and in-person classroom medium to specialize in the more intensive and costly cultivation of non-algorithmic skills, especially the sort that are not teachable.

Recalling that skill acquisition is just one part of the skill development equation we turn now to the other element: application in the context of the workplace.

The Elusive Goal of Skill Transfer

That skills, however acquired, will be usefully applied is implicitly assumed by all educational processes and institutions from kindergarten to doctoral programs, open online courses to informal seminars and workshops, and coaching sessions to on-demand corporate training sessions. The critical outcome measure of learning is the transfer of a skill acquired by a student, trainee, or participant to the context in which it is useful. The efficacy of skill transfer can be gauged by the answers to questions like the following:

- Is a sales executive who has learned the basic principles of incentive-based compensation systems applying them to the design of the team's compensation package?

- Is a student who has learned basic methods of cash flow management applying the learned recipes and heuristics to the management of household cash inflows and outflows?

Do those who develop—as a group, in a highly socialized setting within the precincts of the executive training suite of a leading business school—a heightened awareness of the emotional landscape of an outcome-focused group meeting successfully export this awareness to the management of meetings in their respective organizations? Does it matter to the success of the skill transfer if the geographic context is Seoul and discussions are conducted in Korean? Is the skill transfer limited to groups that are equivalent in size to the training group?

Does reasoned, informed, structured discussion of the strategic predicament that faced Dropbox's founders upon receiving series A financing dispose discussants to apply the structuration schemata used by the discussion leader and dialogical ability developed via a good case discussion to the deliberations they will engage in when they launch their own companies?

What if the learners' home organizations are a large retail chain, car parts manufacturer, or pharmaceutical company? Will what is learned from a case discussion of Dropbox apply in *those* settings, or does an equivalent awareness have to be developed in case discussions of companies in *those* industries?

More pessimistically, might the radical difference between the "make believe" "civilized" setting of the executive classroom and the "reality-laden," "messy," "political," "perverse," "emotionally charged" setting of the corporate environment preclude the transfer of *any* skills developed in case discussions beyond the boundaries of the executive classroom?

Do Skills *Transfer*? Is to Say, Does One Ever *Truly* Learn?
Given its centrality to executive development programs, the assumption of skill transfer warrants particular scrutiny. The transfer of basic and largely cognitive

skills, has been central to cognitive psychology, learning science, educational psychology, and, more recently, the brain science of learning and adaptive behavior. Yet the subject and discipline of skill transfer have received little attention or emphasis in writings on executive and professional education or the design of professional and executive education programs, for reasons that will shortly become apparent.

Seminal work on skill transfer in education dates back to Thorndike's twenty-five-year inquiry into supporting conditions and mechanisms, and *implications* for the nature of education, of skill transfer (see, for example, Thorndike and Woodworth 1901). Thorndike's original work tested a simple case of skill transfer. He had students learn to estimate the area of a large rectangle (123 x 221 blocks, for instance) by tessellating it with smaller rectangles (20 x 20; 10 x 10; 5 x 5; 1 x 1) provided as a set of building blocks. He found that over repeated attempts students produced tighter estimates of the area of the larger rectangles, but that this ability did *not* transfer to a problem in which the rectangles were replaced by triangles, in which error rates of students in the experimental and control groups were barely distinguishable. Thorndike consequently concluded that "improvements in any single mental function rarely bring about equal improvements in any other function, no matter how similar."

More textured versions of Thorndike's transfer tests (Reed, Dempster, and Ettinger 1985) distinguished a problem's textual context from its underlying structure while maintaining the same general solution principle. A target problem was modified in several ways.

Target problem: A small pipe can fill an oil tank in twelve hours and a large one can fill it in eight hours. How long will it take to fill the tank if both pipes are used at the same time? This problem was modified as follows:

A. *An equivalent problem—same imagery, same structure*: A small hose can fill a swimming pool in six hours and a large one can fill it in three hours. How long will it take to fill the pool with both hoses?

B. *A similar problem—same imagery, different structure*: A small pipe can fill a water tank in twenty hours and a large pipe can fill it in fifteen hours. Water is drawn from the tank at a rate that would empty a full tank in forty hours. Suppose both pipes are on and water is drawn from the tank. How long would it take to fill the tank?

C. *An isomorphic problem—different imagery, same structure*: Tom can drive to Bill's house in four hours and Bill can drive to Tom's house in three hours.

Assuming they use the same route, how long will it take them to meet along the way if they both leave their houses at the same time and drive toward each other?

D. *An unrelated problem—different imagery, different structure*: An airplane can fly from city A to city B at an average speed of 250 mph in three hours less time than it takes it to return from city B to city A at 200 mph. How many hours did it take it to return?

The experimenters found that students could transfer solution procedures learned from the target problem to equivalent, but not to isomorphic, unrelated, or *even similar* problems (Reed, Dempster, and Ettinger 1985). This finding suggests that skill transfer relies on a level of specificity in both the context in which a problem is solved (a case of price competition in the soft drink industry) and that to which the solution is transferred (imminent price competition in the bottled drinks industry, with slightly different numbers), and on the similarity between them. This flies in the face of the notion that education provides anything resembling a "lifetime skill set" and speaks to the importance of maintaining a set of teaching materials and instructional cases sufficiently updated that the target problem (the one that informs a case discussion) is never far (in structure *or* imagery) from the modified problems to which participants are expected to transfer the learned skill. Such findings, subsequently reproduced across a large number of problem situations, influenced Thorndike's pessimistic view of education as an unsuccessful attempt to transfer a set of higher-level skills and principles across different situations and contexts and buttressed a retreat to a view that education should teach students, in the words of Detterman (1993), not "how they need to go about applying the knowledge" or "how they need to know," but "what" they need to know—that is, mere information transfer.

The implication for executive development today of the notion of "education as imprinting of facts" is, if anything, even more profound than it might have seemed to educators and psychologists working post-Thorndike. An undisputed characteristic of the Web in its present embodiment is the complete commodification of information and knowledge. If the primary and most important function of education is to transfer information and knowledge (the latter being rules for applying the former to specialized, context-dependent problems), organizations worldwide should immediately retarget their current $180 billion (in 2015 dollars) investment in corporate training entirely to online platforms that codify and convey information as needed by each manager and to large databases of "answers" to as many questions that executives might have as possible.

Traditional pre–Web 2.0 educators and learning scientists troubled by the failure of attempts at skill transfer throughout the past century have produced a large body of empirical studies aimed at elucidating specific conditions under which transfer takes place (or not), and the mediators and moderators of skill transfer over the learner's life cycle. Skill transfer, it turns out, *does* take place—in some situations, for some skills, for some people, with some probability and conditional upon some combination of factors that have to do with trainer, trainee, subject matter, specific skill, and learning context.

Sternberg and Frensch (1993) propose that the transfer of a skill (for example, a cash flow management method) has to do with its being remembered and applied in situations in which it is useful (for example, a division's cash flow planning). This suggests several factors that influence skill transfer:

A. The way a learner encodes conveyed information (as names, numbers, symbols, or associations) matters a great deal to when, where, and how it will be remembered (Tulving and Thomson 1973), and hence to which contexts the skill will be transferable. In a paradigmatic experiment, students exhibited enhanced ability to apply heuristics and methods of manipulating algebraic expressions learned in algebra class in a physics class, but learning the same methods in the physics class did not enhance students' ability to solve "identical" problems in algebra class (Bassok and Holyoak 1989).

B. The way information is organized at the time of learning influences whether or not it is recalled at the right time and place and for the right reason (Tulving 1966). Lists of seven-digit numbers that exhibit symmetries (456-7654) used to encode them are more likely to be remembered than numbers that lack symmetries or possess symmetries hidden from the learner.

C. Contextual triggers and mental frames often determine information's relevance to context, which, in turn, determines the degree to which it is productively recalled (Anderson and Bower 1973; Luchins 1942). Viewed as a "supply chain optimization" problem, dealing on a busy Monday morning with urgent phone calls from suppliers, the engineering team, and the production team relies on specific associations of callers' names and roles with the components of a supply chain that were learned in an operations management class.

Distinctions like these may be music to the ears of empiricists, who can justifiably continue to look for ever more complicated conjunctions of causes, mediators, moderators, and effects, but they entail stark practical choices for designers of executive education programs. One example would be the choice between aiming for "higher immediate relevance of a skill" in order to enhance its transferability via contextual and framing effects and striving to transfer knowledge at the highest possible level of abstraction so as to exploit encoding effects and maximize transferability to a large number of specific situations. Another would be the choice between strict preorganization of material to achieve a higher probability of recall, and employing large numbers of wide-ranging and not readily categorized examples across a range of industries to maximize contextual triggers. Not only do we not know the answers to such questions, but professional and executive education have not even begun to ask them in earnest.

TRANSFER OF EXECUTIVE SKILLS IS EVEN HARDER TO CAPTURE

Much more than how information is organized matters to whether and how it is transferred. How subject matter is represented and taught (case discussions, lectures, small workshops, guided online sessions); the specificity of participants' skill development goals (learning *what* versus learning *how to*; learning to *do* something versus learning to *be* a certain way toward others); and the combinatorial interaction between context and content (learning to act or speak or communicate adaptively in various cultural, hierarchical, political, technological, and geographical contexts) all deeply influence the success of an executive learning program participant's "personal learning project." Providers of executive learning and development experiences must attend not only to how information and knowledge structures are presented and discussed but also to the modality of presentation; the time value of the skills *being* taught; the differences in the functional, social, and temporal contexts of use; and the difficulty of articulating and measuring the skills to be developed and of transferring them to participants of varying ability whose backgrounds reflect a wide range of contexts.

Barnett and Ceci's (2002) typology of the "differences that make a difference" in skill transfer and expected difficulty of transferring any particular skill can, with suitable modifications, shed light on the skill development value of different forms of executive learning, and perhaps more broadly of corporate training. The anticipated difficulty of transferring a skill (of applying it in a context that is different from that in which it was acquired) is best represented as a "near-far" problem, entailing, at one end of the spectrum, the transfer of a skill from one context to another that is highly similar (near), and at the other, to one very different (far).For example, learning to solve mass conservation problems involving two specific bodies in physics, for example, should transfer "easily" to solving problems that involve two bodies of different masses (near transfer), but may not transfer as easily to problems involving three bodies (farther), N bodies (farther still), inviscid fluids (even farther), or relativistic masses (much farther). Mapping the wine industry as a value-linked activity chain involving exchanges of goods, services, and money to reveal the value-added and likely bargaining power of each participant may transfer easily to an analysis of the maple syrup business (near transfer), but not as easily to an analysis of the blood plasma and derivative pharmaceuticals business (farther), telecommunications semiconductor business (farther still), video game graphics engine business (even farther), or the business of using high-powered computational devices to mine for new Bitcoins (much farther). Transfer may thus be nearer or farther in terms of the "knowledge domain" in which a learned skill is to be applied. Knowledge domains more similar to those in which a skill is learned will present less challenging ("near transfer") environments, whereas a program that claims to add "lifetime value" must ensure that a learned skill can be applied in many, and highly different ("far transfer") knowledge domains.

Relevance is the driver of "closeness" and "distance" for skill transfer, but it is not related to content alone. This is because the near-far distinction operates not only in the knowledge domain but in other domains as well (Barnett and Ceci 2002).

Temporal transfer relates to the probability of applying a skill to contexts near or remote in time. It is a measure of the "extinction rate" of a newly acquired skill. College students' cognitive mastery of subject matter is known to "peak" around the time of the final exam and rapidly diminish thereafter. The usefulness of executive skills, however, is highly correlated with longevity, that is, with how habitual their exercise becomes.

Spatial transfer relates to the application of a skill to tasks performed near (different classroom, same school or organization) or far (different school or different facilities of same organization). Physical context can be an important determinant of an executive's ability to exercise a new skill. New modes of communication and expression, for instance, may be highly dependent on the topology of the space in which they are employed (for example, seminar room versus classroom versus large hall).

Social transfer relates to the application of a skill to tasks performed in social settings that differ from those in which the skill was learned. *Is* the skill to be transferred, for example, from a focal group of managers in the same enterprise engaged in a joint seminar to one manager's team or working group (near) or to a team in a different company (far)?

Functional transfer relates to the application of a skill to settings in which its function is different from the one that guided the use cases used to teach or help someone learn it. A case discussion of the choice of a new *database* technology minimally teaches discussants to frame managerial and executive situations as problems and dilemmas that can be addressed using particular methods and techniques. The function of this skill in the executive learning classroom is to enable the discussant to participate in a high-level, disciplined dialogue with peers about the case at hand. Will the skill transfer when the functional context changes, when the objective is, for example, to generate new database solutions, evaluate alternative solutions, or engender idle, conceptual conversation aimed at concealing glaring errors of fact and analysis?

Knowledge Domain transfer relates to the application of a skill to knowledge domains—including professional domains—that are more or less different from the one used to teach or help someone learn the skill in the first place. Learning to analyze oligopolistic dynamics in the context of the Coke versus Pepsi "wars" may entail that the skill is far more transferrable to similar industries ("consumer packaged goods") than to industries that are further away from the prototypical example used ("airlines").

Modality transfer relates to differences in *how* a skill is learned (for example, online, through structured interactions among participants) and applied (for example, in teams and groups, in heavily socialized settings, in an emotional landscape colored by political and economic interests and the moods and desires of group members) or between the ways in which a concept is presented (symbolically, textually) and the ways in which it needs to be applied (graphically, orally).

Relevance is a six-dimensional entity! References to "useful, applicable, relevant knowledge" that populate the marketing materials of many business schools and consultancies are often a misleading oversimplification:

- First, what is to be developed and imparted is not "knowledge"—various Google Search engines, Google Scholar, Wolphram Alpha, and Wikipedia are all faster, better, cheaper substitutes—but rather know-how or *skill*.

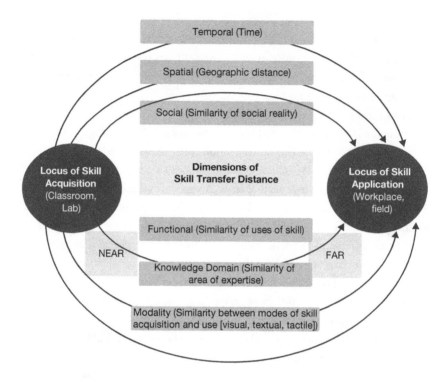

Figure 1.2. The "Near-Far" Challenge of Transferring Skill from the Locus of Acquisition to the Locus of Application

- Second, relevance is not a simple metric, but a six-dimensional measure (see Figure 1.2) that captures the probability that a skill will be applied in contexts that are more or less removed—along six different dimensions—from those in which the skill was acquired. And, given the fact that executives and their organizations should start out wary and skeptical about providers' claims about the applicability of the skills they help learners acquire, the burden of proof is squarely on the suppliers' metaphorical shoulders.

Now imagine you are trying to redesign, from scratch, the entire executive education industry—motivated by a desire to create the optimal skill development regimen for executives using the gamut of learning and teaching technologies, techniques, teachers, coaches, and trainers and equipped with the foregoing analysis of the transferability of skill. The six independent ways in which the distance between the locus of learning and locus of application can be measured entail six dimensions of what it means for a skill to be "relevant." If we

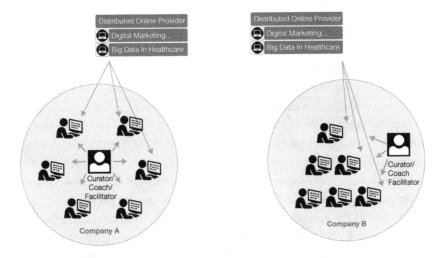

Figure 1.3. The Skills-On-Demand Model of Executive Development

take this (six dimensional) distance to be the key impediment to skill transfer, then there are two ways in which executive learning providers can stay "true to advertising" in the quest to develop relevant skill sets for executive clients: (1) make all transfer local—thereby decreasing transfer distance (model 1), and (2) make learning transferrable to distant domains—increase the reliability of transferring skills acquired to distant domains (model 2).

Let us consider each.

Model 1: Skills on Demand

Discounting as too difficult and costly, and hence unlikely, the prospect and ideal of far transfer—of skills imparted to executive clients on campus, in person, or within a group being applicable much later, in varying social, technical, professional, and physical surroundings and via different modes of expression— results in the deployment of Web 2.0 technologies of learning and interaction by large numbers of curators and facilitators working within their respective organizations to create a seamless fabric of executive learning opportunities that yield skills that are "relevant by design" because they are taught on the job, in the very context in which skills are applied (Figure 1.3). No longer are functional skills (such as "accounting," "strategy," "finance," "operations," "marketing") taught independently from the specific context in which they are to be applied. Basic language systems and models and methods are efficiently taught via online forums and learning management system platforms specially curated for organizations, individual executives, or groups of organizations, that require a specific skill or capability set, and the application of skill to the context in which it is useful is individually and closely guided for each participant by internal coaches and functional experts. Participants immediately see the relevance to the problem at hand of each skill delivered by the learning platform, and elaborated by coaches when needed.

The relevance gap is closed by *making all skill transfer near transfer*. If and when individuals change industries, or roles within an organization, or organizations within the same industry, this distributed, low-cost, interactive "learning on demand" platform follows them like a personal learning assistant, living partly in the cloud and partly in their talent management group in the form of curators of content, facilitators of discussion, and local gurus who guide the application of content to context. Model 1 is embodied in the personal learning cloud, which we will discuss in greater detail in Chapter 3.

Model 2: The Core Skill Development Hub

Alternatively, the learning environment of executive development is designed to maximize the probability of long-lived relevance across the range of physical, professional, social, functional, temporal, and modal contexts of executives' professional and personal lives. To "teach with the explicit goal of maximizing far transfer" (Figure 1.4), core skill development programs are designed using techniques most likely to produce a reliably transferrable set of core skills and maximize the degree to which this skill set is robust to changes in the context in which executives will exercise them. Specific options for doing so will be discussed in Chapter 4.

To cultivate a skill set sufficiently abstract to carry across industries and cultures, the skill development hub model employs techniques like intensive, personalized and timely developmental feedback; collaborative construction of the substantive content of discussions; relentless practice in applying learned skills to a wide range of contexts and predicaments; cases and collaborative projects highly specific in terms of details of time, place, industry, market, and product or service; and classroom and seminar-hall learning focused on argumentation, managing constructive dialogue among people with potentially different views and aims, structuration of ill-defined predicaments and situations

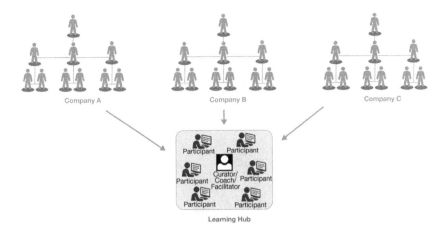

Figure 1.4. The Core Skill Development Hub Model of Executive Learning

as well-defined problems with finite solution search spaces, iterated elimination of dominated solutions on the basis of sparse and noisy data, and so forth.

The skills-on-demand model of executive learning possesses an overwhelming advantage in efficiency, especially with respect to the development of algorithmic skills and learning that bridge the gap between content and context through continuous availability and on-site customization and curation of content. The skill development hub model has a significant advantage in the development of relatively less context-sensitive skills that are fundamentally relational, communicative, and nonalgorithmic in nature. Skills that are difficult to articulate and translate into recipes benefit from high-end, focused, heavily social learning environments supported with constant reinforcement by savvy facilitators and motivated peers that accommodate cocreation of learners' personal learning maps and goals. Because not all—and perhaps not even most—learners are aware of the skills they are trying to develop, the presence of learning facilitators who can help articulate core skill development goals will be a key feature of the learning hub model.

If there is an optimal segmentation of the market for executive skills along the lines of achieving relevance by narrowing the content-context gap or increasing applicability across domains, of developing algorithmic and functional

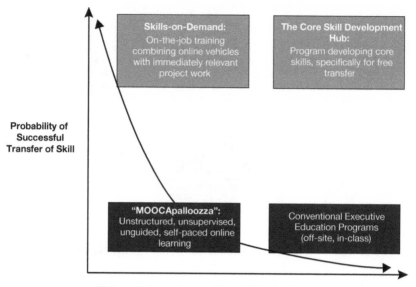

Figure 1.5. Mapping the Executive Learning Landscape Through the Lens of the Near-Far Problem in Skill Transfer

skills through distributed local learning environments and core skills through intensive on-campus learning experiences, all of which can be accomplished by two "corner" models, what then is left of the traditional classroom, a staple of executive education programs across geographies and cultures inherited from the about-to-be disrupted college and MBA programs worldwide?

The situation is pictured in Figure 1.5. As context moves away from locus and content, the case in traditional classrooms and other depersonalized learning environments, the ability to make learning relevant through proximity or deep personalization is lost. As Terwiesch and Ulrich (2014) correctly appreciate, the classroom star is eclipsed by the Internet (online) star, and rendered obsolete by the combination of online subject matter experts whose presentations are curated and made relevant by local coaches, learning facilitators, and gurus residing, working, living, and breathing in the context in which content is delivered to learners.

As the marginal attraction—particularly post-COVID—of leaving home and office to participate in executive learning on the campuses of major providers of learning experiences decreases in proportion to the availability of a ubiquitous *personalized skill development cloud*, competition among providers will increasingly focus on developing the skills least susceptible to digital distributed delivery in ways that are most likely to make them relevant to the greatest number of contexts, namely by designing *learning experiences specifically optimized for the transfer of precisely the skills one cannot "just teach,"* the learning of which must be facilitated in an intensely personal environment.

EXECUTIVE DEVELOPMENT PROGRAMS
ENTER THE DIGITAL MATRIX

Executive development programs have entered a period of disruption catalyzed by the digitalization of content, dense connectivity, and ubiquitously available communication and driven by renewed demand for high-level executive and managerial skills. Unlike other segments of higher education, the executive education market is heavily subsidized by the organizations employing the executives that participate in them. To understand the ongoing transformation of the industry, we map out the (multidimensional) objective functions of executive participants and their organizations, and show how the trio of disruptive forces (disintermediation, disaggregation, and decoupling) that have figured prominently in other industries disrupted by digitalization (media, travel, publishing) are likely to reshape the structure of demand for executive development.

What Learners and Organizations Want: Mapping the Sources of Value and Drivers of Demand

"What does the client want?" is one of the most basic questions anyone who seeks to understand a market must ask. But in the case of executive development, "the client" is not a single, uniform entity. Following are some reasons.

Clients have mixed and varied motives. First, executives' and managers' motivations for engaging in leadership development programs are many and mixed, varying by industry, life and career stage, hierarchical position, and professional background. Some are interested in developing specific skills, others in discovering more about themselves and building their own skill development plan or in plotting out a new course for their lives. Some want to signal their credentials to constituencies within and outside their organizations. Some want to build new connections or refresh old ones. And for many, multiple motives may be operating in cooperative or competitive combination.

The users are not the buyers. Second, any analysis of the executive development industry must capture specific sources of value for the organizations that typically pay the costs of learning and development of the executives that participate in these experiences. Their motivations and value drivers differ from those of the participants. Organizations invest in executive development to enhance their own capabilities, improve coordination, signal commitment to a particular course of action, reward and incentivize behavior, or signal the creation of a new capability. They may be driven to invest in the development in their executives by any subset of these motives. Some executives are aware of the mismatch between their objectives and those of their organizations. As one executive with an apparel brand's umbrella company said, "We must separate the benefit of learning to the individual from what will benefit the firm in the short and long term. Today's culture at large is less forgiving of missteps that are valuable development experiences." Many are not. Most seem aware of a mismatch but are hard-pressed to specify it. Frequently, those who are aware of the tension believe others are not aware of it, or do not believe others are. Our task, then, is to produce both clarity and mutual knowledge—so that everyone knows what everyone else knows.

The (apparent) ends are often means to other ends. We customarily ask, "What do users want?" but far less frequently, "Why do they want it?" In the case of a complex experience good that is a development program, it is essential to examine the value participants attach to the heavily socialized aspect of learning within groups and teams or from on-campus experiences offered by business schools and other organizations, and the ends being pursued by the organizations that invest in programs that train executives in groups or cohorts or try to promote greater coordination among executives across hierarchical levels of divisions. We seek insight into the mechanisms by which executive programs' stated and otherwise revealed sources of value for participants and organizations may further other—often less clearly discerned—objectives.

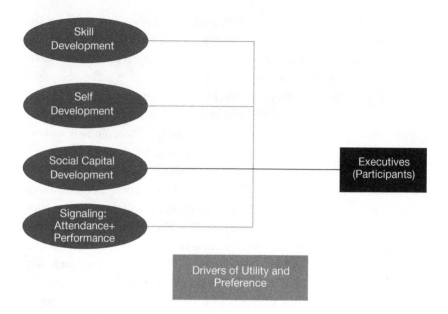

Figure 2.1. Drivers of Utility for Individual Participants in Executive Development Programs

Because we have probed into the "why of the what"—the reasons why executives and organizations make the choices they do in executive development programs—we hope that our inquiry will shed light on the degree to which alternative paths to development substitute for and complement one another.

Mapping the Sources of User Value for Individual Participants

Participants in executive development programs comprise—mostly but not exclusively—middle managers contemplating moves within or between organizations or industries, seasoned executives at the CEO-1 (CEO minus one) and CEO-2 levels seeking to acquire skill sets and capabilities that will enable them to take their organizations to the next level of performance, and individuals with solid academic or professional credentials who want to develop specific "business" or "managerial" skills (Figure 2.1).

Skill Development

Skill development is the most obvious starting point in analyzing executive programs' value to participants, and it is indeed the (stated) source of value that shows up most frequently in our interviews with executive program participants. We construe skills broadly, to include cognitive, meta-cognitive, and noncognitive as well as individual and relational skills and break up the skilling motivation into several components.

Retool

Executive program participants value the development of skills that will plausibly contribute to their professional development and career progress within and outside of their organizations. These include applicable knowledge of new functional domains—such as financial risk management in the Basel 3+ era, cybersecurity or digital marketing in the cloud computing environment—as well as skills related specifically to executive tasks and functions, such as defining and structuring strategic, operational, organizational, and interpersonal challenges and turning them into solvable problems. Executives must (in virtue of their roles) be able to marshal the dialogical and discursive skills required to persuade others through arguments—and challenge and question others' arguments; understand and shape the emotional and visceral landscape of dyads, teams, groups, and entire organizations (perceptual and affective skills); and manage and optimize the intrapersonal allocation of time and energy to competing tasks and objectives (relational and X-factor skills).

Executive program participants range from highly specialized individuals to top management team members, and are distributed throughout the managerial and executive population. Whatever the ends being pursued, whether enhanced ability to manage across knowledge domains and interpersonal styles or the honing and refinement of the executive skill set, a pressing and complex challenge that faces every executive development program is to ensure the transferability of skills from the context of the learning vehicle, be it classroom lecture, case discussion, online material, or small group session—to the context of its application within the organization.

Rethink

Executive programs also provide participants with a valued space in which to refresh their skills and abilities, and perhaps discover gaps and opportunities to develop *skills they did not know they were lacking*, as well as to reflect on the applicability and relevance of new skills and capabilities to personal and organizational problems and scenarios.

Self-Development

Self-development is an important and distinct dimension of value—often overlooked or subsumed under "skill development." Our surveys and interviews with executives, chief learning officers, talent development advisors, and professional development professionals reveal that participants often value a *developmental* outcome and process that is neither tightly nor causally linked to the development of a professional skill or skill set. This value is consistent with the long-standing view that the *personal transformation* associated with leadership development programs operates not only at the levels of knowing (know-what, know-who) and doing (know-how), but also of acting in particular ways toward other people in various settings (know-be-do) (Snook, Khurana, and Nohria 2011). Several components of the self-development value of executive programs stand out.

REFRAME AND REBUILD

Participants often value the opportunity to reframe, reconceptualize, or reinterpret their own professional and personal lives in ways informed by deep and meaningful alternative life designs or models (Moldoveanu 2011), often in the company of others who share the same goals, and under the guidance of coaches and mentors with significant experience in self-transformation and guided behavioral change. Such self-transformation projects and experiences may *not* be instrumental to the performance of a specific organizational task or function, but are often guided instead by an inner quest for greater connectedness, authenticity, integrity, coherence, presence, or some combination thereof. "People who have been questioning their career come back refreshed and re-energized," an executive from an agribusiness company told us. "They see their purpose and want to do good."

REFRESH AND RECHARGE

"Well-being enhancement" is associated with executive programs that blur the line between wellness retreats and "learning and transformation" gatherings. Executive programs generally interrupt routinized flows of actions, thoughts, feelings, and behaviors that dominate quotidian professional lives, providing "regenerative space" in which new ways of being can evolve and develop. Participant well-being is presumed to benefit from the interruptive and disruptive forces that attend a personal holiday from the routines of daily life, both at work and at home. Observed an executive from ABN AMRO, "For me, the benefits have been the time it has afforded for reflection and the time allowed for role playing and experimentation."

Social Capital Development

Social capital ("know-who") tends to be boosted by participation in development programs that afford executives opportunities to get to know one another and build relationships. Networking is important in an economy in which professionals often return to school for skills but may graduate without a job offer. One attendee—a deputy dean for a large university's School of Continuing Studies, noted that building connections has become a larger part of continuing education. "We aren't able to guarantee a job for every person, but we can guarantee that you will meet people who are succeeding in the field you want to get into, and that's very important," he said. "Among elite schools, executives [still] want to have face-to-face programs," remarked an associate dean of executive education at another university. "It's the network effect. Global elites want to be here [that is, on campuses]."

The networking value of executive development programs includes both "knowing" and "being known." It is observed in the deepening and strengthening of interaction, friendship, trust, collaboration, and informational ties with co-workers and close associates on the job, development of new intraorganizational connections that span divisional, functional, and often cultural and national boundaries, and cultivation of reliable within-industry connections with structurally, hierarchically, or functionally equivalent others.

Such ties can have widely varying instrumental and developmental utility for participants. These include pursuing, in the context of a professionally relevant substrate of activities that might include joint participation in case discussions, projects, and group-level exercises, closer relationships with superiors or functional equivalents in their organizations in order to achieve greater levels of visibility or facilitate cooperation and collaboration across functional silos and hierarchical boundaries. Alternatively, connections might be sought with executives elsewhere in the same industry, whether for expanding the capabilities of the focal business through collaboration with peer firms or to enhance opportunities for advancement, perhaps in a different organization. Relationships with executives in different industries can be relevant to the future activities of a participant's employer, or to the participant's own future career plans.

Signaling

Economists (since Spence 1973; 1974) and sociologists (since Simmel 1923) have argued that the decision to pursue personal development can be understood as a signaling move. The decision to invest time in an expensive execution education program signals to the market participants' own information about how competent, talented, and hardworking they themselves are. "Who could possibly know you better than you know yourself?"—is the (rhetorical) question asked by most signaling model proponents. Useful information about participants is provided by their very admission to a highly selective program and by their performance within and completion of it acknowledged by a *certificate* and transcript, and possibly more textured records of activities and interactions with instructors, facilitators, other participants, and course content including concepts, models, and methods. Program selectivity and overall status independent of selectivity affect the value of signaling, which involves two components.

SIGNALING I—SELECTION AND SELF-SELECTION

The signaling value of participation in an executive development program is proportional to the cost of the investment (time and money) and the program's inherent selectivity. The dollar cost of programs is typically borne by employers, the investment of time by participants. Because employers cover the cost of attendance, they often determine employee eligibility. That participants must both *qualify* for a program and be selected by their organizations to be supported to participate in that program effectively doubles the signaling value of participation. Selection value is diminished by high admission rates, even if program costs remain high. Signaling value is greatest for low-admission-rate, high-price programs, and the length and intensity of programs can function as a signal of the executive's own belief in her or his skills and abilities.

SIGNALING II—CERTIFICATION AND CREDENTIALING

Certificates and diplomas that acknowledge completion of a sequence of learning or development experiences signal the acquisition of a demonstrable skill. This adds currency to participants' personal capital that is quite independent of the signaling value that accrues to having been selected by one's parent organization, and subsequently applied, and been admitted to an executive development program. The value of certification as a signal of skill varies with the skill set in question. Cognitive-functional-algorithmic skills are more readily certifiable (even if their applicability to out-of-the-classroom settings is uncertain) owing to their amenability to quantification via exams, tests, and quizzes. Noncognitive, nonalgorithmic, and X-factor skills are less so on account of the challenges faced in measuring and speaking about them in a common language system.

The signaling tokens (for example, admission, performance, credentialing) bestowed by executive development programs allow participants to redefine the skills and capabilities profile they present to their own organizations and to the outside market for talent. A software designer might exploit participation in a leading "agile development" program to rebrand as a development team manager in the Web 2.0 environment, a mortgage-backed securities executive with a set of digital badges attesting to completion of targeted financial risk management training programs as a risk management expert in the post-2008 era. Faced with the diminishing "half-life" of organizational membership and of the signaling value of degrees, executives are increasingly turning to the nimble, rapidly evolving fabric of certificates, "micro-" and "nano-degrees," and digital badges proffered by some programs and many "aggregator" platforms like Coursera, edX and LinkedIn Learning to reposition their skill set and value within their organizations and the broader market for executive talent. A human resources manager might use such a credential to signal a newly acquired skill set in coaching and leadership development.

Distribution of Objectives and Sources of Value Among Executives:
Three Differences That Make a Difference

The objectives with which participants come to executive development programs, albeit varied, mixed, and multiple, exhibit trends with respect to how they vary with origin ("who they are"), functional expertise ("what they do"), and hierarchical level ("whom they manage"). These trends become key "modulators" of the demand characteristics of executive programs worldwide.

"Who They Are": Geographical Distribution

Although the market for executive skill development programs has matured in North America (where they originated) and Europe, demand is rising in growing and emergent economies, in Asia in particular. The difference between the $2.9 billion per annum (in 2018 dollars) Asian companies spend on leadership development and the $10 billion spent annually by North American companies understates actual demand for executive skill development in the "zero-experience" sector, in which participants often pay the tuition for programs that provide bridges to the socioeconomic, organizational, and cultural landscapes of other (predominantly North American) work environments, and that includes the "Executive MBA" market more heavily supported by payments from participants than its North American counterpart.

"What They Do": Functional Focus and Expertise

Participants who seek to develop additional technical-algorithmic-functional skills are interested in the most efficient mode of acquiring them, and unambiguously signaling to the market that they have acquired them. "Risk management," "social media marketing," "real estate lending," "health care logistics," and "the technology and economics of BlockChain and BitCoin" are exemplary of functionally framed certificates that attest to acquisition of a skill base, accretive to existing credentials and certifiable capabilities that afford explicit differentiation in the market for functional skills. Implicit in these skills is a lexicon that enables those who acquire them to decode events in the field and to predict their impact on business and the market, conversational capital that enables these individuals to speak confidently and competently about these events to others within the organization, and a repertoire of well-defined problems experts in the field are called upon to solve, together with a family of reliable or at least standardized methods for solving them. Participants focused on developing "relational" and "communicative" skill bases typically attach more value to the self-developmental and self-transformational aspects of executive development programs and expanded opportunities they afford for social capital development and amplification.

"Whom They Manage": Career Cycle and Hierarchical Distribution

Discernable in association with the career and hierarchical modulator of executive program demand are three established segments—alongside an emerging fourth segment of participants.

1. Participants contemplating a first switch to a managerial career, typically two to ten years out of college and unwilling or otherwise unable to apply for and enroll in a Master of Business Administration (MBA) program, are likely to seek to develop functional business skills that will enable them to take the next step in their careers, and hence to weigh skill development programs that result in high-signaling value certificates and diplomas more heavily than the development of managerial or leadership skills. This bias may be due to the ease with which functional and algorithmic skill acquisition can now be certified. But it may also be due to imperfect awareness and understanding of the very

significant value of noncognitive, nonalgorithmic skills currently labeled as "soft" to the value of a junior manager's life prospects and personal capital. Participants in this segment also typically attach greater importance to the skill development, certification, and signaling value than to the networking value of executive development programs.

2. The motives and objectives of mid-level and senior managers with significant (ten to fifteen years) experience in leadership and managerial roles will vary widely, but they will typically attach greater importance to executive programs' development of specific, critical leadership skills and attendant network and social capital amplification than to the development of specific functional skills and certification value of the programs. As a group, they tend to be far more attuned to the potential to develop "difficult-to-articulate" skills that will serve them in key managerial roles and frequently value the potential for intra- and interorganizational expansion of their professional and personal networks.

3. Senior executives (CEO-1 [CEO minus 1] and CEO-2) typically favor the opportunities for self-transformation and reflection afforded by executive development programs, not least because of the dialog and interaction they facilitate among participants at similar life and career stages. The experience, exploratory, and transformational value frequently outweighs the networking, signaling, certification, and functional skill development components of such programs for these individuals.

4. The growing gap between the skill base possessed by college graduates and that sought by employers, even for entry-level positions, and encompassing communicative, relational, and X-skills -as well as functional skills the acquisition and transfer of which are measurable across contexts, accounts for the emergence of the fourth, very large, segment of the executive learning market, the *zero-work-experience* group just graduated from college or university and cognizant of the need to tool up with skills not acquired in school. Analyses of the wage distribution of recent graduates, by major and discipline, region, country of origin, and economic sector, sheds little light on the demand characteristic exhibited by this segment of the executive development market. Early returns from programs delivered in both online (HBSOnline) and in-person (Wharton) settings suggest that the no-experience crowd is specifically focused on precisely the functional and relational skills and network amplification their college experience did not provide.

Mapping the Sources of Value for Participants' Organizations

An estimated 75 to 80 percent of the cost of executive programs is paid by employer organizations—and that represents a sizable outlay. In 2012, U.S. corporations spent an estimated $13.6 billion on leadership development activities, and the top six hundred companies worldwide an estimated $10.2 billion on external providers of leadership development (authors, compiled from Bersin and Associates 2008–2013). That spend grew at 5 percent per annum over the seven years that followed (compiled from Bersin and Associates 2013–2019). The field of established "executive development programs" associated with business schools and dedicated organizations stands at about $1.2 billion a year (in 2015 dollars), and the most rapidly growing component of the "skills-on-demand landscape" of the $41 billion worldwide learning industry is that for business and executive skills (compiled from Docebo 2014 and 2017). Moreover, the scope of "leadership development" has also expanded to include value-added activities in which "standard" providers of executive education programs do not engage.

As we will see, the sources of value associated with the development of new organizational capabilities; the facilitation of communication, coordination, cooperation, and collaboration; and the spatio-temporal concentration of the executive development "activity set" figure prominently for organizations— even as they do not figure nearly as markedly in the objective functions of participants (Figure 2.2). Given organizations' role in funding and shaping the evolution of executive development, it is important to unpack, with the same level of precision as that employed for individual objectives, executive programs' sources of value to organizations.

Capability and Competency Formation

Just as participants want to build skill and signal the fact they have built it, organizations are keen to build organizational capabilities and competencies— strategic and operational agility, absorptive and integrative capacity over new technologies and market segments, cross-cultural collaboration, and strategic innovation. The urgency not only of possessing, but of being able to quickly develop such capabilities is heightened in an economic environment characterized by fast hard-asset depreciation and a strong dependence of returns to capital on the productivity of labor. Explained an executive at a large tech com-

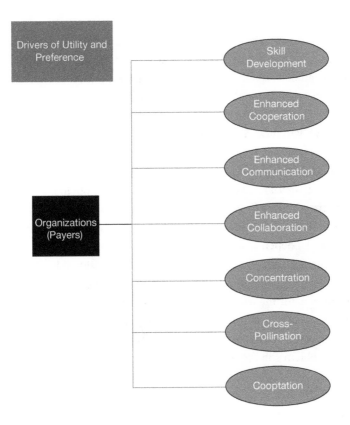

Figure 2.2. Components of Utility and Value Drivers for Participants' Organizations

pany: "We want our leaders to have a broad perspective. Business challenges constantly change, and the ability of people to drive results needs to be constantly developed. In this kind of quickly changing world, we need execution, decision making, leadership, and adaptive learning." Explained an executive at a tech manufacturer: "My company's roots are in manufacturing, but we've now added in aligned services. The transformation requires different competencies....For example, clients for services require leaders with broader business competencies than purely manufacturing. This kind of change is leading our company to break employees out of their home-grown units for broader exposure, including through executive development programming."

That organizational capabilities are clearly not equivalent to random collections of specific individual skills and capabilities is as evident in old economy businesses like manufacturing (Milgrom and Roberts 1990) as in the new information-and-knowledge economy (Garicano 2000). Organizations depend for their success on *specific* managerial and executive skill sets in complicated ways: organizational capability is embodied in specific combinations and collections of technical-functional, affective, and X-skills. The complex nature of the relationship between employee skill and organizational capability explains—in part—the high variance in the payoff to organizations of investments in individual skill development.

The fact that the dependence of organizational capabilities on some combination of managerial and executive skills is intuitively obvious to most chief talent officers accounts for much of the continued emphasis on development programs and activities. However, there is no single explanatory model that accounts for the dependence of organizational capabilities on the quality of executive, managerial, and employee skills at the individual level. The challenge of turning a set of high-functioning individuals into a high-performance group is often daunting. Heterogeneity of problem-solving skills seems to be correlated with better group-level problem-solving performance (Dunbar 2001; Moldoveanu and Leclerc 2015)—an insight also demonstrated by analytical models of problem solving with heterogeneous groups of agents (Hong and Page 2001), and the "moneyball" effects of "star" team performance of a set of "non-star" individuals have been documented empirically, but these examples rest on highly specific assumptions and historical cases that scarcely support drawing broad conclusions. The point is not that organizations are not well advised to invest in executive skill development, but that many additional variables influence the skills-to-capabilities link and their interplay becomes even more complex when rapid adaptive shifts in the capability base are required.

Communication, Coordination, and the Cultural Value of Connectivity

Joint participation in executive learning programs can help teams, groups, divisions, and organizations develop common-language systems including common nomenclature, models, and methods that facilitate coordination. New concepts become focal points in intraorganizational coordination games that replicate a business's culture (Kreps 1990) and communication (via the creation of a shared *code* of intraorganizational communication) (Arrow 1974; Bolton and Dewatripont 1994). The value to organizations of the "conversational capital" developed by executive development programs is therefore separable and in fact separate from that of "capability development." It can also be realized independently of the development of specific skills in participants: it is possible for one to speak knowledgeably about credit default swaps, Gaussian copulas, and Ito processes as models of the time series of stock prices without being able to *explain* these terms to the satisfaction of a professional risk manager, or to *make use* of the models and methods normally associated with their usage in order to perform an organizational task. Coordination and communication can thus be viewed more broadly as a core set of organizational competencies that facilitate a wide range of more specific capabilities requiring efficient and reliable communication and effective and fault-tolerant coordination.

Cooperation and Collaboration

The value of facilitating connectivity among intraorganizational participants in executive programs transcends that of reducing the cost of communication and collaboration and enhancing the expressivity and applicability of face-to-face and electronic conversation. Experiential, feedback-intensive, problem-solving-oriented development programs help participants develop an *esprit de corps* based on a deeper understanding of *who*, *how*, and *when* to trust, and more reliable estimates of others' integrity and competence (Moldoveanu and Baum 2014)—essential to the instantiation of the well-functioning "collective mind" that high-performing organizations strive for. Organizations leverage the trust-building effect of enhanced connectivity to boost the efficiency and effectiveness of cooperation and collaboration (based on greater trust in integrity and competence). Mentoring relationships emerge consequent to same-organization executives at different hierarchical levels co-participating in executive programs. As an executive at Samsung explained: "Our company is still relatively young....Lots of new people are coming from fast-moving consumer goods sectors, with their own strong cultures, and need to learn ours. The company emphasizes relationships to navigate the company, and mentoring helps. Top leaders spend more time on culture in development, which can then trickle down."

Concentration: The Value of Localizing Intervention

Executive development and learning occurs "all the time" in organizations—through coaching, mentoring, dispensing of informal advice, and annual and monthly task- and behavior-related individualized feedback in dyads and groups. Targeted, localized executive learning interventions and development programs enable organizations to *concentrate* their learning and development activities in the four-dimensional space spanned by space, time, people, and skills so as to more easily track, measure, observe, and shape the leadership development process. Concentration optimizes development efforts in order to maximize their impact and the observability of outcomes. Concentration of developmental activity becomes important when an organization needs to produce a new skill or capability base "on demand" as a result of a rapid shift in strategic focus or market conditions. Observed an executive at a chemical company that uses executive programs for fast restarts that track changes in market conditions: "There are evergreen needs, what we expect of company leaders at every level, a base set of skills and values. Then there is the more dynamic set that is aligned to the current business strategy, and that changes fairly quickly. These things have to be developed fast, changed fast, and not fallen in love with. Boards are asking for a refresh around strategy every three years."

Cooptation

Executive development programs' signaling and perquisite values function as talent management and retention tools and mechanisms. Through choices of *who attends*, *what they attend*, and *who pays for what*, organizations shape executive, managerial, and employee incentives - including those that affect individuals' decisions to stay or leave. Observed an executive in a foreign government agency: "External training is used as a retention tool, as we are lower paid than other parts of the civil service." Added an executive from Japanese e-retailer Rakuten: "Japanese companies have often used exec ed programs as a reward for work well done," and an executive from a European bank noted: "Going to an external program is also a viable alternative to higher pay, both because it broadens your skill set, but also because EU banking compensation is not going to rise any further in the near term."

Cross-Pollination

Inasmuch as *executive* education program participants learn from each other as much as from content, instructors, coaches, facilitators, and context, the cross-organization and cross-industry learning and skill transfer components of such programs serve to inform sponsoring employers about broader "best practices," "good routines," and "great ideas." Observed an executive in a Japanese conglomerate: "We are not so familiar with the competitive, harsh discussion and debate in Western corporate decision making. We send executives...abroad or create a similar program in Japan in order to immerse them in such an environment." Added an executive from Baosteel: "We have one three-year training program aimed at encouraging those on our succession list to be more entrepreneurial. We send them to visit private sector Chinese companies over the course of three years. Those people improved quite a lot; most are now leaders of the subsidiaries."

Distribution of Sources of Value Among Organizations: Three Differences That Make a Difference

Like executives who participate, organizations that invest in executive development programs can also be *segmented* according to what they value and why, using a set of distinctions that perhaps is less obvious than those at play in understanding the motivational landscape of participants.

ORGANIZATIONAL MINDSET: TALENT AS A COST VERSUS TALENT AS AN ASSET

Whereas "human capital" shows up as a cost ("headcount") on accounting measures of organizational performance, "talent" is proclaimed by leading organizations to be their most important asset, the key to further and future innovation, differentiation, profitability, and survival. These two interpretations are simultaneously at play in most organizations, and patterns of investment and promotion that favor one over the other, and consequently determine the mindset with which the development of employees, managers, and executives is approached, serve as a basis for differentiation.

"Talent as an asset"-minded organizations, inclined to emphasize the proactive development of managerial and leadership skills and organizational capabilities, are likely to make investments that highlight the skill and capability development and collaborative capital enhancement dimensions of the typical organizational objective function, and therefore favor programs high in demonstrable self-development of participants and development and transfer of applicable skills to their work environments.

"Talent as a cost"-minded organizations, which tend to favor the coordination and communication cost reduction and the cooptation components of the organizational objective function, favor programs that are not very different from organizational events and retreats—social lubricant injections that decrease communication and coordination costs within the organization. Both mindsets seem to function like a Kuhnian "paradigm" (Kuhn 1962), wherein a scientific theory is true or valid within the boundaries of theoretical constructs and experimental and validation practices of the discipline that "speaks its language." An executive at a multinational CPG, echoing Henry Ford's "whether you believe you can or you believe you cannot, you are right!" remarked: "If you believe in it, you invest in it. If you don't, you don't. And all the measurement stuff in the world can't justify what we invest in."

Organizational Structure: Centralized Versus Decentralized Talent Development Processes

Organizations are differentiated on the basis of the degree to which their talent management processes and functions are centralized, as measured by the degree of concentration of decision rights (initiation, ratification, implementation) related to the development of their managerial and executive talent base. Organizations with highly centralized processes and functions tend to favor executive development programs that aim to develop identifiable and measurable skills and capabilities (which represent "deliverables" in the year-end reports of chief learning officers, chief operating officers, and vice presidents and directors of human resources departments) and that decrease communication and coordination costs within the organization by reaching broad constituencies of employees. An Asian oil and gas company's centralized approach to rotation for development was explained by one of its executives as follows: "Our People Development Committee [PDC] comprises members of the senior leadership who meet periodically to discuss mass talent mobilization. For top talent, this function is performed by the Talent Council, which is similar to the PDC but includes more senior members. They look at the list of top talent and assess them on their leadership competencies and other criteria including their performance and verbal feedback from their reports. It's a combination of many factors. The Talent Council then matches top talent to available locations for assignment." Organizations with decentralized talent development processes and functions, by contrast, defer specific objective functions to their divisions, subsidiaries, and teams, which may vary according to differing degrees of intradivisional centralization of development-related decisions.

Organizational Practice: Formal Versus Informal Talent Development Processes

Organizations are also differentiated on the basis of the formality of their executive and leadership development functions and talent management functions more generally. Relatively formal talent development processes are reflected in internal corporate universities' awarding of certificates that attest to certifiable levels of expertise in particular skills and domains and the development of intraorganizational "knowledge" (in the sense of Garicano 2000) or "skill" hierarchies that track executives' individual internally or externally achieved degrees of certification. Such organizations are likely to value the certification and certifiable skill level achievement dimension of executive development and learning programs. Grainger's process was explained by one of its executives: "When I get assigned to a VP, my job is to collect information on their performance, summarize it on one sheet, share insights and feedback received with the executive team, and then sit down with that person to discuss. Out of this process, we identify additional development required, including intense programs, like programs offered at Harvard, or EMBA programs, etc. Out of those reviews we also decide who will participate in Harvard programs. We also exchange ideas with leaders on what else they can do to improve competence and capability for current and future roles."

Integration of executive training and education with a business's strategic and operational goals can amplify the formal aspects of the talent development organization. How this emerging feature plays out was explained by an executive at an agribusiness company thus: "It was very simple in the past. I go to the president of the company, talk about the needs across the business, and he gives me a budget. We agree that we keep the budget in his office so that money isn't redirected when we're under stress in the business. That's worked very well. Now we're integrating the budget more into long-range planning. For high potentials, I see us continuing to fund through the president. But we're thinking about a system of chargebacks to business, having them fund our work through an allocation process."

How the Digital Matrix Is
Disrupting the Market

Executives and organizations value learning and development programs differently (Figure 2.3). Apparent similarities mask divergent motives and incentives that the disruptive forces of digitalization have uncovered and rendered transparent.

For example, organizations and individuals both value targeted interventions and learning experiences that develop skills. However, individuals value those that enhance career-long prospects within their organizations, industries, and beyond, whereas organizations value those specific to organizational objectives and that can optimally be combined and synthesized into organizational

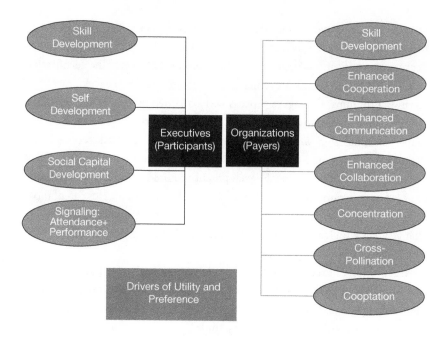

Figure 2.3. Summary of Executive Programs' Sources of Value and Demand Drivers for Executive Participants and Their Organizations

capabilities. Individuals and organizations both value self-transformation and "well-being enhancement," albeit with nuances that highlight different motivations. Individuals value the transformational and restorative dimensions of such programs, whereas organizations see them as modes of cooptation and concentration of the executive development process or as a means by which teams can develop the collaborative capital required to solve specific problems, having shared memorable times together.

Development of greater levels of connectivity is also valued by both participants and their organizations. So too is the formation of intraorganizational networks with densely connected topologies that optimize communication and coordination costs and build collaborative capital that helps both individuals and organizations pursue objectives more efficiently. But then distinctions arise: individuals often value specifically the development of personal networks beyond the boundaries of the organization and its industry that boost immediate and more distant career advancement prospects, which, clearly, organizations do not. And whereas organizations and individuals both value the cross-pollination value of executive programs as "memetic" sources of new organizational routines, technologies, and ideas, individuals often in addition value interactions with executives in other organizations and industries as sources of additional options in the market for their talents. The signaling and certification aspects of executive development programs are valued by both organizations and individual executive participants, but they are significantly sharper for individual participants seeking to enhance resumes and credential bases.

What Happens When Executive Programs Enter the Digital Matrix?

The "market-based solution concept" for coupled and potentially competing objectives and incentives of users and payers is simple enough: apportion the cost of programs to individuals and their organizations in ways that mirror what is valued by each by requiring that the costs of programs that emphasize individual (personal network expansion, self-exploratory self-development, individual skill development, individual signaling) over organizational (individual skills the transfer of which measurably augments organizational capabilities, development of collaborative capital) value be borne by participants. What has kept organizations from adopting this solution to date is that the sources of value for individuals and organizations are blurry and ill-defined, and typically *bundled, intermediated,* and *coupled* in most executive development programs. A program offered by a top-ranking business school offers a hard-to-separate mix of personal skill development, organizational capability formation, personal network amplification, and collaborative capital, all or mostly paid for by the organization. Business schools aggregate a variety of learning vehicles (modules, courses, classes, content) that couple different sources of value (development of conversational capital and of a high-level dialogical skill) and intermediate between instructors (faculty members) and participants.

Enter *disaggregation, decoupling,* and *disintermediation,* the trio of forces responsible for digital disruption precipitated by the informational and computational "tectonic shifts" of the past decade and the culture of sharing, transacting, collaborating, and learning enabled thereby. Lower and ever decreasing search costs; ubiquitous access to broadband links and learning management systems that together form the evolving "personal learning cloud"; executive reputation registries platforms that track with great precision individuals' value to the organizations that employ them (for example, SalesForce.com); and the "quasi-free agency" of instructors, trainers, and business school faculty members who can deliver content through various platforms collectively afford *organizations the option of paying only for what they value*, leaving *individuals to pay for that which they value but their organizations do not.*

Now, organizations can design skill development programs that solve the *"far transfer of skill problem"* because they are delivered internally and at the level of groups and teams that must work together to turn individual skill into organizational capability. Cooptation and concentration value can be maximized by making such programs selective with respect to who (and whose team) is admitted and predictive of promotion and advancement. Organizations can leverage the wide base of freelance executive mentors, coaches, and instructors, and an evolving personal coaching cloud to reduce the cost of executive development offerings. The forces that drive the digital vortex figure prominently in delivering the market solution to the "mixed motives" and "multidimensional value drivers" problems. The divergence in the objectives of users and payers positions the industry for immediate disruption simply on the basis of presenting payers an unbundled menu of easily searchable options, thereby reducing the bargaining power of aggregators and intermediators. How this is likely to come about can be shown by unpacking the effects of each of the three forces.

Disaggregation

The disaggregation of different components of executive development programs is facilitated by the abundance of information regarding the quality of instructors and offerings in any one program, or offered by any one provider, as well as regarding the specific "feel" of the learning experience. (As we shall see later, client ratings and feedback in the field of executive development, to date, are not very useful as indicators of the degree to which programs help participants build the skills their organizations can turn into capabilities they value). Disaggregation enables the provisioning of executive development *à la carte*, allowing participants and organizations to choose individual program components that maximize their specific objectives and very often *on demand*, as required by organizations that need to develop certain capabilities quickly. Business schools, talent development organizations, and large-scale consultancies have traditionally offered programs composed of *bundles* of lectures, case discussions, and opportunities for interaction that facilitates both networking and learning. Profitability in such a model is driven by providers' ability to bundle into high price-cost margin offerings low-cost content and experiences (such as repackaged lectures and case discussions from MBA and undergraduate business programs) and carefully selected high-delivery-cost ("premium") activities (personalized coaching, project-based learning, feedback-intensive group sessions). In a disaggregated regime low-cost, commodified components such as lectures and teaching note-scripted case discussions, quizzes, tests, and problem sets are offered separately, leaving participants and organizations to select only the highest value-added components from any one program, and to mix and match components from different programs. A disaggregated environment makes it possible for organizations to measure the outcomes and sources of value of each component of an executive development program, and to pick those components that maximize the organization's development objectives, leaving participants to cover the cost of modules, programs, and components that maximize objectives they have that are not shared by their organizations.

Decoupling

Decoupling increases the "choicefulness" organizations and participating executives have regarding their development experiences even further. A classroom lecture discussion, a standard feature of programs run by business schools in both custom and open-enrollment settings, can be decoupled into a "transmission" component—the presentation itself—and a "feedback-deliberation" component that serves to clarify and deepen, through a process of public dialog, participants' understanding of the content presented. The *transmission* component can be replicated at negligible marginal cost in distributed learning environments with the added advantage of enabling participants to slow down and replay content that at first seemed unclear, and prestructure the discussion component by grouping, classifying, and ranking participants' queries, questions, challenges, objections, and rebuttals in advance of a far more focused and higher-value-added in-person, or Zoom/MSTeams/Hangout-mediated discussion. Decoupling intensifies the effects of disaggregation and supports ever finer distinctions among, and refined choices of, specific aspects of learning interaction that maximize the objectives of individuals and organizations.

Disintermediation

The disintermediation of the field from a state in which instructors, be they faculty members, master trainers, coaches, or other senior executives, must provide their services through their home institution to a state in which they can choose the platform and the venue in which they will teach entails that client executives and organizations can choose to pay for individual instructors according to the reliability and utility of the results they bring about. It both liberates instructors from having to act through intermediaries (for example, executive program organizations that are part of business schools that are part of universities) that compensate them according to policies aimed at promoting horizontal equity and liberates executive participants and client organizations from having to acquire entire programs or modules, often taught by instructors of different levels of quality, while paying a large premium to cover the operational expenses of the intermediator. The new "demarcation line" that emerges for most clients of executive development experiences is the specific need for the kind of certification that can be provided by a university or by a professional organization that can grant continuing education units. If the inferences we made from our study are valid across the industry, we expect that organizations seeking to develop capabilities—regardless of participant certification—should and will be more likely to take advantage of the evolving disintermediation of the industry and contract directly with talented instructors that have demonstrated they can help learners acquire and apply the requisite skills, leaving executives seeking to "signal with credentials" to pay for university- and professional-service-organization-run courses that enhance their personal signaling value.

(3)

DISRUPTING THE LANDSCAPE
OF SUPPLIERS OF EXECUTIVE
DEVELOPMENT PROGRAMS

Even as the demand for executive skills continues to grow, executive development worldwide has entered a period of disruption caused by the digitalization of content, connectivity, and communication. The current offerings of many executive education program providers fall short of creating new skills in executives and developing fresh capabilities for organizations. Based on a study of the programs offered by the business schools, consultancies, corporate universities, and online education platforms, we analyze the advantages, and the constraints, of existing programs; map out the vehicles they use for skill development—such as case discussions, lectures, simulations, coaching sessions, live projects—in terms of their potential to develop executives for the future; and examine the impact of the forces of digital disruption—the disaggregation and disintermediation of activity chains, and the decoupling of the sources of value in education programs—on the future of executive education.

The Emerging Landscape of
Executive Education

We have contrasted the objectives of the managers attending executive development programs with those of the organizations that sponsor them, and described the fast-changing landscape of the executive education industry in order to answer important questions about who wants what and why. We now analyze the major providers of executive education programs, so we can better understand the industry's supply dynamics and map out substitutes and complements of the sources of value that organizations and participants find in executive development programs. Doing so helps us understand the impact that the disruptive forces of digitalization—disaggregation, disintermediation, and decoupling—are having on the education providers' cost structures. To facilitate the comparison among offerings of different providers, we distill the executive development offerings available at present into a set of learning vehicles, ranging from classroom-based lectures and case study discussions and simulations to on-site and off-site skill-oriented and developmental coaching to online learning vehicles that try to impart the right skill to the right person at the right time and analyze each learning vehicle with an eye to its likely effects on skills developed and applied.

Mapping the Landscape of Executive Education Providers

Executive education comes in many forms and is delivered by an increasing number of organizations ranging from external providers—such as online certifiers and aggregators, consultancies, business schools, and universities— to internal suppliers such as organizations' human resource (HR) and talent-management functions and corporate universities. Most providers offer several products. Business schools, for instance, offer as executive MBA programs, custom programs, continuing education programs, and so on. Each of them has a different cost structure, participant profile and value proposition, so they occupy different positions and compete differently in the market.

Executive education as we know it now began after World War II, when leading U.S. business schools—such as Harvard Business School in 1945 and Columbia Business School and Northwestern's Kellogg School of Management in 1951—started offering nondegree business education programs. Most were residential programs, with participants living and working with their peers on a university campus for a short interval (weeks), often during the spring or the summer. The prototype appears to have been Harvard Business School's World War II–era fifteen-week production management course that retrained senior managers so they could switch from their civilian posts to wartime roles.

From the 1950s to the 1980s, executive education consisted mostly of university-based programs. Participants learned the latest theories of management and the techniques with which to apply them, largely by studying cases and listening to lectures. The faculty tended to decide what courses would be offered on the basis of their research interests. "For the attending executive, the experience itself was seen as both a reward and as preparation for their promotion to senior levels," points out an industry study by Jay Conger and Katherine Xin (Conger and Xin 2000). Companies relied on university-delivered programs to develop executives in functional areas, such as marketing or finance, as well as in broader policy-related issues, such as environmental regulation (Crotty and Soule 1997).

A shift took place in the early 1990s, when companies started using executive education programs to bring about organizational changes, rather than responding or catering to managers' developmental needs. The popularity of "custom programs" subsequently soared: more than half the members of the University Consortium for Executive Education (UNICON) reported that over 50 percent of their revenues between 2005 and 2010 came from custom programs (Lloyd and Newkirk 2011). While the shift from open-enrollment, classroom-based programs to custom programs designed for and with the cooperation of client organizations increased the popularity of business school executive education programs, it also enabled new kinds of organizations, such as strategy and human resource consultancies, to enter the field (Figure 3.1).

Let us focus on each class of provider and bring into focus key strengths and challenges.

Business Schools' Executive MBA and Open-Enrollment Programs

By "business schools," we mean the faculties of business administration or management at established universities—and "established universities" means universities that are recognized as such. Universities are notoriously hard to set up, and startup costs in both time (institutional hurdles) and funds (infrastructure, certification) are currently prohibitive. At one level, business schools serve as selection and certification engines. They provide signals—through their selection criteria and records of achievement—to the employment market, regarding the skills executives are expected to have acquired from the courses they have taken. Business schools are also social capital amplifiers, offering participants the opportunity to form relationships in their own and other industries while attending programs together.

Business schools' Executive MBA (EMBA) and open-enrollment programs use both on-campus and mixed-mode (classroom and on-the-job projects) teaching. These programs of cohort-based study vary in length. Some run for

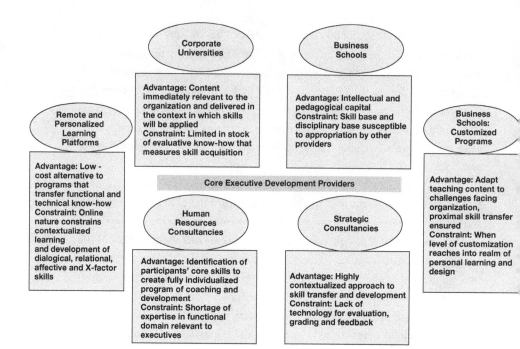

Figure 3.1. Map of Executive Education Development Program Providers

up to eight weeks, some are broken up into multiple modules over two or three years; programs that focus on developing a specific topic or skill usually extend from two to five days. By contrast, custom executive programs are usually in-person programs commissioned by a single company and conducted on a campus, at the company, or at a neutral location such as a conference center or retreat. They are developed and taught in one of at least three ways: by business school faculty through the school's executive education departments; privately, by business school or other faculty acting individually, in ways that are not intermediated by the business school that employs them; or by independent consultants and nonfaculty instructors. They typically last between one and two weeks.

CORE DIFFERENTIATORS AND VALUE DRIVERS

Business schools differentiate themselves from other executive education providers by their intellectual and pedagogical capital. Since the 1970s, their faculties have comprised mostly academics with doctoral degrees in the social sciences, such as economics; psychology; and related subdisciplines such as finance, accounting, marketing, and strategy. These academics have established different degrees of legitimate expertise—or cognitive jurisdiction (Moldoveanu 2009)—over the functional disciplines of business—such as strategy, marketing, finance, human resources, and organization behavior (Figure 3.2). Unlike business school curricula before 1970, when classroom discussions of managerial problems were led by current or former executives, the curricula of EMBA and most open-enrollment programs today are carved up along disciplinary lines. Different academic disciplines have established their intellectual jurisdiction over the teaching of functional topics: psychology and sociology over leadership, operations research and microeconomics over operations management, economics and sociology over strategy, and so on.

Because of their standardized curricula, business schools find it difficult to differentiate themselves from one another (Moldoveanu and Martin 2008; Datar and Garvin 2010). However, they differentiate themselves from other types of education providers by their pedagogical tools and tropes. Academics at the business schools have learned to turn the empirical data and theoretical frameworks associated with academic disciplines into frameworks and methods that help solve business problems—and which form the substance of the teaching notes and course designs that are the essential canon of business school teaching.

Business schools also differentiate themselves by the selection and evaluation practices they deploy to measure candidate quality and skill acquisition: batteries of precourse (admission) and postcourse (exams and quizzes) tests associated with teaching in the standard formats of higher education. They have developed expertise in evaluating the acquisition of cognitive and technical skills by formulating questions that produce the "right" spread among respondents' scores—which enable employers to differentiate among graduates according to their performance and legitimate the signaling value of the certificates and diplomas business schools award.

Challenges and Constraints

Business schools' standing and current role in executive development face several challenges.

- First, their pedagogical and teaching tools are optimized for the development of the cognitive, technical, and algorithmic skills associated with functional

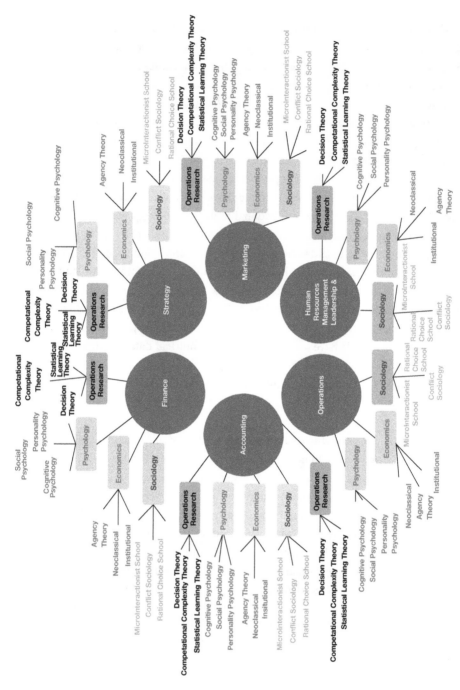

Figure 3.2. Map of the Division of Labor in Business Schools

disciplines, rather than built specifically for the development of relational, affective, communicative, or X-factor skills. Organizational decision makers on executive development have realized that the "one stop shop" for executive skill development that business schools were thought of is no more. They are increasingly seen as providing an increasingly small piece of an increasingly complicated nexus.

- Second, business schools focus on teaching canonical models and methods that constitute a standard managerial toolkit, which is usually suited to address only well-defined and well-structured business problems (Moldoveanu and Leclerc 2015), whereas executive predicaments and "situations" arise without preset labels: they are not "designed to be solved by the formulaic application of a model hatched by economics or other disciplines"—as one high-ranking executive in the higher ed space told us.

- Third, business schools' learning "form factors"—the low instructor-to-learner ratio and the structured and strictured interaction formats—are optimized for large classes that economize on the time of faculty, graders, and teaching assistants, and are often imported without much change into the (much smaller) executive classroom. As a result, business schools' executive development offerings limit the opportunities for the development of communicative, relational, affective, and X-factor skills that are increasingly in demand in organizations, and which require intensive, iterative, personalized, and specific feedback.

Organizational and institutional inertia in academic settings are likely to restrict possibilities for significant changes in response to the new landscape of executive development. Business schools' learning "production functions"—the specific combinations of learners, content, context, and instructors that produce learning experiences—are not easily adaptable to the demands for new skills or new ways of learning. With few exceptions, they must fit in with the academic machinery of the business schools' parent universities. Their learning production functions depend on a workforce—academics trained as researchers and investing substantial time and effort in doing research—that has high fixed costs and a high overhead: revenues from teaching must subsidize the costs of research. The structure can be modified only in the long run because of academics' tenure-based employment and compensation systems. Consequently, business schools' responses to the disintermediation, disaggregation, and decoupling unleashed by the digital economy seem to be heavily constrained.

The external, industry-related competitive challenges business schools face in the executive development field are matched by challenges they face from within—brought about by an increasingly fractious and disintermediated workforce. Even as business schools are strategically and operationally viscous—if not inert—the employment agreements of business school faculty are far less restrictive than those of instructors working with other executive education providers. Tenured academics are quasi free agents, with their contracts allowing them to teach, consult, and lecture without restrictions. This contractual freedom has enabled a significant secondary market for their services—allowing consultancies and corporate universities to appropriate the business schools' pedagogical skills and disciplinary base by hiring their faculty to teach at higher rates than those they could command teaching on behalf of their own institution's executive program. This trend renders business schools increasingly vulnerable to a dynamics of disintermediation-reintermediation we find increasingly common in business education.

Business Schools' Custom Programs

Most business schools offer executive education programs that are customized to organizations or to a specific function in an organization. They are offered either on campus or on the client's premises, and they attempt to bridge the gap between acquiring and applying a new skill by adapting teaching content and learning tools to specific challenges facing each organization. They also try to bridge the gap between the relative inability of open-enrollment programs to generate collaborative capital and organizations' need to turn individually acquired skills into organizational capabilities by creating internal cohorts of learners.

CORE DIFFERENTIATORS AND VALUE DRIVERS

Core differentiators of the business schools' custom programs are their intellectual capital, base of pedagogical know-how for specific sets of problems and scenarios, and evaluative practices. Because they have been codified and routinized over decades, those practices can make the business schools' custom programs more efficient than those offered by rivals—particularly those whose core business is not skill development and the certification of skill acquisition.

CHALLENGES AND CONSTRAINTS

The skills that business schools claim to cultivate are constrained by academics' own stock of skills and the methods they have developed for measuring skill acquisition—such as tests and exams. This separation often results in a gap between the skill development outcomes of "customized" education and those required by organizations. As customization increasingly entails the personalization of learning and the codesign of courses, the business schools are constrained by their institutional structures and skill bases. Consultancies, corporate universities, and even facilitator-moderated, cohort-based, online courses are not subject to those constraints. Moreover, as noted, academics' pedagogical skill bases are best suited to situations in which problems are well defined and data are "given" and available—rather than contentious, missing, obscure, obscured, colored, and distorted as it often is in the "noise of action"— and the skills required to solve them can be specified and tested by standard instruments. These capabilities are often badly strained when problems are ill-defined or their definition is contentious and "data" are not in any sense "given."

Strategy Consultancies' Executive Education Offerings

Strategy consultancies, such as Accenture, BCG, Bain, Deloitte, and McKinsey, provide an array of executive development experiences for their clients. They often provide training as part of consulting engagements, with learning occurring as part of the interventions. For the past ten years, large consultancies have also offered "capability development" and executive training as a standalone offering—for example, the McKinsey Approach to Problem Solving—in which the course is customized to tackle specific capability gaps or is offered to a variety of organizations trying to develop a similar capability.

CORE DIFFERENTIATORS AND VALUE DRIVERS

Consultancies' offerings stand out because of their sharp focus on specific challenges facing an organization and the applied problem-solving capabilities the management consultancy brings to the learning experience.

- While in faculty-led programs in the business schools learning occurs through teaching and evaluation, in a consultancy-led capability-building-oriented program learning takes place through facilitation; mimesis; introspection; feedback; and the discovery of gaps, difficulties, opportunities, and common ground by participants.

- Management consultancies' educational offerings are shaped by the capabilities and skill bases they attempt to develop—as opposed to discipline-based content. Among their offerings we find programs with titles such as "Managing Yourself," "Coping with Complexity," "Managing Diversity," and "AI in Financial Services"—as opposed to "Pricing Derivatives," "Strategic Negotiations," or "Advanced Financial Statement Analysis," which business schools are more likely to offer. These programs trade signaling value—which requires standardization and constancy over a period of time—for a contextualized approach to skill development, usually on the job and specific to the task at hand.

- Consultancies' executive development programs are significantly more "organizationally aware" than are those offered by many of their competitors. There is significant focus on tapping organizational sources of value by developing a common language that reduces organizational coordination costs. When all participants are also teammates, the process directly contributes to building the collaborative capital needed to turn individual skills into organizational capabilities.

CHALLENGES AND CONSTRAINTS

Management consultancies are not constrained in the scale, scope, timing, location, or content of their development programs by the rigid contracts, high-cost structures, and institutional forces that impede adaptive change in business schools. However, they are limited by a shortage of pedagogical skill and prowess—being a solver of business problems does not always translate into being a successful facilitator of learning how to solve business problems—and often by a lack of clarity about the marginal rate of substitution in the value they place on senior partners engaging in "teaching" versus "consulting" that seems to be wired into their organizational structure. As one senior partner in a large consultancy put it to us: "We cannot start our own business school because every partner would want to teach in it, and we do not know how to say no, or how to compensate them for teaching." They are also—currently—constrained in the ability to provide the signaling value that accrues to certification because they lack the evaluation and certification practices fundamental and familiar to business schools.

Human Resource Consultancies' Development Programs

Human resource consultancies, such as Mercer Consulting, Optimum Talent, Hay Group, Korn/Ferry, Kienbaum, and Egon Zender, have for some time offered individual and team-level evaluation, selection, and coaching services to companies. In the process, they have developed the ability to identify the causes of challenges and problems individual executives face; uncover competency gaps; build data-intensive portraits of leadership abilities through focus groups, surveys, and 360-degree performance evaluations; and identify relevant causes and conditions when collaboration breaks down among the members of top management teams.

These consultancies have complemented their diagnostic services with coaching, training, and therapeutic interventions at the individual and team levels and started offering individual and team-based executive development programs aimed at remedying leadership, relational, and organizational challenges surfaced by their clients. The programs are flexible in duration and delivery style and can be adapted to meet specific requirements of clients and participants.

CORE DIFFERENTIATORS AND VALUE DRIVERS

HR consultancies differentiate themselves by their focus on the specific needs and characteristics of participants and teams.

- Unlike admission tests and intake questionnaires—which rarely inform program design in business schools in spite of the wealth of information they give about participants and are usually not designed to elicit program-design-specific information—the evaluation instruments used by the HR consultancies are used to develop highly personalized and context-specific development programs, which are thereby far easier to customize than those of providers like business schools or even large consultancies.

- These programs target the participants' social and task environments directly, are based on knowledge of these milieus, and are likely to be more successful at connecting to executives in specifically the areas they need help with.

- Such programs also provide a useful feedback channel to the parent organization, which can be anonymized to provide privacy to executive participants but which highlights to the top management team key challenges and skills and capabilities gaps that beset the organization.

CHALLENGES AND CONSTRAINTS

HR consultancies offering executive development programs face similar challenges to those faced by strategy consultancies: a shortage of the pedagogical know-how that can translate into a reliably repeatable and therefore "standard" set of training programs that beget signaling value in virtue of their stability, and difficulty in optimally allocating rewards and incentives to "regular consulting" versus "executive development activities" and accordingly in making and justifying investments in the latter. In addition, HR consultancies have a far narrower repertoire of skill and capability development programs than do their larger and more well-rounded counterparts such as large consultancies and business schools.

Corporate Universities

Corporate universities are usually staffed by full-time coaches, trainers, and instructors who typically work for the organization but can also acquire, on a contractual basis, talent from outside their parent organizations to provide targeted, contextualized learning experiences to groups and individuals. Corporate universities in firms such as Apple and Google routinely recruit leading executives, coaches, and coaching organizations and business school professors as external providers. Learning experiences are matched to the specific problems faced by the organization.

CORE DIFFERENTIATORS AND VALUE DRIVERS

Corporate universities offer contextualized learning experiences that help the parent organization address skill and capability building and cooperative and collaborative capital building objectives.

- They "live inside" and are owned by the organization—mitigating some of the problems of transactionality and misaligned incentives that plague outside providers like business schools and consultancies.

- They include content directly relevant to the organization, delivered in the context in which the skills developed are applied. At Apple University, for example, faculty members facilitate discussions using case studies based on Apple's decisions in the *previous year*—as opposed to problems that are faced by organizations *like* Apple during the previous year (consultancies) or problems faced by Apple or Apple-like organizations three to ten years ago (business schools).

- The membership of learners across the organization can be informed by detailed metrics of their aspirations, traits, and accomplishments. For example, Google EDU serves as an in-house training program for employees. It uses statistics from existing and former employees to recommend courses to managers at different stages of their careers.

- The learning environment is not constrained by confidentiality concerns: executives can freely discuss topics of relevance to the organization and their groups without concerns for undue propagation.

Challenges and Constraints

Corporate universities are expensive—even though costs have been coming down quickly during the past five years and vertiginously during the past year. It is often difficult to justify the investments needed to set up an in-house university when resources are limited. For a corporation large enough to consider setting up its own learning hub, the value of its investment will often seem, *ex ante*, volatile, uncertain, and ambiguous.

- Volatile, because the value of the skills and capabilities deemed worthy of a specific investment can vanish when market conditions change or when executive sponsors drop off.

- Uncertain, because getting together the right talent to curate or create the right content, build the right learning experiences, and provide the feedback mechanisms necessary for learning is difficult: talent is scarce and cooperation among several people with different skills sets—which is rare—is very important to the design and deployment of successful learning vehicles.

- Ambiguous, in that the mapping, measurement, and definition of the right skills and capabilities is not obvious, even for the organization that is the primary user of the skill and the main beneficiary of its own corporate university.

Moreover, any learning hub requires an evolving nexus of coupled activity sets: the development of the base of learning experiences—be it case studies, feedback sessions, or action learning approaches to the redesign of tasks or relationships—relies on the continuous accumulation of cases, learning plans, and most important, teaching or learner-interaction blueprints. Because their endowments and the span of their activities fluctuates with the organization's quarterly or annual performance, corporate universities are often unable to accumulate the pedagogical know-how necessary to make an impact. Barring a handful of exceptions—such as at Apple, Google, Goldman Sachs, GE, and Procter & Gamble—corporate universities have exhibited a tendency to evolve into organizational overhead that provides (usually secondary) support to the HR function instead of growing into learning and development hubs.

The scope and the scale of personal network development and signaling value of attendance and credentials in a corporate university are also limited.

Participants are drawn from within the organization. Their selection is often weighted in favor of organizational capability-development goals rather than the individual characteristics emphasized, for instance, by EMBA programs.

Finally, corporate universities are most frequently deficient in the evaluative know-how (tests, exams, quizzes, problem sets) that allows the instantaneous measurement of skill acquisition. They do not have the pedagogical IP base of business schools, or the learning- and capability-building technologies of consultancies that regularly measure progress in large-scale cross-sectional studies of the industries they serve and have often well-developed internal "feedback cultures" owing to their sharply peaked pyramidal structures requiring the timely justification of frequent up-or-out decisions.

The Personal Learning Cloud

A fully disintegrated and disintermediated solution to a large swath of executive skill-building needs is now looming large—and ominously to incumbents and entrants alike. Drawing on fourth-generation learning management systems and content from leading universities and think tanks, and powered by online learning hubs—such as Coursera, edX, LinkedIn Learning, Udacity, Udemy, 2U, and Degreed—a seamless fabric is being rapidly stitched on the Web of on-demand, open online courses and modules, and micro- and nano-certifications for executives at all levels in their organizations. This "personal learning cloud" (PLC) can now be used for cultivating a broad set of managerial skills—and in particular the technical, algorithmic, and cognitive skills that still account for the majority of credentials in executive education and corporate training.

Online learning vehicles that make up the PLC impart competencies whose acquisition can often be measured using standard remote testing processes. They favorably compete in scale, scope, and quality with open-enrollment courses offered by business schools—in many cases they draw on elite business school faculty members to design and deliver courses and modules. They can be deployed in forms that are either curated by in-house or external coaches and "learning designers" or purchased in bulk from reintermediators such as edX and Coursera that have arisen and grown in part to solve the informational problems posed by the disintermediation of the field. They can be interlaced with interactive developmental activities, such as individual and team-based projects within and outside the organization, to create a pool of conversational, collaborative, and intellectual capital within an organization. Being distributed and ubiquitous, they can be exploited to support learning "adhocracies" such as Singularity University and the Kauffmann Founders School, which use curated online content to support numerous learning and collaboration-oriented gatherings (short courses and conferences) that turn skill development into a continuous, distributed process.

Core Differentiators and Value Drivers

Massive, open, online courses (MOOCs); small private online courses (SPOCs); and the mixed-mode blended programs they support provide a low-cost alternative to programs that aim to cultivate functional and technical skills in a classroom format.

- Costs are low both in terms of dollars spent per hour of instruction, which is a tenth to a hundredth of those of alternatives, and in terms of the time required of executives, as they can participate in an asynchronous fashion, on their own schedules, and not be bound to the place-time constraints of business schools, consultancies, and even corporate universities.

- The courses and programs of instruction they offer are open and modular: they can be appropriated by other players in the space—such as coaches or corporate universities that want to curate online content and monitor the completion of online courses by participants.

- Because digital courses can be quickly appended, modified, or redesigned, the personal learning cloud can be *quickly* deployed to fill skills gaps that regularly—and with increasing frequency—appear in the market, such as cybersecurity, utility blockchain design and implementation, and machine-learning-based data analytics for business, which would take many years, if not decades, to be filled via traditional educational vehicles such as college and professional masters' degrees.

Challenges and Constraints

The offerings of the PLC traditionally have been associated with a limited level of interactivity. Even in synchronous courses, the sort of dialogue that is taken to promote learning at the executive level is constrained. PLC offerings are considered good enough for the development of technical and algorithmic skills, but less so for the development of the relational, communicative, collaborative, coordinative skills that many executives and their organizations seek. Online credentials are also currently perceived as being "second-best" to credentials obtained by attendance of in-person courses, in part because of the lower level of verifiability of attendance and performance. Moreover, organizations large and small are only imperfectly aware of the programs of study and development enabled by the fabric of the PLC—and only a few organizations have developed the internal ability to curate skill development programs and guide executives to developmental goals in the online environment.

How the Response to COVID-19 Accelerates Growth in Usage and Numbers of Use Cases of the Personal Learning Cloud

However, these constraints have been both loosened and rendered less relevant as the PLC has received a massive boost from societal responses to the COVID-19 epidemic starting in March of 2020, from efforts to make educational credentials immutable and verifiable, and from the emergence of the personal coaching cloud.

The modal response to the COVID-19 pandemic in the Western democracies—social distancing and the proscription of gatherings large enough to enable a class, seminar, or workshop to convene—have changed the dynamics of how "learning is taught." Online delivery of courses has become an imperative for most colleges and universities and caused a step change in the ways in which universities—and therefore business schools—deliver learning experiences. Tens of thousands of courses have been placed online, with varying levels of quality. Existing course bases in the PLC—from leading institutions offered online through platforms like Coursera, edX, ExecOnline, XED, Emeritus, and 2U (formerly GetSmarter) have become increasingly viable plausible substitutes. These (re)aggregators of educational content are accelerating the disintermediation of teaching talent (away from their home institutions) and riding a sudden increase in demand that allows them to justify higher investments in the near term. In addition, new, generic white-label platforms such as Thinkific and Learnable have emerged to equip any instructor (or senior executive with a calling for teaching) with the ability to create, deliver, deploy, and process payments for her courses, without having to go through a parent institution—like a business school or a university. In the process, they have also essentially reduced the cost base of setting up a corporate university—an organizational learning hub that concentrates learning activities in one place—by another factor of five to ten.

The Higher Ed Trust: A Blockchain for Executive Credentials

Hand in hand with an increase in demand comes a significant change in the signaling value of online experiences: a digital "higher education trust" has taken shape during the past two years. It will allow every executive learner to certifiably, verifiably, and securely guarantee his or her credentials to an employer, or to the financial backer of his or her education. The new trust rests on the assumption that any "educational program" is backed by a series of transactions between the learner and the provider that are simple, "mechanical," and therefore easy to track: applying to a program, being admitted, taking a course, completing the course, getting a grade, graduating from the program, and so forth. These transactions can be traced, tracked, and verified so as to guarantee that the answers to the following questions are true:

- Are you who you say you are?

- Have you done the work you claim to have done?

- Have you reached the level of accomplishment entailed by the completion of a learning experience?

Once verified and aggregated, these transactions function as safeguards and backings for what we are currently calling a "degree" or a "credential" of any kind. A common, verifiable, credible, trustworthy record of a learner's accomplishments, maintained in perpetuity by a distributed ledger, is an immutable record of her or his passage through a learning and credentialing process. Anchored by a digital trust, the PLC begets real bite in the employment market: learners' records of completion and achievement in courses or classes taken online have the kind of value that edX and Coursera have been aiming at for more than a decade.

Two major efforts are now under way for building the "educational trust base" of the future:

- The MIT Digital Credentials Coalition is building a distributed ledger that will allow all learners to possess a certified, verifiable, shareable record of their learning accomplishments—which will furthermore allow educational institutions and employers alike to perform the analytics required to ascertain the degree to which completion of a particular course helps the student acquire the skills and abilities that are necessary for a job. It is a learner-centric and learner-oriented platform that places decision rights on creating and sharing educational credentials squarely in the hands of each learner, while at the same time allowing educational institutions to verify—and certify—the claims that a learner makes about his or her background.

- The White House–initiated and U.S. Department of Labor–backed Independent Learning Record platform—more recently backed by large corporations such as Walmart, SAS, LinkedIn, and IBM and potentially backed by IBM's HyperLedger (Blockchain) platform—allows learners to document—in an unfalsifiable fashion—their learning journeys, including formal and informal educational experiences, courses taken and exams passed, internships undertaken and experiential learning opportunities, in a way that moreover makes the learning record fully exportable—and always verifiable by would-be employers.

Even as the signaling value of PLC credentials increases, so do the depth and breadth of the learning experiences that executives and managers engage with online, buoyed by the boost to remote interactions that the "distancing economy" has effected.

The Personal Coaching Cloud

Just as important in an era when learning in a classroom setting has received a large setback from which it may not recover easily is the emergence of a "personal coaching cloud" (PCC), which promises to redress the weaknesses of the PLC with regard to the development of relational, communicative, and executive skills. The coaching industry has been in steady ascent since the early 2010s, and has become an $11.8 billion industry by 2020. Some hundred and fifty thousand business coaches worldwide provide in-person counseling, feedback, and personalized learning plans to executives and managers, which are geared to their jobs, functions, and predicaments. Large organizations use both internal coaches—usually part of the HR departments—and external coaches and coaching organizations to help high-potential managers and executives achieve their skill development plans.

The coaching relationship is such that executives can receive guidance, feedback, and self-development interventions that are suited to their specific predicaments, roles, and situations, as opposed to the generic, catch-all advice and guidance usually offered by executive education providers. The coaching relationship is primarily and primordially relational. It relies on a special and privileged relationship between coach and executive, wherein the former understands the latter's challenges and context and offers guidance, prompts, questions, and feedback that are adapted to and adaptive to this context. The PCC provides a critical complement to the PLC in an era in which relational, communicative, and executive skills are increasingly important but most interaction occurs in an online setting and may well reflect the fact that the development of such skills requires personalized, attuned, intensive feedback—a skill base most providers of executive development programs lack.

The coaching market has been at a growing rate (30 percent from 2011 to 2015; 45 percent from 2016 to 2020) in part because of the degree to which the sort of skill development vehicle most needed in the executive realm is one that is adaptive to the predicament of the learner and her organization, and geared toward the development of skills that are difficult to specify and observe—let alone measure—in standard class-based or classroom-based environments. The PCC is buoyed, as well, by the massive growth in online footage and transcripting available from Zoom, Microsoft Teams, and Webex—which allow coaches first-hand access to real, and real-time, "performances" from executive learners in authentic managerial and communicative environments—and by the explosion in platforms such as Gong that enable organizations to monitor and give feedback to employees on their performances in activities (such as sales calls) that are critical to the organization's success.

How Executive Education Providers Interact: Mapping Substitutes and Complements

In Figure 3.3, we show, along the organizations' and participants' value-vectors, how different offerings complement and substitute each other. Because digitalization allows companies greater visibility into both the educational offering and the ROI on the learning-relevant outcomes, developing a substitutes-and-complements map should, we believe, guide an efficient restructuring of the executive education industry.

Participants' Value Substitutes and Complements
SKILL DEVELOPMENT SUBSTITUTES AND COMPLEMENTS
The substitutes for skill development vary with the type of skill and the context in which it will be applied. At one end of the spectrum are functional skills (for example, financial statement analysis) that are predominantly cognitive (involving reasoning and calculation) in nature and algorithmic (do this first,

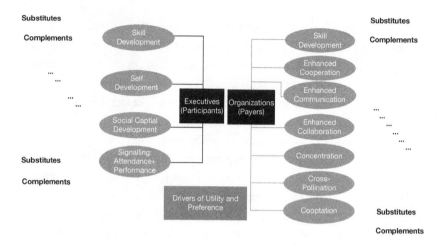

Figure 3.3. Map for Charting the Substitutes and Complements Among Executive Education Program Suppliers

this next, with the outputs of one step usually figuring among the inputs to the next, and the set of rules applied to each input usually fixed by the protocol or algorithm designer) in terms of usage. In this space, there will be growing competition between the traditional lecture-and-case discussion, with the associated evaluation protocols, and online vehicles, with or without on-the-ground coaching in the application of the skill in the focal context. (In addition, these skills are the most likely to be automated by machines present and future).

Skills that are either noncognitive (such as empathic accuracy, presence, and resilience) or mixed (dialogical, deliberative, and discursive skills) lie at the other end of the spectrum. Those are best developed in the social environments of action learning, small group discussions, and coaching interventions that enable participants to develop skill sets whose measurement or instantiation cannot be automated. At this end, the competition is between in-house corporate development programs—which include coaching, mentorship, and guidance—and customized, intensive, off-site programs that provide developmental paths for individual executives. Across this spectrum, the successful development of skills hinges on the synergies between the forces of socialization, guidance, coaching, and discussion that operate in conjunction to produce the conversational capital that promotes the internalization of concepts and higher levels of skill acquisition, and ensures the more effective transfer of skills to the relevant context.

In the same way, complements differ across the spectrum of skills development. At the cognitive-algorithmic-functional end, there is a great deal of complementarity between large-scale, online, skill-to-desktop platforms and classroom-based instructional techniques. The former use functional specialists and coaches to guide participants' application of the skills they've learned to their work environments while the latter use a community of practice—such as the alumni of past programs—as a mutual aid and self-help group.

At the nonalgorithmic relational end of the spectrum, the social medium of skill development—participants who serve as sources of guidance and feedback for each other, for instance—complements the coach, intermediator, or facilitator as well as the content. A community of managers willing to provide feedback, having gone through a master-trainer program, is often a prerequisite for sustaining the transfer of skills to the organization.

Self-Development Substitutes and Complements

The self-development value of executive programs can be derived from a variety of experiences offered by education providers. The experiences include personalized coaching and mentoring imparted on the job or at retreats; on-site mindset transformation exercises conducted by individual trainers or consultancies; and off-site workshops and facilitated sessions, in which participants help one another in the context of a transformation project.

The self-restorative—"refresh and recharge"—objective of executive development programs lies at the boundary between wellness retreats that incorporate a self-development dimension and conventional off-sites that afford participants a physiological and interpersonal medium in which they can disconnect from their daily routines. The complements to the self-development exercises are coworkers who want to transform their style of interacting, or a set of like-minded participants who desire to engage in a process of self-development, guided by an expert. The group-related aspect of self-transformation and self-development is well-known to executive education coaches and group therapists (Yalom and Vinogradov 1993). To achieve the refresh-and-recharge objective requires a dynamic between the environment and the process that enables participants to sustain a state of disengagement without slipping into the "vacation" mindset created by retreats that focus only on bodily well-being.

Social Capital Enhancement Substitutes and Complements

The development of function-specific intraorganizational networks can be enhanced through facilitated e-learning programs. The participants in these programs can, for instance, be broken up into groups of like-minded learners who can share similar aims and problems, or participants from the same function, who can share learning experiences. The development of interorganizational and cross-industry networks can be facilitated by creating cohorts from different organizations, which are then guided to the acquisition of functional skills through different media. It can also be achieved through off-site programs that recruit participants from various industries or from different companies in the same industry. The development of intraorganizational networks that cross structures, functions, and hierarchical roles can be facilitated by intensive, thematic, on-site development programs as well as cross-functional, cross-hierarchical knowledge platforms that encourage collaboration, not just communication.

Social capital development depends on the conditions under which participants come together. Joint relevance, joint purpose, and joint attention are key to forging meaningful relationships within and between organizations. As we argued in Chapter 1, focusing on networking as the sole source of value undermines an executive education program. Executives will come partly to learn a meaningful skill and partly to meet others, but they are less likely to do so if there are no clear learning objectives or development goals: the content of the skill development process critically complements the socializing function of executive education programs. Equally important is the presence of a trust and legitimacy conduit—a teacher, facilitator, instructor, or master coach—who, trusted by all the participants, functions as an arbiter in interactions.

Signaling-Value Substitutes and Complements

Executive education programs are all substitutes for one another to the extent that they communicate to the talent market, and organizations, commitment by participants and organizations to development. Similar-status programs, reflected by their price points and selectivity, will substitute for one another more readily than programs of lower status and selectivity. Today's leaders in executive development—Harvard, Stanford, Wharton, Duke, INSEAD, and IMD, among the business schools that offer large-scale open-enrollment programs; McKinsey and BCG, among the management consultancies; and London Business School, Columbia, Kellogg, IE, and CEIBS among the EMBA program-providers—enjoy a significant advantage in terms of providing signaling value.

Alternatives to the premium programs—such as online nano-degrees and certificates procured from online education platforms—vie with one another for audience and market share. However, given the burgeoning popularity of online degrees and courses, and the combination of cognitive skills, technical skills, and X-factor skills needed to complete an online course without external reinforcement, it is possible these courses will acquire significant signaling value in the future. The higher value of online *certification* should compensate for the lack of *signaling* value in registering for such courses, and will only increase if secure, verifiable tracking of credentials via a distributed ledger or Blockchain comes into place.

At the high-certification-value end of the spectrum, the substitutes will be programs in which the links between the developed and the requisite skill can be measured. The value of standardized certification is often predicated on the problematic assumption that skills can be transferred to contexts outside those in which they are developed. Here, there is substitutability between EMBA programs that rely on uniform content and large open-enrollment programs (Harvard Business School's General Management Program and Professional Leadership Development program, for instance). At the low-certification-value end lie customized programs that cannot easily be compared to, or distilled into, a common skill base; but which they can compensate for by measurable results in the acquisition and transfer of valuable new skills.

The emergence of online education providers has increased the transparency of the skill sets that executives acquire because the new providers break up a skill into learnable chunks. For instance, the increased popularity of nano-degrees in computer science indicates the importance of breaking a composite set of professional skills into bite-sized chunks—such as Java programming, database programming, and machine-learning basics—that employers can track. The certification value of the programs increases because of the greater transparency around the specific components of the skill being developed and the participants' level of proficiency. Similarly, the way online courses break up skills into concentrated bits accessible asynchronously may increase their value tomorrow, allowing them to compete head-on with EMBA and large-scale open-enrollment programs.

Educational signals are multidimensional signs of participants' inherent abilities and acquired skills and as such are often ambiguous. The signaling value of admission to a skill development program is determined by the quality of the sponsoring organization's selection process, the program's selectivity, and its perceived status. A manager selected by a Fortune 100 organization to participate in a well-recognized, top-ranked, open-enrollment program will gain a higher signaling value than one selected by the same organization to participate in a lower-status program.

Certification value is subject to the existence of multiple complements. The transparency of the skill sets inculcated by a program will interact with its rigor and status to produce different levels of value. An increased level of transparency must include methods of measuring the skill set's acquisition within and outside the development context, and the degree to which the skill base is well-established (for example, balance sheet analysis is a well-established skill) and measurable using standardized testing instruments.

The completion of some programs can explicitly certify the development of a skill and, at the same time, implicitly signal the possession of a more important skill: the X-factor skills which signal that the executive possessed the discipline required to complete the program. In such cases, the complements of the high-certification-value programs should include the X-factor skills required to complete the program, even if they aren't explicitly mentioned by the education provider: plowing through a difficult, well-designed online program requires the self-supplied "get up and go" behavioral blueprint and the stick-to-it discipline that organizations usually (try to) refer to using the catch phrase "self-starters."

Providers' Value Complements and Substitutes

Let us now examine how executive education providers complement and substitute for one another on the metrics most relevant to organizations.

Substitutes and Complements for Capability and Competency Formation

In most organizations, there seems to be little awareness of which skills will deliver the capabilities they desire. Notwithstanding, there is general agreement that skill development in executives is a necessary condition for the enhancement of organizational capabilities—which require the coordinated co-exercise of many individuals instantiating new skills to a problem of interest whose solution is valuable.

At one end, EMBA and open-enrollment programs with canonical curricula that develop generic, just-in-case, "canonical" skills substitute for one another. Such skills are usually sought by organizations that don't quite know what is needed to turn individual human capital into organizational capability: they simply index people with the right level of discipline and self-confidence to make an investment in their own future that has uncertain returns. At the other end of the spectrum, organizations that know what skills they require to build their capability bases choose between training exercises and capability-building interventions designed to impart organizational skills to a team of participants. For organizations discovering on-the-fly the skills they need for fresh capabilities, skills-on-demand programs—which include online platforms and on-call coaches and functional knowledge experts—can substitute for open-enrollment programs.

The development of new organizational capabilities is usually related to the acquisition of specific skill sets. For example, agile response capabilities are a (convex) combination of technical skills (database design and management, information technology infrastructure maintenance); new technology and operational skills (new CRM system, new inventory tracking database); and a set of relational, affective, communicative, and X-factor skills that support the coordination of large teams and the development of trust with minimal communication. The means to develop those tightly coupled capability sets must be heavily socialized (within a group) and contextualized (within the organization), but the capabilities that are less dependent on the coordination of multiple skill sets (compliance with a new ISO process framework, for instance) will increasingly depend on the use of online learning technology.

Substitutes and Complements for Communication, Coordination, and Cultural Value

Professionally relevant conversational capital can be developed by executives participating in on-site or off-site programs, and can also be generated by creating carefully chosen organizational cohorts on online platforms that participants can use for communication via a shared new language system. To overlay a new language on existing sets of practices requires a pedagogical design that targets maximal applicability across a broad range of scenarios akin to designing for the maximum transferability of skills to far contexts, and support of the new ways of communicating, often using the distributed learning infrastructure of Web 2.0, to render concepts and "mere ways of speaking" into effective norms of communication and coordination (Moldoveanu 2002).

Substitutes and Complements for Cooperation and Collaboration Value

The habitus, or disposition, to work together to solve a problem is critical to the development of both collaborative practices and cooperative norms. Executive development programs that bring participants from the same organization together to work on problems of joint relevance—for instance, custom programs based on action-learning principles and problem-solution-centered programs delivered on the job—will be substitutes for each other at the high-touch end of the spectrum.

Those at the low-touch end—online learning platforms—fare relatively poorly in terms of the development of collaborative capital since the level of intimacy afforded to participants is, by design, low. However, new generations of collaborative and joint learning platforms are enabling managers to achieve ever higher levels of rhythm and intimacy. They may in the near future provide effective alternatives to the high-touch interventions required for trust-building.

The degree of complementarity between program content—jointly and uniformly, not just individually—and the elements of context—opportunities for learning that provide credible tests of trustworthiness and the ability to trust—determine whether the informal networks spawned by participation are immune to subversion, decay of interpersonal ties, and attrition. These complements entail both design and support for the interactions among participants at dedicated forums, the mapping of projects, and tracking platforms that together nurture an organization's collaborative capital.

Substitutes and Complements for Concentration Value

The concentration value of executive education programs is maximized when they increase an organization's ability to track skill development and optimize the allocation of roles to executives with newly developed skill sets. That is being further enabled by the development of skill-transfer measurement systems, which allow organizations to measure the benefit of the skills learned at the levels of the group and of the individual executive. Synchronous online programs deliver cohort- and group-based developmental experiences to managers throughout an organization in a specific location, at a specific time, off-site or on-site, so they are a substitute for traditional offerings. Meanwhile, the burgeoning demand for skills on demand and the evolution of learning management systems are also rendering small, cohort-based, private, and mediated online courses increasingly viable as alternatives to face-to-face offerings.

Substitutes and Complements for the Cooptation Value of Executive Programs

Executive development programs substitute for one another to the extent they are all subsidized by organizations that (usually) nominate executives to participate in them. The incentives for the selected participants include recognition between, and across, organizations. High-prestige, high-status programs that offer participants significant developmental or well-being benefits will be substitutes for each other on this dimension. Programs that optimally combine the benefits of well-being and skill enhancement, along with recognition, ensure that their certificates become recognizable signals whose value frequently transcends organizational boundaries.

Substitutes and Complements for Cross-Pollination Value

Cross-industry recruitment can quickly inform an organization about practices and ideas—and opportunistic hires can substitute for any program along this dimension. Strategy consultancies such as McKinsey and BCG can function as cross-pollinating agencies that can inform, for example, an insurance company about successful billing and collections practices from the telecom industry, a media company about content-management practices in the software industry, and so forth. In the face of viable substitutes, the realization of the learning objectives that participants in executive education programs share must rely on a rich, interactive environment that facilitates interparticipant learning. Executive programs that deliver on that metric will create environments that afford participants repeated opportunities to discuss, learn, observe, try, and reflect in ways that allow the emergence of good ideas and best practices to diffuse across a base of participants that comes from many different organizations.

The Learning Vehicles: How Are Skills Acquired and Transferred?

Skill development and skill transfer being the *raison d'être* of executive development, it is important to examine executive education programs to understand their capacity to develop and transfer the skills and capabilities organizations seek. We will evaluate the teaching components of the executive education programs to see how well they help develop and transfer skills (see Figure 3.4). Since the personal learning cloud—asynchronously available learning experiences such as videotaped lectures, quizzes, problem sets, and so on—has become a viable, low-cost learning option, the skill acquisition and skill transfer

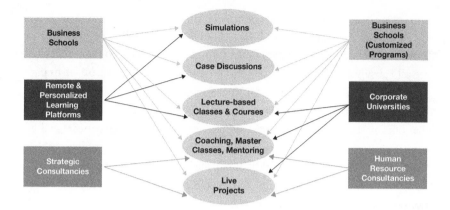

Figure 3.4. Map of Skill Acquisition and Transfer Vehicles

characteristics of every other learning vehicle should be benchmarked against it. Future-looking providers should also take into account the burgeoning development of the personal coaching cloud, which is quickly making inroads into the market for skills that are best developed through dense, feedback-oriented interactions.

Lecture- and Test-Based Courses

Lecture-based classes and courses that lie at the core of the EMBA and open-enrollment programs offered by the business schools are characterized by structured presentations related to an instructor's area of expertise, and participants' interest is clarified, challenged, applied, and extended in discussions guided by the instructor and influenced by the participants. Presentations may be preceded by work, and sequences that form a course module may be followed by work (problem sets, tests) designed to measure the extent to which skill acquisition has been achieved. The presence of diverse participants in the classroom amplifies the impact of the content, as participants learn from each other's questions, answers, and responses.

SKILL ACQUISITION: WHAT IS LEARNED?

Lecture-based courses are focused on helping executives acquire functional, cognitive, and algorithmic skills, amenable to testing and grading systems, and honed by centuries of application in the higher education system. The skills are acquired because ideas (models, methods) are imprinted via discussions and exercises, and measured by participants' performance on quizzes and exams.

Skill Transfer: Where and How?

The literature on skill transfer suggests that even the best-designed content and learning materials, when delivered in lecture and test formats, don't generate skills that transfer to contexts spatiotemporally, socially, or functionally far removed from the locus of their acquisition. Different ways of teaching are associated with better skill transfer results (Billing 2007), but those are mostly project- and practice-based methods that "invert" the classroom, eliminating the epistemic privilege that the lecturer normally enjoys. The personal learning cloud threatens to substitute lecture-based courses by deploying user-optimized regimes of chunked learning and spaced learning (Kelley and Whatson 2013). Such learning techniques can outperform classroom-based courses on skill acquisition.

Case Discussions

Case discussions are a subclass of discussion-based teaching, the roots of which can be traced to the writings of John Dewey, one of the originators of the Oxbridge method of engaged debate as a means of developing judgment through relentless, disciplined, open dialogue. The case discussion, now and for a long time closely associated with the Harvard Business School, is the dominant method of classroom teaching in most MBA and EMBA programs globally. Some form of discussion-based learning shapes pedagogical design in most of the open-enrollment and custom programs run by the business schools.

Implicit in the case study discussion is a data-rich, nuanced narrative of a managerial predicament, which usually reflects the perspectives of multiple actors with incompatible or conflicting interests and personal dispositions inducing different framings of a "raw situation," and punctuated by a "crisis point" that requires the learner to frame the problem, as well as to propose and argue for (justify, explain, rationalize) one or more solutions. The purpose of a case discussion is often to promote the acquisition of a language system and to develop an associated set of models and methods necessary to understand the situation or predicament, as well as to acquire a sort of proactive disposition for articulating assumptions and proposals and defending them in public against questions and challenges. It emulates an executive team in which participants identify sufficiently with the described circumstances to engage in a discussion. That generates a counterfactual exploration and learning environment, in which participants are afforded the opportunity to explore, through structured dialogue, what might have, could have, and should have been done by the executives in the case study.

Because they are frequently meant to function as simulations of deliberations on executive teams, case discussions often take the form of the creation of a "business communication lab," where participants generate, advocate for, or respond to inquiries and requests for clarifications, and defend or modify their opinions in response to challenges or actionable options for the organization featured in the case. They can experiment with their own "executive ways of being" by trying moves and countermoves in a language game constrained by their knowledge and the case's informational base—as well as by the instructor's deftness and acuity in managing a discussion of this type.

The role of the case teacher, instructor, or facilitator varies greatly across instantiations of case discussions in the field. It can range from being a light-touch coordinator of the discussions and a gentle prompter of queries, objections, and challenges to being an involved framer of the discussion through the precise wording and timing of questions, and the active arbiter for the verbal game that unfolds. He or she may be the collator and interpreter, after each segment, of the discussants' insights.

Skill Acquisition: What Is Learned?

A case discussion's objectives start with the appropriation of the "language" system (such as for entrepreneurial finance, CEO succession, managing software product development when technologies are changing quickly, and so on) that makes the protagonists' predicament intelligible and helps develop a set of cognitive, affective, relational, and communicative skills that (ideally) transcend the context and enable participants to become better public "dialogicians," inquirers, deliberators, discussants, and enforcers of standards of probity and intellectual honesty that constrain the often relentlessly pragmatic ways of being of business people.

The discussions typically reference include other participants' arguments, defending or modifying ideas while responding to objections while always remaining open to a good counterargument. The acquisition of those skills depends on the quality of the discussion space that the classroom leader creates by framing the different loci of the dialogue as well as the timing of his or her feedback regarding participants' ability to sustain executive-level discourse.

SKILL TRANSFER: WHERE AND HOW?

Skill transfer involves multiple contexts, as we have seen earlier, including knowledge (that is, the proximity of the participant's situation to the experiential circumstance of the protagonist); sociocultural factors (such as the participant's association with one, or more, teams, organizations, or industries); physical locations (on-site or off-site); and temporal factors (such as whether it happens immediately after a discussion or much later). Logically, the cognitive skills associated with the mastery of the functional and technical language systems of a case study are likely to transfer most effectively from case studies that are about a participant's organization or industry, are about a predicament that is relatively recent, and are taught on the premises by a facilitator familiar with the host organization to a group of executives from the same organization that must work together in the near future.

At the far transfer end of the spectrum lie EMBA and open-enrollment programs' case discussions. Participants, drawn from several organizations and industries, iteratively build, through discussion of cases about *other* organizations and industries, competence in dialogue and discussion. That competence is contingent on the presence or the acquisition of a set of individual-level communicative and dialogical skills. The transfer of those skills to the relevant setting in the participant organizations can be difficult because it is far removed from the locus of acquisition; different groups, roles, topics, and functions of public discourse make the transfer a challenge.

Electronic learning environments focus on the interaction between participants and text (or video). Those environments cannot easily replicate the skill-building environment of a case discussion led by an expert facilitator. Textured, contextualized case discussions, delicately choreographed by expert facilitators whose awareness includes the physiognomic characteristics and gestures of participants, is not substitutable by the learning cloud—yet. The discussion forums that are part of remote learning environments are, for the most part, unable to exercise the sort of dialogical scorekeeping required by high-level language games. However, the new interaction fabric that is being prototyped online has evolved beyond linearly displayed, temporally asynchronous sets of interactions between users. Increasingly, the new digital environments offer sophisticated ensembles of users, facilitators, and materials. They are orchestrated in ways—that heed participants' connectedness and insight into each other's affective and cognitive states—that transcend the classroom environment of the traditional case discussion.

Simulations

Simulations are learning environments constructed to replicate the "bare bones" structural, relational, and dynamical features of business environments within the guided, deincentivized setting of a workgroup or class. Roles are assigned to participants as are rules to their modes of interaction, which may be trading games, negotiation simulations, market share competitions, and so on. The participants infer successful patterns of action ("skilled behavior") from their performance in the games.

Simulations can affect learning either through top-down pedagogies, where the principles of successful behavior are articulated *ex ante* and exercised during the simulation, or bottom-up pedagogies, whereby the principles, including many not contemplated by the designer, are inferred, often through dialogue. Viewed through this lens, a case discussion is a specific form of simulation; specifically, the simulation of high-level executive dialogue about a managerial predicament. The difference is that the rules and mechanisms of successful behavior are (most frequently) not explicitly communicated during a case discussion.

SKILL ACQUISITION: WHAT IS LEARNED?

In a simulation, skill acquisition occurs primarily through the group practice of procedures and the feedback about the success of various behaviors in the context of the simulation. For instance, a simulation of oligopolistic competition in a commodity market will involve teams that enter their strategies into a central clearinghouse that assigns payoffs based on stochastic demand fluctuations and the interdependent strategic choices of other teams.

Simulations can also seek to develop higher-level cognitive skills: forecasting the evolution of nonlinear environments through the well-known "beer supply chain game," a staple of MBA operations management courses; interactive reasoning in cooperative and competitive game scenarios through oligopolistic market simulations; whole business simulations that are based on multi-agent models of an organization's functions, competitors, suppliers, and clients; and affective and relational skills through mock negotiations and rehearsals of pitches, "exit interviews," and "hiring interviews."

SKILL TRANSFER: WHERE AND HOW?

The skill transfer capabilities of a simulation depend, as with case discussions, on the transfer distances and the learning and interaction mode (socialized, feedback-intensive, or multimodal). Simulations that target the development of specific skill sets (for example, demand forecasting in a buyer-seller system) are more likely to succeed when one of two conditions are met. First, the simulations are heavily contextualized; that is, they are conducted with data from the host organization, and the participants are debriefed in ways that inform the organization's future practices. Second, the simulations are pre-optimized for transfer by being repeated in different environments to establish the robustness of the behavior patterns they endorse. The transfer properties of simulations that aim to develop complicated, partly undefined bundles of cognitive, affective skills are often dependent on social context. For example, learning how to emote to counteract power moves in an EMBA classroom simulation of employer-employee dynamics may have little impact on the participants' ability to emote that way during a team meeting. Although the transferability of non-cognitive and relational skills is far from understood, it seems plausible that the transfer of those skills is even more dependent on the proximity between the loci of acquisition and application than so far assumed.

The replicability of simulation-based learning experiences in the personal learning cloud depends on the skill sets that organizations need. Web environments, particularly 2-D- and 3-D-gaming environments, seem well suited for developing simulations aimed at cultivating predictive, analytical, perceptual, and even X-factor skills—which can be achieved by imposing time limits on critical decisions that affect participant outcomes. The imminent generational shift in the executive population demographics to the Millennials and Generation Z are likely to extend the degree to which gaming environments will be accepted as substitutes for simulation-based classroom experiences.

Capstone and "Live" Projects: The Field-and-Forum or Action-Learning Approach.

The recent growth in the use of "live" projects and "live" cases in both MBA and executive programs is likely a sign of the skill-transfer gap in executive education. "Live" cases are two levels closer to reality than traditional case studies, which document situations that have been already resolved and can, therefore, be easily researched online. They are also more "real" than the raw cases introduced by the Yale School of Management in 2000, which describe a situation that participants must address by studying original data and documents. "Live" cases are neither fully developed nor have they played out completely. Like co-consulting projects, they are current, are not easily summarized, and unfold as participants and facilitators engage with the situation. They are typically structured either as consulting projects for participants, when run alongside a company by a business school, or as co-consulting engagements, when a consultancy is trying to solve a client's problems and involves some of the client's executives in the problem-shaping and solution-generation process.

EMBA programs are starting to adopt the field-and-forum approach developed by management consultancies such as McKinsey & Co—which brings participants together for intensive co-consultation and mutual feedback along specific dimensions of a problem, but without any limits on the kinds of problem that are admissible. Consultancies and business schools also employ action learning approaches, whereby participants, under the guidance of facilitators, engage in structured inquiry designed to bring about organizational change (for example, the project management discipline enforced by a new platform) or solutions (a new product design). In the process, the participants learn from both their successes and their failures by registering and keeping track of their actions and the resulting outcomes.

Skill Acquisition: What Is Learned?

"Live" cases and co-consulting projects help the development of skill sets such as data modeling, decision making, and project planning, as well as structured inquiry and the subtle art of asking questions that are sufficiently open to encourage honest answers and sufficiently pointed to stimulate answers that are informative . They can bridge an important gap at the cognitive-functional-technical end of the spectrum between the ability to solve a problem that has already been formulated to everyone's satisfaction and the ability to formulate a problem, sometimes iteratively, in a way that the solution secures agreement from several parties. At the other end of the spectrum, the affective-relational-communicative skills required to navigate, as a team, the uncertainties in a "live" case make the approach useful for developing the framing, interpretation, co-reasoning, and co-creation skills usually associated with facilitators rather than participants.

Skill Transfer: Where and How?

Because they introduce indeterminacy and immediacy to the learning experience, live cases shift the locus of learning closer to the locus of application than is the case with simulations and packaged case studies. The predicaments in "live" cases are usually not defined, and participants' actions—including their queries and questions—change the predicament of the organization and the nature of the problem. Because they happen in a realistic scenario—one that resembles the context in which a real transformation or executive problem-solving project takes place, they instantiate the kind of involvement of participants that bodes well for the transfer of skill (see, for instance, Gray and Orasanu 1987; Alexander, Broadfoot, and Phillips 1999). Due to the differences in distance from the locus of intervention, there likely are significant differences in skill transfer between "live" cases that involve participants' organizations (as is the case with action learning and field-and-forum interventions) and those set in other organizations in which executives participate passively, as happens in MBA and EMBA capstone projects.

Transformational Interventions: Coaching, Master Class, and Mentoring Programs

Many executive development programs offer individual and small-group-centered coaching, or other personalized feedback-intensive self-development modules. They are meant to help individuals and teams acquire higher levels of awareness and skills not amenable to development in structured environments. They are usually relational, affective, and communicative skills such as the ability to express yourself precisely during contentious conversations to ensure that the points of view of team members radically different from the majority are not overlooked, or the ability to give pointed, precise, actionable, legitimate feedback to someone whose self-concept or self-appraisal is likely to be contradicted by the substance of the feedback. Such interventions have become more common in executive development programs that are tightly focused on the development of interpersonal skills, and are frequently offered by HR consultancies as well as by business schools and larger consultancies.

Skill Acquisition: What Is Learned?

Tailored interventions and coaching programs and sessions differ from other executive programs in that their focus is often emergent: it evolves as a function of the developmental needs of each participant. Being tailored to individual, team, and context, feedback regimes cannot be easily standardized. Skill acquisition can thus be measured only with respect to program participants' skill level differentials, whether determined by self-assessment or polls of peers, colleagues, direct reports, and hierarchical superiors or feedback from the organization, which makes it challenging—but not impossible—to make claims about the skill development outcomes of such interventions. The popularity of one-on-one and one-on-few formats for developmental interventions suggests that they are highly valuable to participants and their organizations, even though it is often, understandably, difficult to distinguish between the thera-peutic and skill development value of these interventions.

One exception comes to us via dedicated coaching circles that are com-mitted to increasing the ability of executives to deal with precisely the chal-lenges that an executive faces. For example, Cultivating Leadership is a loosely structured organization—a circle of fifty practitioners distributed around the world—whose members are jointly committed to increasing executives' abil-ity to deal with conflict, complexity, and ambiguity in the scenarios they face. The circle functions both as a support system for executives in their daily tasks and challenges and as a capability enhancer via a set of programs targeted at executives' teams and meant to build the sort of emotional resilience, cognitive resourcefulness, and ontological nimbleness that are required of humans who must often "swivel without duplicity"; that is, accommodate and integrate across different ways of being that sharply contrast with and contradict one another and reach resolutions that make various stakeholders feel not only "at peace" but genuinely understood and motivated—often in virtue of being accurately understood. The circle's interventions are meant to be transformational rather than informational: devoted to "enlarging the vessel" in which new skills are kindled and developed, as opposed to seeking to impart or imprint new infor-mation. Participants in their coaching and development program for a large bank speak of "being less attached to control and to being right or having to find all of the answers by themselves" and come to see the value of "seeking multiple, diverse perspectives and...thinking and working systemically."

Another notable exception is the master class (Moldoveanu and Martin 2008) or self-development lab (Moldoveanu 2014; Moldoveanu and Djikic 2017). In master classes, dedicated coaches, trained in psychodynamic processes and communications skills, work with individuals and small groups to develop the skills related to executive performances such as the executive committee meet-ing, the pitch, the analytical presentation, the board meeting, and so on. Each involves specific combinations of text, subtext, and context aimed at achieving targeted developmental interventions in individual and team environments (such as second-by-second analyses of taped presentations by an individual and group discussions). The modules emphasize learning over teaching, and use individualized, timely, and pointed feedback to help participants achieve higher levels of intra- and interpersonal competence.

The skill-transfer properties of coaching sessions and interventions can be described only with reference to specific skills. Skills such as the acute and astute articulation of the perceived emotional states of the self and others, which are often the objectives of coaching interventions, are highly susceptible to the social and functional context of their application, as are team-level interventions that enhance the degree to which difficult dialog and conversation is possible. Contextualized, on-the-job interventions will exhibit the highest levels of skill transfer and impact, on account of the co-membership of participants in pre-existing teams and groups that undergo an "opening up" of their communicative space and prowess as a result of a well-designed, "cathartic" intervention. As one Cultivating Leadership partner commented: "We use the trickiest and most exciting issues that each leader faces, [which allows us to] focus on places where the leaders need to stretch—and we help them see the immediate value of the tools we offer." Personalized, socialized contextualization of learning— as we will see in Chapter 5—appears to be where the industry as a whole is heading.

How Shall the Building Blocks of Executive Development Programs Evolve?

As the organizations that pay for the participation of executives in executive development programs acquire the capability to deliver on-the-job training that co-locates skill acquisition and skill application, off-site training programs will need to reinvent themselves—quickly. Otherwise, they will not be able to increase the frequency of skill transfer given the distance between the locus of acquisition and the locus of application. They can manage that by changing, shaping, and modifying their core vehicles (case studies, lectures, coaching, and so forth) used to develop skills and capabilities.

Figure 3.5 depicts the diminishing returns to executive development as a function of the distance between where skills are acquired and where they will be applied, and identifies the trajectories along which the various skill development vehicles must change. As executive education programs come to grips with the effects of diminishing returns to skill development, and as talent and learning officers come into possession of an expanded and searchable set of development modules—whose ROI on learning can be measured—executive

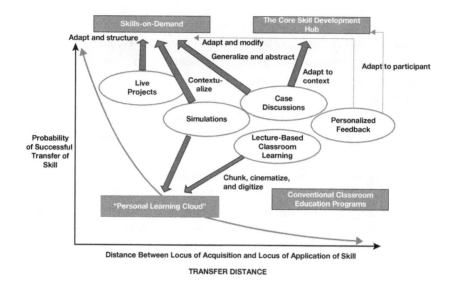

Figure 3.5. Mapping the Trajectory of the Evolution of the Building Blocks of Skill Development

program designers and developers face a choice: they can either retreat—or adapt.

Providers of executive development can adapt in one of two ways. They can push learning content and experience to the job, using personalized learning vehicles and platforms to develop skills only in the context of executives' worlds, thereby minimizing transfer distance. Alternatively, they can redesign the learning experiences they offer in off-site settings (for example, the business school classroom) to maximize the transferability of acquired skills to the job and the role.

Lectures and low-interaction content (including quizzes and exams) can be transferred to the personal learning cloud, which will enable low-cost reproduction of the learning experience on an individual basis. Standard options, such as rewind, repeat, slow down, speed up, and participant-level analytics with respect to performance, and the customization of content to learning style (adaptive learning mechanics) will increase their value, both to the executive and the organization.

Case discussions can shift toward greater contextualization by documenting situations about the participant or organization and being delivered in-house.

They can also move toward greater levels of abstraction and generalization by cultivating specific conversational and dialogical skill sets—as we will show in Chapter 4.

Simulations can be contextualized to organization-specific situations and offered internally, specifically involving situations salient to the tasks of participating individuals and groups. They could also be transferred to remote, multiplayer, online settings, in which user interaction and behavior can be mapped, tracked, and analyzed. That will allow simulations to be synthesized into learning experiences that are integrated with online lectures and quizzes.

"Live" projects can exploit the greater visibility into, and the ability to track, executives' tasks, routines, and interactions to become even more contextualized to the situations that executives face in the organization they are working in.

Personalized feedback-based interventions, such as coaching, can be deployed in "live" settings, using videos from sales, marketing, and executive meeting calls (for instance)—as opposed to material that is contrived or specially created for the purpose of feedback sessions. They will benefit from the rapidly proliferating technological capabilities afforded by tracking, polling, sensing, and sampling platforms, such as Gong. They could also be redesigned to undertake psycho-dynamically informed, deep dives into participants' patterns of relating, emoting, communicating, and interpreting, triggered by measurements of participants' verbal and nonverbal communication that reveal deep-seated fears and anxieties or, alternatively, domains about which participants feel exceedingly positive and animated.

The Effects of Disaggregation, Disintermediation, and Decoupling on the Competitive Landscape of Executive Education

Let us now consider the impact of the three disruptive forces on the cost structures, competitive landscape, and innovation paths of executive education programs.

As executive education, along with higher education, financial services, and health care, enters the digital era, the activities, tasks, business models, ways of doing business, and trade-offs in the industry as well as the various modes of learning—visual, textual, behavioral, online, in-person, group, and so on—need to be analyzed afresh to determine the equilibria that are likely to emerge.

Cost Curve Effects: Changing Nature of Communication
and Redesigning the Canon of Learning

There are two components of the impact of the emerging infrastructure of teaching materials, methods, instructors, and platforms on the production, and thereby the cost structure, of executive education providers.

First, there will be a quantum reduction in the costs of optimizing instructor-participant interaction. What separates the seeker of a skill from its possessor is clearly a combination of guidance, content, practice, and feedback. The first two are in the purview of the instructor, the coach, or the faculty member who selects, curates, and adapts content to participants' needs. The content may be aggregated from many different courses and learning experiences (lectures, quizzes, and so forth) designed to mediate the skill-acquisition process.

The burgeoning PLC repertoire of cases, lectures, modules, platforms, and apps affords education providers distributed access to the content and experience base of the industry, function, or role for which participants are seeking to develop new skills. It also helps education providers optimize the learning experience across the modules that catalyze learning. For instance, by using online vehicles, the standard chunking of content delivery to eighty-minute classes, each with a sixty-minute lecture and twenty minutes of discussion, could be reconfigured into more efficient twenty- or thirty-minute online lectures, themselves chunked into modules of no more than six minutes each, which deliver content far more efficiently by editing out instructors' classroom idiosyncrasies.

Online lectures also come with inverted classroom experiences that afford opportunities to apply the models, methods, and heuristics that the participants have learned to real problems and predicaments. The availability of a stock of content and experiences, and the means to tailor those experiences to learning outcomes as well as the context of the interactions, enables instructors to fragment and recombine learning experiences to suit both organizations and participants. They can also selectively develop those components of a routine that provide high value along a specific dimension of discussion-based interaction (moral deliberation, strategic prospecting, for instance) that was previously embedded in an uncustomized set of interactions in case discussions or discussion forums.

Second, there will be a large reduction in search costs to businesses and online providers for the right providers of skill development experiences. The personal learning cloud, enabled by the Web 2.0 environment, affords a quantum reduction in the costs organizations incur while searching for content and experiences from providers. Until now, when a business school used teaching materials developed by faculty members in other business schools, it incurred large sunk costs associated with sampling and experimental deployment. In the new environment, though, it will involve no more than disciplined surfing, informed by user feedback and usefulness metrics, often supplied by client organizations themselves—an example of the combined power of disaggregation and disintermediation, working at the level of each provider's offerings.

Content that matches pedagogical purposes and learning outcomes can be made available by the PLC in customized forms. A provider can search for the most relevant lectures, discussions, testing materials, and simulations produced by its instructors, whose presence in the classroom is often no longer necessary to deliver the content. That shifts the provider's cost curve downward by minimizing the inefficiency of scheduling specific instructors to teach specific content at specific times.

In a disaggregated environment, a provider can optimize content and learning experiences across the range of learning vehicles that other providers have created. For example, an open-enrollment program can design learning experiences that involve its instructors delivering content created by other providers. The provider can slice up the value bundles provided by each instructor and optimize its cost structure and value proposition using the entire stock of teaching and learning materials created by its cadre of instructors. It can replace any one specific instructor with a combination of other instructors and a skilled facilitator.

Value Chain Transformation: Reconstituting the Network of Buyers, Sellers, Aggregators, Intermediators, Payers, and Participants

The era of undifferentiated or ill-specified skills taught across contexts, users, industries, and modes of delivery is over. Content, learning experiences, and instructors—mentors, coaches, faculty members of established business schools—can be selected and combined to provide the optimal development experience for an organization's workforce. That effect will be particularly pronounced in the case of academics delivering, as free agents, learning experiences to paying organizations. The academics can take advantage of the PLC to create personalized learning experiences around their core pedagogical capabilities.

As bargaining power in the market shifts from providers to talent-development organizations, large-scale "super aggregators"—such as edX, Coursera, Harvard Business School Publishing, McKinsey, and other large consultancies—will become potent marketplaces for content and learning experiences. As content becomes commodified, the evolution of learning experiences and content-management technologies into experience design and management will become a critical differentiator. In such an environment, learning-as-an-app, or on-demand learning, will become a capability that enables the traditional content providers to claim more of the value from transactions in the education market, as we will show in Chapter 5.

In the information technology industry, Microsoft, Apple, Google, and Facebook have created environments incorporating information-, knowledge-, and analytic-sharing capabilities that enable entire organizations to get on the same page, not only technically and technologically, but also interpersonally and culturally. In the same way, the emerging online learning powerhouses will create executive learning environments that will afford individuals, teams, and groups many opportunities to collaborate, cooperate, and communicate more effectively and efficiently, which in turn will enable companies to turn the individual skill differential of executive learning into the capability differential that characterizes the learning organization.

Innovation Effects: Divining the Unpredictable

No discussion of a tectonic shift in the landscape of an industry would be complete without considering some imponderables. Those include emerging organizational forms, models, and modes of executive development that are currently not on the radar screens of buyers, sellers, or researchers.

The personal learning cloud, coupled with machine-learning-enabled predictive algorithms and the potential to measure learners' emotional states and behavioral patterns, portends the emergence of adaptive learning environments. Such environments can exploit the latest learning science—such as affective state-dependent learning, spaced learning, dialogical learning, and punctuated learning—to create dedicated learning pods that will impart far more effectively, in a distributed on-demand environment, skills previously thought to require special kinds of classroom-based interaction.

Just as the Web ecosystem of online modules, interactives, snapshots of "live" predicaments, and spot quizzes is already taking the place of textbooks, case studies, and exams, so too will a rich set of user-and-content-specific modes of interaction, based on access to learners' states of mind and body, supplant the traditional listen-read-write-speak modes of teacher-based learning. At the same time, those modes will expand the range of skills that can be learned, and increase both the reliability and the distance over which skills can be transferred and applied. The ways in which predictive analytics, personalized networking, and wearable learning will engender these effects can already be spotted.

As the evolution of executive development is driven by the disaggregation and disintermediation of content and learning experiences at greater levels of granularity, it would be logical to examine the building blocks of executive education programs—lectures, cases, case discussions, simulations, and so on—and their value to the skill and capability formation dimension of organizations. With the job of optimizing learning experiences shifting from education providers to chief learning officers and their talent-development organizations at one level, and at another level, to coaches, instructors, faculty members, and other learning facilitators, it will be instructive to take a closer look at how skills are developed, acquired, and transferred by the dominant modes of teaching and learning, which is the focus of the next chapter of our study of executive education.

WHAT IS TO BE DONE?

The Chief Learning Officer's Compass and the Program Designer's Guide

Executive education worldwide has entered a period of disruption catalyzed by the digitalization of content, connectivity, and communication—while the demand for managerial skills is growing, the number and number of kinds of providers are increasing, and the opportunities for innovating in the space of content and learning experiences are growing rapidly. The forces of disintermediation, disaggregation, and decoupling are independently creating an unprecedented increase in the nature, number, and visibility of options for companies seeking to increase their skill and capability base.

In this chapter we will draw on our own experiences in leading executive development organizations—comprising both hands-on design and management of programs and learning experiences and strategic and tactical prospecting of an industry in which we have each played a role and take a proactive view of the predicament faced by decision makers in both client organization and executive development programs. We will articulate a compass for chief learning officers, chief talent officers, or chief executive officers who want to chart effective routes through the emerging landscape of executive development, and a guide for executive education providers, who will have to adapt quickly to the new demand characteristics, technological options, and cost curves. We show how the feedback loops connecting suppliers to organizational clients have to be reengineered if education providers want to stay connected to their clients and learn how to adapt their offerings to the changing marketplace.

Mapping the Skills Gaps

Skill development—comprising both skill acquisition and skill transfer—is the fundamental source of value in executive education for both companies and executives. No executive would attend an education program if the only benefits it offered were social signaling, networking opportunities, or interesting conversations—in spite of the real value these entail. There are many other cheaper, more effective substitutes available for those purposes in the times of podcasts, digital rendezvous sessions, and impromptu thematic conferences. In Chapter 1, we identified the key skills (Figure 4.1) executives and organizations seek, and canvassed both the technical and cognitive skills associated with functional expertise and the relational, affective, perceptual, and X-factor skills affiliated with the kind of human practices we identify with "leadership" or "executive work."

Our dialogues with executive education clients suggest that while companies attempt to monitor skill transfer—because they value it as it represents what they pay for—most executive education providers do not: they only track participants' satisfaction with their programs—which may include self-reported measures of skill acquisition—but they do not educate respondents about *what skills are*, about *what kinds of skill* there are, and how skills can be observed, identified, and measured. Unsurprisingly, instructors and the service provider organizations that usually employ them tend to believe they have succeeded in their programs if participants rate the program highly on a catch-all "skill acquisition" measure—along with other metrics that measure "entertainment value" (such as "facilities") and "networking value." But organizations believe that the programs they funded *have failed* if executives don't use most or all of the new skills they're supposed to have acquired when they return to work.

Bridging the Skills Gaps

The gap between the skills that organizations need and those that executive development programs provide—the "skills gap"—appears to be linked to the incentive misalignment and poor choice of performance measurement variables. As we showed in Chapter 2, because organizations pay for the programs their executives participate in, the payers for the experience good that is an executive development

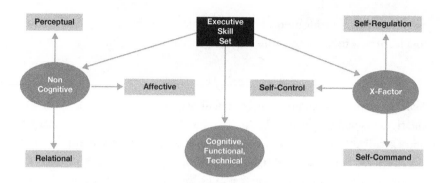

Figure 4.1. The Executive's Skill Sets

program are not the consumers of that good. The motivation of payers and consumers largely differs—overlapping solely with respect to skill development (but may differ once again with respect to the range and nature of the skills sought). Performance measures used by organizations and executive programs providers predictably differ. Organizations care about performance enhancements attributable to the acquisition of a skill by an executive in a program she or he has enrolled in, and the application of that skill in the context of an organizational process or task. Executive education designers and providers care about the subjective evaluations of participants. Thus "fixing" the skills gap is a simple to understand but hard to implement matter of straightening out the feedback loops that inform organizational choices of suppliers and program designers' choices of instructors, content, and means of delivery. We will unpack the feedback loops that are required to bring about a narrowing of the skills gap later in this chapter.

What of the skills transfer gap? Two approaches to bridging it stand out. One relies on bringing learning to the workplace, the other relies on making off-site learning maximally transferrable to the workplace.

One approach education providers can take to bridging the skills transfer gap is to develop programs that build skills in the same context in which they are to be applied, inside each function and team. "Teaching", in this approach, is based on projects and problems an organization currently faces. The practice of new skills takes place in the same context in which they are to be used: participants face the same predicaments everyone in their organization faces when trying to apply a new skill. The evaluation of programs and participants' skill sets incorporates the values and learning objectives of the organization—rather than those of individual participants or of program designers. The growing popularity of this approach is attested to by the rise in the number of corporate universities, the increase in the number of programs that deliver online content to on-the-job learners, and the large number of custom programs that management consultancies and business schools now offer.

Another approach is for education providers to develop programs that use teaching pedagogies that are *designed for skill transfer*—across companies, industries, and countries. Such pedagogies must take into consideration the need for contextualized and socialized learning, allow customized feedback to each participant, and alternate the learning of abstract principles with their application to concrete and particular. An on-campus program becomes a learning laboratory in which traditional teachers and instructors may give way to learning facilitators who are skilled not only and not primarily at the exposition of content, but rather at making content salient a long time after an executive has left the program.

As programs proliferate and become more easily researchable, better information about education providers becomes available at a lower cost and customers can specify and seek to fulfill their learning objectives more precisely—the middle of the market will hollow out, leaving the "high value" and "low cost" segments at opposite ends of the price-cost margin spectrum. The demand for education programs that neither teach skills in the context of their application nor facilitate the transfer of skills across contexts will likely fall. As companies become adept at figuring out how to help their executives learn new skills and acquire new capabilities, they will likely devise ways of calculating the return on investment of educational experiences, which will allow them to select for the highest–Learning ROI programs. This trend will also lead to the demise of programs with low returns.

Mapping the Sources of Value in Education Programs

Digitalization is enabling organizations and executives to choose among modules, workshops, and classes at higher levels of granularity than before to create *a la carte* learning experiences. The ability to see—online and remotely—what is likely to happen inside classrooms; to experience the delivery of teachers and "star instructors," before paying to enroll executives in their classes; and to collect detailed information about modules' learning outcomes is allowing CLOs as well as executives to choose and pay for only the learning experiences they deem useful. "Web 2.0" is a key influence on the disaggregation of executive education programs as it enables a far more textured and intensive optimization of educational programs than was possible ten or twenty years ago: due to the Web 2.x ecosystem of ubiquitous com-

munication and distributed inexpensive computation, the opacity has been elimi-
nated and the mystique of the "exec ed classroom" is gone, leaving demonstrable
skill development as the determinant of the value of a program.

Mapping Education Programs Suppliers and Their Offerings

From business schools and universities, through general and specialized consultancies, corporate universities, and other learning organizations, to the
emerging personal learning cloud—we mapped out in earlier chapters the suppliers of executive development programs with respect to their core offerings.
That enabled us to show how education programs differ and, given participants'
and organizations' objectives, helped identify the challenges and opportunities
that education providers face today (Figure 4.2).

We saw that universities are being displaced as monopolists over the canons of
teaching, learning, and evaluation and challenged in their roles as intermediators and
aggregators of the skills and courses of their faculty members in the executive development space by consultancies, online education companies, and corporate universities,
all of which are adapting teaching to the environment in which skills are used. Human
resource (HR) development firms, for instance, are using their human capital evaluation and development know-how to tailor more effective programs on-site, on-project,
and within teams, utilizing the large base of online courses and modules as a starting
point. Web-based learning platforms that aggregate the content of universities' best
faculty members pose a rising threat to traditional education providers, as they allow
individual faculty members to collect "teaching rents" that are not under the control
of their home universities. As the focus of executive education is moving from skill
acquisition to skill development—which includes skill transfer—skill development is
brought in-house, inside organizational projects—to the teams that need them most
at the time at which they need them. The decline of many business schools' open-
enrollment programs signals they are being supplanted, primarily by the growing
offerings of the "personal learning cloud"—the fabric of on-demand, cohort- and
certificate-based learning courses that have become ubiquitously available.

The Supply Landscape Is Undergoing a Tectonic Shift

The greater visibility offered by online platforms and courses, the rising competition among course providers, and the comprehensive feedback from participants all point to the need for a more transparent treatment of offerings. In
Chapter 3, we unpacked the basic elements of executive education programs
such as the core learning vehicles and experiences including lecture-based

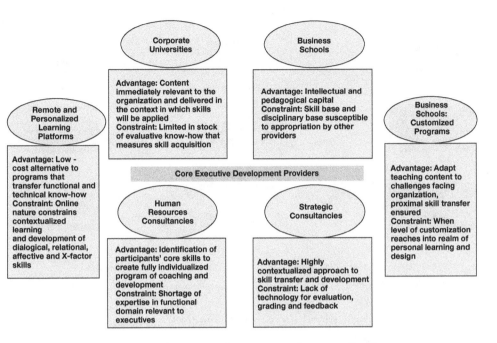

Figure 4.2. Comparative Advantages and Constraints of Executive Development Providers

classes, case discussions, simulations, live projects, team and individual coaching sessions, and master classes (Figure 4.3) and analyzed each component with respect to its skill-acquisition and skill-transfer properties.

The increase in the transparency of executive education programs enables both CLOs and participants to choose the best programs that fit their budgets. They can do so across all the providers and programs in the market as well as the different ways in which skill sets can be developed. Because data on the available options are more granular today than they were even ten years ago, CLOs can take a mix-and-match approach to designing programs. They can bring together the best of academic-created and practitioner-developed content, and combine them to develop the skill sets their organizations need. Companies' talent-development functions can focus on the key differences between programs to make their choices. They can ask: How much *better* at skill development and skill transfer than the personal learning cloud is an in-person-delivered learning experience? How should the personalized learning fabric of the personal learning cloud be *augmented* to maximize the organization's development needs?

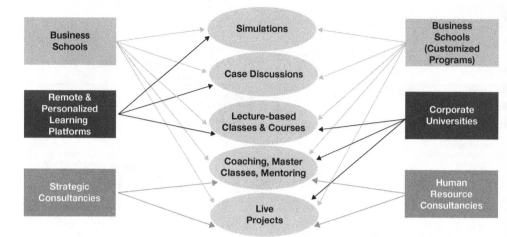

Figure 4.3. Executive Development Unpacked: Core Experiences and Vehicles by Which Executive Learning Happens

The Chief Learning Officer's Compass

Figure 4.4 shows a battery of critical questions a CLO needs to answer before investing in an executive development program.

To contract with programs that will help their executives develop useful skills, corporations have to specify these skills precisely. If you do not know where you wish to go, it does not matter what direction you take. If a chief learning officer cannot define the skills his or her executives need, it will not matter which provider or program he or she turns to. However, just as understanding machine learning is more than learning how to rattle off a few terms and names, learning and using a skill is much more than knowing a topic. To specify the skills their companies need, CLOs must look under the "subject hood" of course offerings, beyond "topics," to the skills instructors purport to help participants learn. But the task is not easy. Courses and learning experiences are described in terms of subjects and knowledge areas ("financial accounting," Blockchain for financial services, and so on—these form the "subject hood" of a program)—which makes them opaque regarding the skills (for example, programming simple contracts in Ethereum and iOS; creating pro forma income statements and balance sheets in Excel; writing supplier agreements in the fashion industry) that participants can hope to acquire and bring back with them. It is not enough for a CLO to ask: What new terms of art will our executives learn to reference in a discussion by participating in the program? or What new frameworks will they contribute to the conversational capital of the organization? The question CLOs should ask

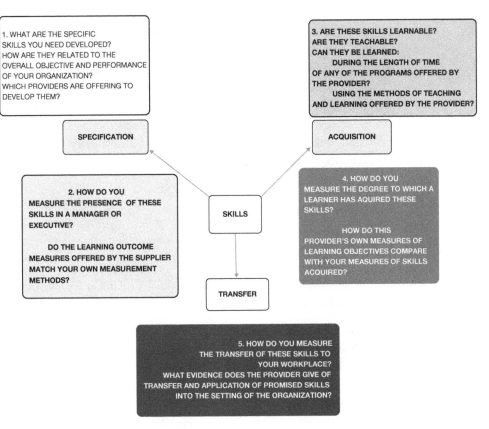

Figure 4.4. The Chief Learning Officer's Compass

is, rather: What do we need our executives to learn *to do* and to what extent are they likely to learn to do that in *this* program? Selecting programs on the basis of useful skill demonstrably provided—not by (academic) topic covered—is a heuristic CLOs can no longer afford to ignore.

Thinking of an executive as a *bundle of skills*—rather than as a repository of domain-specific knowledge with certain traits, proclivities, and certified educational background—allows CLOs to map the use and value of skills in the organization's problem-solving processes. Specificity has its costs: CLOs will also need to specify the relative value the organization places on different kinds of skills—on dialogical and collaboration skills, say, as opposed to technical and design skills—and to identify the organization's willingness to pay for developing certain skill sets.

Knowing where you want to go is difficult unless you know where you currently are—which is why maps are not much use if they do not come with a compass. The CLO must ask: How do we know if we possess, or don't possess, those skills and capabilities? Most educational measurement systems are designed to ascertain *know-what*—executives' ability to recall cognitive structures—which can be measured via tests and exams. But the measurement of skills, especially those with a noncognitive and X-factor skill, requires new methods of measurement that CLOs will have to identify and sometimes design.

The other end of the compass's needle helps CLOs become more precise about the ways in which a program will help participants acquire the skills that the organization deems important.

- Are those skills teachable?

- Are they teachable by standard methods such as lectures, discussions, and quizzes?

- Are they learnable though guided practice and feedback even if they are not teachable by standard methods?

Importantly, skill acquisition measures must help CLOs distinguish between programs that have, and haven't, enabled skill acquisition. To act responsibly, CLOs need to measure skill development in participants not only before every program but also after they return to work, upon completing them, in order to be able to answer the following:

- What has changed?

- How has it changed?

- Is there evidence of the application of the skill after attending the program?

- Are there data suggesting individual skills acquired have turned into organizational capabilities?

Compasses are meant to function as a prosthesis for intuition and supply an orienting instinct, and the CLO's Compass is no exception. It is meant to guide attention to the questions most worth asking—and the measures most worth heeding when making choices. It will help CLOs make informed decisions in a crowded marketplace in which education providers often obscure the value of the complex experiences they provide.

The Executive Education
Program Designer's Guide

Education providers that want to cope with the current disruption of the executive education industry also need to rethink what it means to skill up executives—from first principles. That means understanding what an executive development program is about at its core. To help in doing so, we decomposed an executive education program into two different components, the *context* of learning and its *content.*

Context—the cultural, geographic, and organizational factors that shape learning outcomes—is critical to addressing the skills transfer gap. At the same time, because knowledge engines, learning management engines, and personalized learning platforms have made information, data, and facts free to users, the content of learning—the combination of know-how and know-what that together constitute the substance of any program—must also be reconsidered. Education providers that hope to persuade companies and executives to leave their work and families for long periods to attend on-campus programs need to design learning experiences that justify large investments of time and money—including opportunity costs. The programs that merit attention must be fundamentally different, and more valuable than experiences that can be remotely replicated—such as lectures and exams.

A compass for executive education providers comprises a set of questions whose answers provide the foundations of a strategy for developing a program, and which can be grouped as follows.

Context-related questions relate to the times and places of interactions among learners, their interactions with facilitators, the relationship between the program content and the participants' skills and predispositions, and their work experience, such as the following:

- How is the program's context designed to maximize skill acquisition?

- How is the content designed to maximize the transfer of skills to work contexts?

- To what other contexts can these skills be transferred?

Content-related questions relate to the thematic and topical subject matter presented and discussed in a program including case studies, notes, visual materials, and online materials:

- What are the skills the content is designed to cultivate?

- How does the content help cultivate those skills?

- How is the content designed to maximize skill acquisition by participants?

- How does it maximize skill transfer to work contexts?

No program designer can afford to ignore the critical questions that will be on the minds of his or her clients:

- What are the specific skills that the program seeks to develop in participants?

- How do participants acquire those skills during the program?

- How are those skills measured by organizations?

- How is their acquisition measured by the program?

Accordingly, the Program Designer's Guide leads its user to make explicit the ways by which participants acquire skills, the mechanisms by which their transfer to the workplace is maximized, and the ways in which skill-based outcomes are measured (Figure 4.5).

We have found that few education providers fully understand the kinds of skills that client organizations need—or the best ways of developing them. Upon closer examination, we found that the information gap arises because feedback from payer and client to provider in the executive development field is broken, suggesting this is a good time to redesign the feedback loops that inform executive program design.

Feedback is essential to learning and adaptation—as suggested by research in organizational design (Sterman 2000) as well as learning science (Moldoveanu and Djikic 2017). The importance of feedback to "learning" is also suggested by the rapid advances in machine learning and deep learning algorithms that make proficient and efficient use of feedback from their own performance on training data sets to create software agents able to classify patterns—from large sets of sparsely connected and individually "dumb" entities (McKay 1993; Haykin 2014).However, feedback in the executive development industry is currently limited to evaluations of instructors by participants, which often degenerate into popularity contests and the development of indices that relate to feeling good and being treated well.

The kind of feedback that does result in adaptive change and transformation

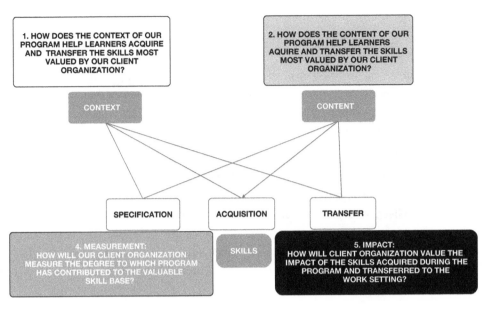

Figure 4.5. The Program Designer's Guide

is precise, personalized, textured, timely, and actionable and takes place along and across six loops (Figure 4.6).

1. Feedback from the participant to the instructor regarding the effectiveness of the methods, experiences, tools, and techniques she or he uses to facilitate the achievement of the executive's learning goals (F1).

2. Feedback from the instructor to the participant about the latter's progress along the trajectory that brings the participant closer to his or her skill development objectives (F2).

3. Feedback from the participant to the program as a whole regarding the degree to which the design of the program—including instructor selection, sequencing of learning activities, learning practices, content, context, and experience—brings the participant closer to her or his skill development objectives (F3).

4. Feedback from the client organization to the education provider regarding the degree to which the program has brought about the development of executive skills and organizational capabilities that are relevant and valuable to the organization (F4).

5. Feedback from the education provider to the client organization regarding the most reliable ways in which the organization's skill and capability develop-

ment needs can be met and its stock of skills and capabilities can be measured (F5).

6. Feedback from the education provider to the instructor—based partly on feedback from the client organization and the executive learner—on the degree to which the instructor's pedagogical design and presence furthers the learner's skill development goals and the organization's capability development needs.

The Web's informational ecosystem makes the acquisition and tracking of feedback along these loops simple enough that the obstacles to implementing them can only be organizational or institutional. They are decidedly *not* technological. Given the degree to which continuous, distributed, parallel, multi-user feedback systems have disrupted most industries outside education and health care, the latter would be well advised to create the feedback loops which we have argued are requisite to their own adaptation and survival.

Addressing the Skills Transfer Problem

Solving the skills transfer problem drives many education providers—new entrants ensconced in the worlds of client organizations, such as the strategy consultancies, as well as incumbents such as business schools equipped with a large body of teaching, facilitation, and measurement materials—to bring learning inside organizations, where skill acquisition and skill application can be co-located. The literature on skill acquisition and skill transfer shows that learning takes place most effectively when there is a tight acquisition-application loop: when the executive applies what she or he has learned immediately in the context in which the skill is meant to be used.

Executives have more of an incentive to learn a new skill when they need to solve a concrete problem than when tackling a problem designed solely to test their theoretical mastery of the skill. They are also more likely to apply a skill when the language system and the social environment in which they have learned it are the same as that in which they must apply it. The organizational uses of language, the specific ways in which words glom onto events and objectives, and how words parse out domains of relevance in the context of meetings are all different in companies from the ways in which the same phenomena play out in classrooms among learners unfamiliar with each other's ways of communicating.

A skills-in-context approach to redesigning executive education programs will have several components:

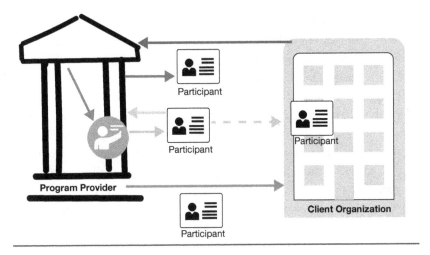

F1: Feedback from participant to instructor
F2: Feedback from instructor to participant
F3: Feedback from participant to program
F4: Feedback from client organization to program provider
F5: Feedback from program provider to client organization
F6: Feedback from program provider to instructor

Figure 4.6. The Feedback Loops That Should Guide Executive Education Program Design

Contextualizing content. Content is becoming ubiquitously accessible through the personal learning cloud, comprising courses, modules, and interaction platforms that can be turned into programs, courses, or mini-courses that may be offered in open, semi-open, and closed environments. As a result, the ability of education providers to tailor content to the specific and timely needs of every organization will increase to the point at which the latter can address companies' skill-related needs on the job in real time.

The standard fare of MBA, Executive MBA, and open-enrollment executive education programs will be broken up into short and targeted education programs that promise rapid skilling for tasks that are relevant at that point in time to the executive in his or her work. That is the approach several online learning platforms—including LinkedIn Learning, Coursera for Enterprise, and Skillsoft—have taken. The skill transfer gap between content and context narrows when participants only engage with the content designed to meet task specific and organizationally relevant needs. Both virtual and local experts become available to help participants contextualize their learning to the organization's task base and culture. In this scenario, the certification power of the business schools' programs will likely be supplanted by "digital credentials" that can be stored on online ledgers or utility blockchains.

Imagine you are an executive education program developer who wants to offer a short skilling program on viral marketing. Ten years ago, you would have been forced to design, staff, and market an on-campus program consisting of modules of various durations and intensity. The course may not have been up to date because it could only be staffed by your institution's faculty members and instructors. Their own willingness to bring their context up to date would be a function of many factors, including competence, motivations, and incentives. Fast forward ten years. Now, the personal learning cloud will allow you to curate the best online content—be it lectures, demonstrations, or exercises—in ways that are tailored to the specific needs of the client in terms of its industry, products, technologies, and size. Whereas your earlier offerings would have been constrained by the blocks of time and space that an on-campus offering demands, new cloud-based offerings are far less constrained. Most of the learning can be self-paced. Most interactions will be asynchronous—except for those that will benefit from the presence of both facilitators and participants. Testing participants before and after the program is easily done, and can help the company ascertain the extent to which the program is meeting its learning objectives.

Context on demand. The ability to electronically segment learners into working groups and cohorts—now available in most communications platforms such as Microsoft Teams, Webex, and Zoom—allows the adaptive tailoring of the context of learning to organizational needs at the level of learning groups. A learning group can be created such that its members come from the same team, department, function, discipline, division, organization, and industry—or from several different ones. Adaptive cohorting—a standard feature of today's learning management systems such as Instructure, Blackboard, and Desire2Learn—allows for the segmentation of participants into the optimal learning groups for a particular skill set. Coupling that with project-oriented interventions that help participants apply in real time the skills they're acquiring allows the organization to tailor the context of skill development to its capability-development needs.

Assume you are developing a program that aims to increase collaboration and teamwork among several groups in an organization. Until recently, you would have had to develop an on-campus program to which the client may not have been able to send all the teams and groups that could benefit from it. Since interactions with the participants and the organization would have been constrained by technology, the upshot would, most likely, have been a quick-and-dirty residential program that would not have produced lasting results. Of course, neither you nor the client would realize that—because the program's customer satisfaction ratings, based on feedback from the participants who enjoyed the experience and the time away from work—would have been high. The program you can *now* design can combine technology and pedagogy to get each participant to change behavior patterns that impede the teams' workflows. Individual polling, mutual feedback using dedicated rubrics supplied by subject matter experts, targeted coaching—in person and online—are feasible in a distributed, flexible online platform that any of a number of current learning management engines can provide.

From Know-What to Know-How: A Revolution in Content

Information alone—the subject matter of "know-what"—cannot supply a reason for executives to attend development programs or for their organizations to support them in doing so. Facts change rapidly and are ubiquitously and almost instantaneously disseminated. Providers such as academics can no longer claim that the most up-to-date, relevant, or accurate information is to be found in their classrooms. Moreover, the kind of knowledge academics see themselves as "building," "discovering" or "creating" is largely and increasingly free to the public in the "open publishing" era in which ResearchGate.org and Academia.com makes research dissemination simple and free. Executive development programs cannot base their value propositions on providing participants with topical or disciplinary knowledge, or with specialized information about their areas of interest, even when this knowledge has been developed by their "global thought-leader faculty members"—as many programs' marketing scripts say. Focusing on *skill development* as the driver of value and skills rather than topical knowledge as the valuable output of a development program shows that the know-what to know-how transformation executive education program designers must make requires the ascension of a steep ladder that leads away from "mere facts":

From "Information" and "Facts" to Models and Theories

In the current Web environment, very few facts are not a click away. For a learner, an executive development program based on the pure dissemination of information is nil. Unlike skills, facts (or "data") are not transferrable across situations. They relate to what has been—even if only a few milliseconds ago. Moreover, in an era of distributed silicon memory and dense electronic connectivity, the benefits of memorizing raw facts to a learner's memory are doubtful, as the age-old argument that learning lots of words of a "dead language" (such as Latin) helps develop or maintain the declarative memory required to retain other, useful information loses its force.

What *may be* portable from current learning vehicles are the models and theories used to make sense of data to generate explanations, justifications, extrapolations, and predictions. According to Eric Schmidt—and as of as far back as 2010—we (the 7-plus billion humans alive) currently produce five exabytes of data every two days—which is the equivalent of all the information produced prior to 2003. Data need to be *compressed* in order for them to be useful—and that is what models and theories often do for us. They are the equivalent of the MPEG coders in your HDTV set top box—compressing facts and figures rather than moving pictures and their audio signals. They enable highly efficient communication of very large amounts of information: with just a few coefficients of a multidimensional polynomial taking up a few bytes, one can communicate the equivalent of several petabytes of data.

Executive development programs have outgrown informational dissemination as a pedagogical goal, but have not outgrown the mindsets and the practices associated with a time in which information was scarce and educators held a monopoly on its legitimate conveyance. Many of them operate on the implicit assumption that models and theories are in themselves learnable, useful, and transferrable. However, to be useful, models and theories themselves need to be grounded in ways of thinking and speaking, in the purposes and predicaments of the participant and the organization, and in the code bases and databases on which they work. And the skill corresponding to the predictive or explanatory use of models and theories needs to be contextualized in several ways in order for it to be transferred. A learner must see a model or theory applied to many different predicaments, and to predicaments that have not been presanitized for the purpose of classroom teaching, in order to develop the confidence to use it in *her* situation. Moreover, the rapid development of data-based and data-driven modeling tools—ranging from computational knowledge engines such as Wolfram Alpha to "deep learning" platforms like H2O, TensorFlow, and CaffeAI, which allow the user to build and test his own model, suggests we should reconsider the real sources of learning in executive programs that aim to take the high road to skill transfer.

FROM MODELS AND METAPHORS TO SPECIAL LANGUAGES AND MENTAL HABITS

Experts do not only or primarily add value to executives in the predicaments they face by the stock of models and theories they have at their disposal. They also contribute the special languages, questions, and reasoning patterns that they bring to thinking and talking about predicaments and situations.

"Reliably valid" theories and models come and go. Their half-lives are currently at no more than 2.5 times the one-year half-life of "relevant data" for most business decisions. But the half-life of the special languages and logics that allow scientists to pose meaningful questions, formulate hypotheses, and specify experiments and the equipment needed to carry them out stretches over decades. The language systems of neoclassical economics (such as rational choice theory, rational belief theory, and game theory), network science (derived from graph theory and topology and progressively developed to accommodate experimental findings across subjects ranging from social to metabolic to Web page networks); information and computation theory (derived from fundamental models of information and computation and increasingly used to understand biological, neurophysiogical, and neuropsychological processes that may work at the levels of individuals, groups, organizations, markets, and societies); system dynamics (again spanning mechanical, electrical, fluid, chemical, neurological, and social systems of causal chains) are long-lived, learnable, and teachable *as languages.* They are universal enough to be applicable to a broad range of phenomena and predicaments—which is the hallmark of *transferability.*

Pursuing this opportunity requires a significant shift away from *content* and toward *syntax* and *semantics* as the units of content and toward *context* and *process* as the drivers of skill acquisition. The ability and proclivity (together, "the skill") for inquiring, arguing, explaining, justifying, and synthesizing needs to be developed and rehearsed *in the problem-solving language that is being developed*—and *across* a wide variety of examples, situations, contexts, and predicaments—rather than in the context of one functionally oriented class, module, or course. Content becomes a *pretext* for helping a learner develop a skill. It is a useful part of the *con*text—not the main show. The reliable acquisition of transferrable skills rests on the degree to which the skill is practiced on many different pieces of content—under many pretexts—rather than the degree to which it is "drilled" into the participant in the specific context anchored in a piece of preferred content.

FROM MODELS AND METHODS TO PATTERNS AND FUNCTIONS OF THINKING

As the skills associated with functional specialization in executive training have steadily given way to cognitive skills that are even more abstract ("critical thinking") and applicable in contexts that transcend any specific business function or current academic discipline ("economics," "sociology," "psychology," "operations research"), quasi-discipline ("accounting," "finance," "marketing," "operations management," "organizational behavior"), or pseudo-discipline ("systems thinking," "design thinking," "integrative thinking," "complexity thinking"), the designer of executive development programs that have for decades been shaped by the functional skills canon is challenged to articulate learning outcomes at a much higher level of abstraction than that of the disciplinary "models and methods" we have seen above. This challenge arises in part from the increasingly heterogeneous and amorphous nature of cognitive expertise in business (see, for example, the "complexity competence" that many CEOs in Fortune 1000 companies say they wish they had [Palmisano 2013]).

But it is also related to the higher level of transferability of cognitive skills operating at a more *abstract* level—admitting, thereby, of a greater number of concrete instances. Just as learning the basic logic of algorithmic thinking or algorithm design or a high-level-of-abstraction language like LISP or Python will be applicable to more contexts, problems, and environments for a programmer than will learning Java, Ruby on Rails, or HTML, so will learning basic modes of thinking and reasoning—deductive, abductive, inductive—or of modeling—relational, structural, causal, functional models—be for a set of cognitive skills with a far greater region of applicability than will learning the specific models that finance, managerial economics, marketing, or strategy use to model specific phenomena that occur in specific institutional, economic, and cultural settings. Designers of executive programs are well advised to turn their attention to describing and mapping the skill acquisition and transfer promise of their offerings at a higher level of abstraction and with far greater precision than is currently the case in all programs we are aware of (see Figure 4.7). See Appendices 1 and 2 at the end of this chapter for a proposed decomposition of cognitive skills and functions or purposes of reasoning that executive development programs should try to cultivate.

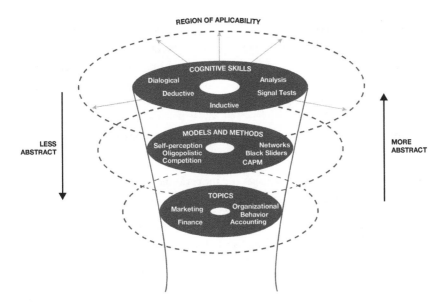

Figure 4.7. Expanding the Range of Applicability by Conceptualizing Cognitive Skills at Greater Levels of Abstraction

FROM MODELS AND THEORIES TO ONTOLOGIES AND WAYS OF BEING

The special jargon scientists use to develop the models from which they synthesize their hypotheses is often only useful to managers as "stylized facts" and "things to know"—rather than "applicable skills." Such jargon is therefore subject to the radical and merciless devaluation that the learning cloud brings to all kinds of "mere information." As Karl Marx pointed out—"[P]hilosophers have so far just interpreted the world. The point, however, is to change it." Substitute "scientists" for "philosophers" and your favorite synonym for "interpreted"—such as "explained," "justified," "represented," "described," "talked about"—and you will have a good picture of the difficulty that "theorists" and "empiricists" alike face in the executive development setting.

Unlike scientists acting in their "scientist" roles, managers and executives are *makers* of organizations, markets, products, relationships, and transactions—not just *explainers* or *describers* of their environments or *justifiers* of the right actions to take in an environment they do not fully inhabit. The critical skill to them is thus not just a representational or explanatory one, but one that is *dialogical and performative* in nature. They need ontologies, not just concepts; tools, not just methods; and prisms, not just microscopes. For instance, executives need not only to be able to talk with precision about the agency costs of alternative contractual employment arrangements or capital structures of the firm (Fama and Jensen 1983; Jensen and Meckling 1992; Moldoveanu and Leclerc 2015) but also to act as principals in a principal-agent nexus of relationships which entails the need to

- Apportion decision rights—by hiring and firing people or changing their organizational roles

- *Set* others' compensation packages and the performance metrics that will determine variable compensation levels and likelihood of promotion

- *Design* the right financial structure of a business or division in order to mitigate adverse incentives created by debt and equity issues

- *Persuade others* of the effectiveness, efficiency, and moral correctness of the decisions they make

- *Defend* these decisions against objections and challenges

- *Monitor and sanction* the implementation of these decisions through a large set of dense interactions with all affected parties

Development programs that aim for far transfer of skill must therefore invest heavily in developing participants' skill in using *and acting with and upon* the insights generated by thinking and talking using the language systems developed in the classroom or coaching setting, across a wide variety of contexts so as to maximize the degree to which participants can *embody and enact* the language in their own contexts.

Redesigning Executive Development by Turning Learning Science
into Pedagogical Practice

"Rethinking" executive programs cannot stop at just asking (the right) questions. Designing new offerings aims to build specific paths by which useful and transferable executive-level skills can be developed in participants. With this in mind, we will now consider the redesign of learning vehicles cultivating skills for maximal *transferability to the work setting*, embodying what we know to date in the science of learning. The question of skill transfer is as relevant for those designing and running on-site (or "on the job") and off-site executive development programs, for in both cases the objective is to turn acquired skills into useable and useful skills. The question is both pressing and urgent for traditional developers of executive programs on campuses and in other environments that are far away from the geographic, functional, social, and technical locus where participants will use these skills.

THE SCIENCE OF SKILL TRANSFER: WHEN AND HOW AND WHY DOES IT WORK?

We marshalled evidence showing that the degree to which learned skills are *applied* to the settings for which they are intended (the "skill transfer" problem) is not nearly as high as commonly assumed, and that skill transfer is rare and improbable, likely leading to a large and *negative* ROI on executive development expenditures. We used established and empirically measures of "distance" (in time, space, social and functional context, linguistic and pragmatic context) to argue that the farther away (in this 6D space) the place where an executive applies the skill is from the place and context in which he or she learns it, the lower the probability that acquired skills will transfer. These findings explain the shift toward "on the job" learning specific to corporate universities, small private online classes run specifically for cohorts within an organization, and development programs run by consulting organizations in conjunction with their solutions and services practices. They also take the mystery out of the steady progress of online "warehouses" of skill development platforms (such as Skillsoft and LinkedIn Learning) and steady decline in attendance to open-enrollment executive education courses run by universities and business schools.

The evidence from learning science also speaks to cases in which skills *are* being successfully transferred across significant geographic, social, functional, and temporal distances—and, more important, to the specific teaching *practices* that are most likely to lead to skill transfer. High-level skills—such as critical reasoning, problem framing, and so on—are the most likely candidates for programs that seek to achieve "far transfer" because, by definition, they are the skills with the longest "half-life" and the farthest reach—they apply to many different situations and predicaments. The literature on the transfer of high-level skills (Gentner, Loewenstein, and Thompson 2003; Billing 2007) reveals that even though skill transfer is rare and challenging, programs that are most successful at transferring high level skills do have a number of common features:

- *They teach general principles and concepts alongside applications.* Successful transfer of skill is aided by methods that clearly specify general principles, methods, and concepts—abstract entities that are maximally exportable to other settings.

- *They use a wide class of examples for each abstract entity.* Skill transfer is facilitated by methods that use large sets of examples coming from many different scenarios and use cases (or "frames")—that highlight their exportability and applicability at the very time they are acquired.

- *They vary the context of applications of abstract terms.* Not only the variety of content, but the variety of (functional, social, technical) contexts of application also helps to increase transferability of the skill.

- *They employ heavily socialized forms of learning.* Heavily socialized forms of learning (discussions, interactive presentations, simulations) help to increase the transferability of the acquired skill as concepts, constructs, models, and methods become part of the communicative and conversational fabric of the learning environment.

- *They employ intensive and immediate feedback.* Intensive, frequent, and personalized feedback helps to facilitate not only the process by which the skill is acquired but also the degree to which it will be transferred to other settings, by creating a "normative corpus"—or easily accessible memory of successful and unsuccessful uses of the skill.

- *They embody the process of skill transfer in the very process of teaching the skill.* Most generally, perhaps, skill transfer is facilitated by learning processes that themselves emulate the process by which a skill is transferred to other use cases, situations, and predicaments. Conceptual schemata, models, and methods are more easily transferred when they are applied to examples and predicaments that are generated by the learners and by other, independent sources (as in "project-based learning") than when they are learned on the basis of a canonical set of "textbook examples" that have been filtered and adapted to best exemplify the use of a schema or method.

Developing Transferrable Skills Through Case Discussions: What, Why, and How?

Case discussions have been a staple of in-person executive education ever since the field started up. The case discussion "blueprint" is likely familiar to the reader. Participants come to the discussion having read a detailed account of a business predicament or situation featuring one or more protagonists faced with making choices that have immediate impact on their businesses. The facilitator of the discussion—often guided by teaching notes and past practices—

creates a "communicative space" in which participants, working together, can reconstruct the relevant fact base of the case; take on the roles of the case protagonists in proposing frames for the situations, options for managerial action, and recommendations for the actions most worth pursuing; and articulate, debate, justify, explain, and deliberate on different courses of action and arrive, through guided discussion and moderation of debates among participants having different or conflicting perspectives or recommendations, at a reflective equilibrium regarding the executive predicament documented in the case. Such reflective equilibria need not entail unanimous agreement: they can reflect principled disagreement, in which opposing stances and arguments are understood even if they are not agreed to.

At their best, case discussions are realistic and compelling simulations of real executive dialogues, debates, and problem-solving sessions in which participants can rehearse the all-important processes of taking on a particular role that is different from their usual organizational role but relevant to it (higher up or lower down on the hierarchical scale; functionally different, culturally different, and so on), advocating for a point of view in the face of conflict, ambiguity, and uncertainty; engaging with potentially sharp dissent or difference from their classmates in real time; and developing an "executive persona" by trying out behaviors (ways of expressing, ways of arguing, ways of listening) that lie outside their everyday repertoire.

At their worst, case discussions become competitions for "air time" among participants who vie for attention, ego gratification, or extrinsic rewards such as grades or emotional validation, in ways that undermine the communicative environment of the classroom, or opportunities for instructors to "score conceptual points" by using the facts of the case selectively to establish the validity of their favorite theories and models—a practice that has come to be known in business school circles as "lecturing by the case method." The communicative environment of the case discussion classroom can be dulled or diminished by inexperienced, anxious instructors following teaching notes and teaching plans mechanically, in ways that curtail, truncate, or eliminate altogether discussions that seem "tangential" to the instructor's conception of the case. The large variance in the quality of case discussions in business schools and other settings—in spite of lots of work aimed at elucidating the pedagogical mission and agenda of case-based learning (Christensen, Garvin, and Sweet 1991; Garvin 2007)—strongly suggests that there is an irreducibly idiosyncratic, "case discussion facilitator"-dependent factor that predicts "how well a case discussion goes."

Of course, "how well a case discussion goes" is currently measured by participant evaluations of the experience in business school classrooms and other settings and is not a "learning outcome measure," a "skill acquisition measure," or indeed a measure of the value of the experience to the executive's organization—which is unusual in a market in which organizations subsidize executive education to the extent that they do. A case discussion facilitator may produce an environment in which participants feel they have "had a good time," or feel personally and collectively "validated" by a socially unthreatening and emotionally smooth classroom presence, or come to think they have mastered a skill set in virtue of having learned some new words and phrases that add to their conversational capital, but in each case, no net new ability has been developed in the participants and no new and useful skill will have been transferred to the organizations that have subsidized the program.

The new "learning fabric" enabled by Web 2.0 and the ubiquitous deployment of learning outcome and skill development measures to executive learning programs worldwide make it possible for CLOs and their organizations to audit and track executive program providers' claims to adding value through learning to their organizations. They can now track not only participants' attendance, satisfaction, and graduation, but also the degree to which they become more (or less) skilled as a result of their participation and the degree to which these skills are transferred to the organization and congeal into organizational capabilities. However, in order for CLOs and their organizations to take advantage of the new capabilities for tracking of skill development and transfer and auditing that technology enables, they need a map of the transferrable skills that case study discussions aim to develop in the first place: "no map" leads to "no measures," and "no measures" leads to "no measurements." Where to begin?

The key to understanding the transferrable skills that case-discussion-based learning develops is a detailed mapping of case discussions at a high enough level of abstraction that we can talk with precision about what the case discussion involved participants in doing *without talking about what the case discussion was specifically about.* One will learn the terms of art in the telecommunications industry of 1999 when engaging in a case discussion of the predicament of Cisco just before the dot.com crash of 2000, but this conversational capital will hardly be transferrable to other industries in 1999, other industries today, or even the telecommunications industry today. Learning key words, buzz words, acronyms, and synonyms cannot be the skill-building value-added of case discussions. What is?

If we think of successful case discussions (case discussions that build trans-ferrable skills) as *simulations of the dialogical environment of executive meetings* that have different purposes (due diligence, deliberation, final approval, plan-ning) and constituencies (product teams, service teams, sales teams, execu-tive meetings, board meetings, annual general meetings) and that employ an identifiable set of genres for the organization of "meeting work"—or the work one does in meetings—(Figure 4.8), then we right away see that case discus-sions (and even case discussions about Reebok in 1984 or General Electric in 1950, that is, those that decidedly do *not* feature contemporary predicaments and up-to-date jargon) can aim to build the highly valuable and transferrable skill set of public reasoning in the forms and genres that are most relevant to a preponderance of business settings.

If case discussions are to become skill development vehicles whose skill acquisition and transfer outcomes can be mapped, tracked, and evaluated, then it is important to map the genres of case discussions to the genres of business communications. As in the case of functionally relevant cognitive skills and generic cognitive skills, it is possible to identify a set of communicative or dialogical skills that case discussions can aim to cultivate and are transferable to far-away contexts.

Inquiry modes involve the iterative probing of the facts of the case and the inferences participants—and the case writer herself—is making from raw experiences, using a series of direct, indirect, and follow-on questions and que-ries. Facilitators may aim to develop in participants both the skill of iterative and attuned questioning and querying and the skill of answering questions in responsive and informative ways. Neither all questions nor all answers are created equal: just as there are cognitive skills and virtues that the develop-ment of cognitive skills aims to nurture, there are specific "inquiry skills and virtues" that case discussions conducted in inquiry mode can seek to develop. The way in which questions seeking epistemic warrant ("How do you know?") and relevance ("So what?") are deployed and answered in real time, as part of the discussion, in ways that admit (or not) to follow-on questions amount to a dialogical skill ("dialogical inquiry") that is transferrable to settings that may have nothing to do with the subject matter of the case. The skill of the facilitator in creating a discussion environment that mimics the emotional landscape of real executive inquiry will influence the degree to which the skill is transferred to the social and functional settings of the participant's organization.

Prospecting is a genre of case discussions that aims to reconstruct an op-

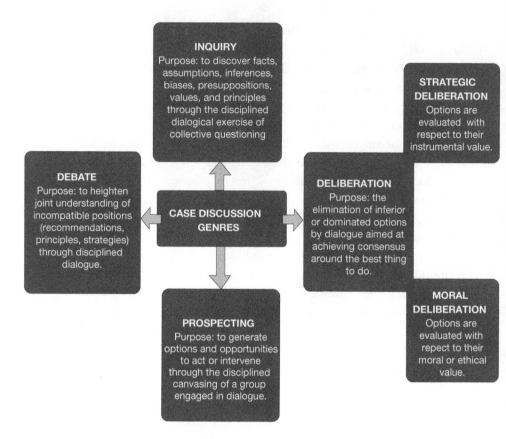

Figure 4.8. Genres of Case Discussions Track the Genres of Business Communication

tion or opportunity set for a protagonist or his organization, which is a special case of inquiry. In addition to questions that seek to uncover facts, inferences, and the reasons for holding them to be valid, prospecting in addition involves a series of counterfactual ("What would X have to have done in order to be in a position to…?") and subjunctive ("What would Y likely do were X to…?") questions that aim to uncover the conditional and contingent dynamics of executive action. Prospecting can be thought of as a set of dialogical skills (asking relevant questions; answering them in ways that are responsive to the question, informative to the questioner, and relevant to the group as a whole) that explore *possible worlds* via modal forms of questioning that can be transferred to similar discussions across a wide range of executive situations.

Deliberative genres of case discussions, whether strategic or moral, seek the iterative elimination of inferior options for possible executive actions. Questions are aimed at enumerating, evaluating, and comparing different options for executive or organizational action; at eliciting participants' beliefs about the likely costs and benefits of each option; and at reducing the number of options by eliminating the ones that are payoff-dominated by all of the others.

Moral deliberation differs from strategic deliberation in that moral principles, rules, and virtues may be invoked to justify the costs and benefits of alternative courses of action, but it often retains the logic of enumeration, evaluation, and sequential elimination, while adding a *normative* dimension, entailing the principled discussion of applicable principles and their value, validity, and ability to resolve moral quandaries

Debate is a genre of case discussion that can be deployed within *any* of the genres we have described above. Given the requisite tension among reasonable discussants (which a facilitator can establish through polling or elicitation of dissenting views to an apparently emerging dominant view), the debate genre proceeds in bootstrapping fashion and features iterative challenges and questions that each side (or the facilitator speaking on behalf of each side) raises regarding the opposing position, and answers and responses that aim to defend, refine, redefine, augment, or renounce the position advocated for.

Having laid bare the building blocks and some design heuristics for an executive program that heeds the importance of jointly reengineering context and content to design experiences that maximize skill acquisition and skill transfer and deliver value in an economy in which skills—rather than subject matter knowledge—will be the dominant source of value, the challenge to program designers and educators is to incorporate an awareness of their pedagogical purpose as learning facilitators and designers of learning vehicles, and not turn their gaze away either from what is possible or from the threat of obsolescence to those that do not take advantage of the new technological and social landscape of learning. Business schools, in particular, have entered dangerously contested territory that will pose existential threats to their executive education programs as well as their main lines of business. And because we are both writing as academics and heads of executive development programs in leading business schools, we believe it is appropriate we end this chapter with a more narrowly focused look at the business school predicament.

Turning the Business School Canon into
a Set of Skill Development Vehicles

Business schools have come to be populated by experts in the applied social sciences, such as economists, psychologists, sociologists, anthropologists, and operations research specialists. Consequently, the evolution of the core canon of business school pedagogy has been shaped by the social science disciplines of the faculty members teaching them, that is, economics in strategy, finance, and accounting; psychology and economics in marketing; psychology in organizational behavior; psychology and sociology in organizational behavior, and so on. The practical, first-person, know-how-know-who-based teaching used in most programs before 1960 has been replaced by a combination of the know-what (models) and know-how (methods) of social scientists—most of whom have little experience in setting up, managing, or working in an organization.

In theory, this trend should have helped executives acquire transferrable skills. The models and methods favored by research-focused academics are abstract, and thus they are more exportable than the intuition and acumen of the practitioner-pedagogues that predated them. Modeling a firm as a nexus of contracts, or as a population ecology of individuals, ideas, technology modules, or product assemblies, or as an evolving network of relationships of influence or interaction entails that one could in principle apply a model to *any* organization. But what works "in theory" does not always play out in practice: as academics trained in specific disciplines have sought to relate and communicate effectively to students from highly varied backgrounds (engineering, economics, arts history), with markedly different modeling and analytical competencies, the canon of models and methods of the social sciences has needed to be diluted and taught via anecdotes and case studies—"lecturing by the case method" often replaces "helping others learn by the case method," with results that have been deleterious both to attempts to teach formal modeling (which is diluted) and to attempts to teach using case discussions (whose aims reach considerably beyond formalization and theoretization).

Moreover, business education curricula, like higher education curricula more generally, have been opaque with respect to the specific skills that they aim to develop and the learning outcomes they hope to achieve. That is partly because of academics' reluctance to allow monitoring and guidance—which allows them to preserve their autonomy and perceived authority over the domains in which they seek to establish cognitive jurisdiction (Moldoveanu 2009).

The veil they have drawn makes it difficult for Learning ROI–conscious CLOs, executives, and participants to audit the claims of education providers that they develop valuable skills in executives. Skills-oriented curricular maps are, right now, hard to come by.

But this opacity is not impenetrable. And if business schools are willing to rigorously and unblinkingly map the skills bases that their core curricula aim to develop in learners, it is possible for them to make a substantial case that the skills they provide can be both useful and potentially transferrable in virtue of the level of abstraction at which science-based business education proceeds. To demonstrate that, we have constructed a map of the core pedagogy of prototypical MBA programs (Figure 4.9) based on an analysis of the functional courses they teach. (We were helped by the fact that the first-year, "disciplinary" curricula of the top fifty MBA programs in the world jointly overlap to the tune of 80 percent). We broke down the content of each course into a set of representations—the models—and a set of procedures—the methods—that together represent the cognitive skill base of the discipline to which they belong. For example, being skilled in the capital asset pricing model involves knowing models (risk-reward frontiers, portfolio variance) and methods for performing calculations (equilibria, dominant and dominating strategies, maxima/minima/mean variance frontier calculations, and so on) using the model's conceptual building blocks. Our decomposition of the skills base of business school curricula focuses attention on the value-added by teaching, and demystifies the nonspecific functional skill base of business expertise, allowing CLOs, executives, and program designers and providers, to design measures of skill acquisition and skill transfer.

Equipped with this map, a CLO or education program designer can identify the specific cognitive skills—models, methods, or combinations of them—that are or should be developed in the participants in a program. The map will also help to identify the sorts of problems that participants will get better at resolving by acquiring those skills. That will enable CLOs and program designers to develop accurate measures of skill acquisition and skill transfer (aka learning outcomes). Such measures will allow program designers to evaluate two things: the extent to which the models and methods used by business schools are optimal, as compared to frameworks from disciplines outside the social sciences, for solving the canonical problems of the field, and whether the problems that the pedagogical core drills and tests for an ability to solve are relevant to the critical challenges and predicaments organizations face today.

COURSE:
Managerial Making Decision

HIGH-LEVEL PROBLEMS
How to evaluate alternative courses of action under uncertainty in single agent and multi agent scenarios

MODELS	METHODS
• Rational Agents • Utilities • Probabilities • Decision Trees • Interdependent Decision Trees (Games) • Irrational agents (cognitive biases) • Risk and Uncertainty • Risk aversion	• Collapsing Decision Trees • Bayesian Updating • Nash Equilibrium Calculations • Expected Value/ Utility Analysis

Applied Problems
- Use decision trees to understand options and incentives of relevant agents
- Represent agent incentives in terms of expected value (utility) and uncertainty in terms of probabilities
- Consider impact of risk aversion on decisions under uncertainty

COURSE:
Managerial Economics

HIGH-LEVEL PROBLEMS
How to evaluate alternatives regarding pricing, production, and investment given different market structures

MODELS	METHODS
• Rational Agent • Supply and Demand • Games • Models of market structure/competition • Production models • Pricing Models • Value of Information models	• Linear Optimization • Equilibrium Calculation • Analysis at the Margin • Nash Equilibrium

Applied Problems
- Use demand modeling and consider elasticities to aid in decisions regarding pricing and production levels
- Understand implications of market structure on pricing, profitability, entry, production and exit decisions

COURSE:
Statistics for Management

HIGH-LEVEL PROBLEMS
How to make probabilistic inferences from data by evaluating relationships among variables

MODELS	METHODS
• Stochastic Systems: random variables • Models of inductive inference • Probability distribution models	• Regression • Sampling • Statistical Inference methods • Hypothesis & Significance Testing (ANOVA, correlation, t-test) • Dummy variables

Applied Problems
- Differentiate between descriptive and predictive statistics
- Use hypothesis/significance testing, prediction intervals to infer from sample to population
- Use of dummy variables to test impact of events or isolate impact of variable

COURSE:
Finance

HIGH-LEVEL PROBLEMS
- How to allocate resources over time under conditions of certainty or uncertainty
- How to maximize firm value based on capital structure decisions and resource allocation decisions

MODELS	METHODS
• Time Value of Money (TVM) • Black Scholes Option Pricing Model • Capital Asset Pricing Model (CAPM) • Fama French Three Factor Model (FFM) • Dividend Discount Model (DDM) • Modern Portfolio Theory • Probability • Principal agent model • Miller Modigliani • Time Value of Money • Prospect Theory • Irrational Agent (Behavioral Economics)	• Discounted Cash Flow Method (DCF) • Net Present Value (NPV) • Free Cash Flow Discount Model (FCFDM) • Regression • Discounted Cash Flow (DCF) • Net Present Value (NPV) • Internal Rate of Return (IRR) • Adjusted Present Value (APV)

Applied Problems
- Value different assets (bonds, stocks, futures, options) based on time value of money principle (cash flows, risk, time)
- Understand debate around shareholder value as the sole corporate objective

Figure 4.9. A Decomposition of the "Pedagogical IP" Base of Business School Curricula

COURSE:
Strategic Management

HIGH-LEVEL PROBLEMS

How to sustainably capture economic value for the firm

MODELS	METHODS
• Porter's Five Forces • Activity-Based Competitive Advantage • Valuable Rare Inimitable Organized (VRIO) Analysis • Society Technology Environment Economy Political (STEEP) • Decision Trees • Game Theory • Competition model (diversification vs. low cost) • SWOT (Strengths)	• Better Off Test & Ownership Test for Diversification • Expected Value Analysis • Unit Economics Analysis • Methods for using SWOT, STEEP, VRIO, Porter's Five Forces to make business unit/firm strategic decisions

Applied Problems

- Represent strategy as a function of value adding and inimitable set of activities based on clear trade-offs
- Understand distinction between two fundamental strategies - diversification (increasing willingness to pay) vs. cost leadership (reducing supplier opportunity cost)

COURSE:
Financial Accounting

HIGH-LEVEL PROBLEMS

How to prepare and interpret financial statements to measure company performance

MODELS	METHODS
• Purpose of Financial Statements (Representative of Reality/ Predictability) • Debit/Credit Model • Financial Statements (Income Statement, Balance Sheet, Cash Flow Statement)	• Financial Ratio Analysis • Discounted Cash Flow Method • Methods for preparing financial statements

Applied Problems

- Differentiate between profits and cash flow
- Differentiate between accounting profit and economic profit
- Perform a 5C credit analysis to evaluate credit worthiness of company

COURSE:
Marketing

HIGH-LEVEL PROBLEMS

How to create, communicate and deliver economic value by satisfying consumer needs

MODELS	METHODS
• Value Need Model of Value Creation • 4P (Price, Place, Product, Promotion) Marketing Mix Model • Product Lifecycle • Experience curve • Purchase funnel • Marketing process model (environmental analysis, marketing strategy, 4Ps) • Growth Share Grid (BCG Matrix)	• Marketing strategy methods (Segmentation, targeting, positioning) • Expected commercial value (ECV) calculation • Market research methods (Semantic Scales, Multi-dimensional Scaling, Conjoint Analysis) • Customer purchase behavior modeling • Pricing process • Resource allocation methods (Economic, rules of thumb, decision calculus) • Strategic Analysis based on BCG matrix

Applied Problems

- Differentiate between profits and cash flow
- Differentiate between accounting profit and economic profit
- Perform a 5C credit analysis to evaluate credit worthiness of company

COURSE:
Organizational Behavior

HIGH-LEVEL PROBLEMS

How to organize and motivate people to effectively accomplish organizational objectives

MODELS	METHODS

• Work Group Model (WGM)
  • Models of Motivation
  • Model of Leadership
  • Models of Interpersonal Interaction
  • Model of Power
  • Models of Org Design
  • Models of Team Process
	• Social Styles Analysis
	• Organizational effectiveness analysis based on WGM

Applied Problems

- Become a more effective leader by understanding components of (e.g., interdependence vs. authority) + role expectations
- Avoid pitfalls of group decision making (decision process, group think, cognitive biases, shared/unshared additional data, etc.)
  information, specialization vs. integration, asking for

Of course, making explicit the skill base—as opposed to the "list of subjects or topics"—that business schools currently can credibly undertake to provide also lays bare the very significant gaps that have emerged during the past twenty or thirty years, as the world's most valuable organizations are no longer natural resource companies (Exxon) or hardware manufacturers (GM, GE) but information, communication, and interaction companies like Apple, Amazon, and Microsoft; the most important skills are no longer merely technical and cognitive in nature; and the nature and working style of the 30MM+ small and medium-sized businesses that together (still) make up the economic backbone of North America have changed both their product and service mix (what they do) and their interaction, development, and talent selection and retention practices. Once we specify where we are, there are opportunities for getting to where we need to go in terms of new skill development needs—and the disciplines that we may be able to turn to in order to address them—for instance,

- Hermeneutic, computational and analytical skills that enable executives to specify algorithms and pseudo-algorithms that researchers, developers, and designers are to embed in a product, platform, or service—and to audit and respond competently to claims and arguments made by highly trained researchers and engineers (computation science, analytical philosophy).

- Dialogical skills that enable executives to articulate complex arguments and thoughts across a wide variety of domains in ways that make different stakeholders, coming from many different backgrounds, feel understood and empowered to speak their minds (analytic philosophy, moral philosophy, communicative ethics, the history and philosophy of science, comparative literature).

- Observation and articulation skills that enable executives to use natural language in ways that refer precisely, specifically and unambiguously, to objects, people, and events and to articulate descriptions of human tasks, states, and traits that can be conveyed to researchers, engineers, and developers in ways that allow the latter to turn descriptions, prescriptions, and injunctions into algorithms, programs, and platforms (analytic philosophy, the philosophy of language, semiotics).

- Interaction skills that enable executives to express—with voice and body and text and visuals—difficult, textured messages that resonate with people at different levels of expertise and interest and potentially from vastly different backgrounds—and engender authentic, connected, meaningful dialogue in which each speaker feels empowered to be maximally truthful and truthlike in his utterances (communicative ethics, the dramatic arts).

- Communicative and analytical skills that enable executives to understand, synthesize, and communicate about complex technological problems, theories, models, methods and their uses and organizational implications both to people who are highly skilled and trained (computer scientists, engineers, physicists, biologists) and to those who are not (natural sciences and engineering, biology, computer science).

Because most business schools are currently almost exclusively populated by people trained in economics, psychology, sociology, operations research, and their efferent "applied disciplines" (accounting, finance, strategy, operations management, marketing, organizational behavior), the skills gaps that an accurate skills map reveals represent an opportunity for broadening, transforming, or replacing the disciplinary base of business academia.

Designing for the Transferable Learning of Conceptualization and Modeling Skills

Understanding the skills base that a curriculum can be used to develop is only the first step for an education program provider that is bent on reengineering its offerings. We will also examine how the teaching of one subject can be reconceptualized and reengineered, so that it becomes a development vehicle for a useful conceptualization skill. The skill of thinking about a situation or predicament through the lens of a set of concepts and constructs brings about greater levels of precision, clarity, and reliability to reasoning and deliberation. It is—both traditionally and more recently, in light of the enhanced powers of algorithms—thought of as a "high level" and "irreducibly human" skill (Moldoveanu and Martin 2008; Lake et al 2017). Because such skills are usually not algorithmic in nature, they cannot be subcontracted to machines.

A conceptual skill is not merely a mental skill. It is also discursive and dialogical in nature; it is used in the production of dialogue and text, and in the interpersonal process of giving and taking reasons and entertaining and answering questions and challenges. Its acquisition depends on numerous interactions between the participant and the facilitator, wherein feedback is provided, both implicitly and explicitly, on the way participants use language to confer ontological ("real") status on experiences and predicaments that were previously categorized differently. For instance, the categorization may have used different metaphors and mental models or answered to different discursive practices, or it may not have been cognitively penetrable at all, but lived at the subconscious or unconscious levels of an executive learner, which insulates it from confrontation with both sense data and counterarguments.

Teaching "Organizational Design" for Optimal Skill Transfer

The goal of the prototype we describe below is to provide a learning platform to teach participants to define, structure, analyze, and think through organizational issues, predicaments, and challenges—that is, ill-defined and ill-structured problems (Simon 1973)—using a dedicated language system. The latter maps the everyday language we find in "executive talk" and the "business press" (power, authority, responsibility, take-home pay, bosses, employees, promotions, perks, year-end evaluations) that forms the core of a lay person's understanding of his or her job to a technical language (decisions, choices, outcomes incentives, decision rights, principals, agents, contracts, specific and general knowledge, capital structures and performance measures). On account of being more precise than the "everyday" language system it replaces, the technical language allows the participant to make more relevant distinctions among causal variables and to carry out the partial or global optimizations of a situation (organizational design) using the variables that are under the participant's control (the decision or policy variables).

The skill that the organization wants participants to master and transfer has several aspects:

- *A representational skill.* The ability to map everyday variables onto the expanded variable set of a problem-solving language (PSL), and to inversely map solutions derived using the variables of the language, such as decision rights and pecuniary incentives, onto everyday language systems and executable actions (hiring, firing, promoting).

- *A symbol manipulation skill.* The ability to piece together a description of an ill-defined or ill-structured predicament using formulas that use the variables of the formal language and the regulative principles of the formal language to arrive at a well-defined and well-structured problem.

- *An optimization skill.* The purposive manipulation of the variables of the problem-solving language to synthesize solutions. That is, design optimal or better solutions to the problems that result when everyday predicaments are conceptualized through the terms and variables of the problem-solving language.

The goal is to help participants develop skills for interacting with their organizational predicaments and peers through the disciplined use of a conceptual lens embodied in a precise and coherent problem-solving language. It aims to transfer conceptual skills to domains that are linguistically (in what field of organizing?), functionally (for what purpose?), socially (in what context: at home? At work? In voluntary activities?), and modally (in what way is the problem presented and solved?) far from the context in which they are learned—which is perhaps the central challenge of education.

Teaching the conceptual structure of organizational strategy can be done in three ways.

A MODEL AS LINGUISTIC PRACTICE AND PRAXIS

Using a theory to represent a situation and to execute change is like speaking a language fluently without having access to a dictionary or a thesaurus (Wittgenstein 1953; Eccles and Nohria 1992; Moldoveanu and Nohria 2002). Analogously, teaching and learning a theory is akin to teaching and learning a language. Theories comprise three sets of components:

- The first relates to terms that denote concepts, such as decisions, payoffs, incentives, contracts, agency costs, coordination costs, and communication costs in the case at hand.

- The second relates to axiomatic propositions that make use of those terms, and can be thought of as formulae that relate terms to each other (S-1: efficient organizational forms minimize the sum of coordination, communication, and agency costs; S 2: aligning individual and organizational incentives minimizes agency costs; and so on.).

- The third comprises hypotheses that result from the conjunction or disjunction of axiomatic propositions and the conditions to which they are applied. For instance, one hypothesis could be "Giving oversight rights to Person X over decisions of type D will reduce communication costs in Team A in this situation."

Theories thus have a semantic component that relates to the mapping of their terms (different kinds of "decision rights") on to plain English (authority or power)—and a syntactic component relating to the combination of the terms into propositions or formulas, using a grammar specific to the theory in question (for instance, "increasing efficiency" by minimizing agency costs, which can be done by generating alternatives for the co-location of decision rights and incentives and choosing the one with the lowest cost). Framed in this fashion, the process of learning to use a concept can be understood as a form of linguistic competence. And just like learning Spanish makes one capable of communicating with a vast number of people, in a large number of situations on many different continents, at different times and regarding several different subjects, learning the language called "agency theory" makes one capable of tackling organizational problems and to articulate organizational predicaments in many industries, at many different times, and facing different challenges.

Dialogue as an Instrument for Feedback and Adaptation

The development of conceptual skills as linguistic skills depends on using structured dialogue to iteratively fine-tune, correct, refine, and adapt the use of the new language of a theory. Errors—both semantic (the use of the wrong words to encode and transmit intuitions and vague propositions) and syntactic (the erroneous application of rules for generating hypotheses from assumptions)—and their corrections are critical to linguistic development. Saying "snow is white" in German (Die Schnee ist Weiss) can be corrected in real time by a classroom instructor (*Der* Schnee ist Weiss). He or she can also supply the regulative principle that makes the correction necessary, that is, "Schnee" is a masculine, not feminine or neutral, noun in German. The error correction, or feedback signal, functions as an important somatic marker (Bechara and Damasio 2005) of the word or phrase. It helps participants remember both the correct form of the sentence and the regulative principle that justifies its usage just as the body remembers the negatively charged emotional experience of receiving the feedback.

Analogously, the use of theoretical terms—such as agency costs due to the misallocation of decision rights of type R to agent A—to refer to, in plain English, the costs of delaying a decision can be regulated through feedback that helps sharpen the use of the language (What kind of delay? Who will bear the costs of the delay? Who should have decision rights over what a reasonable delay is?). This can in turn help learners distinguish between failures of *internal* agency—of self-control and self-command (delaying relative to one's own goals and interests) from the failures of adequately assigning incentives in teams (delaying effort that contributes to group objectives). Classroom discussions conducted in the new language system of are likely to be more successful at transferring conceptual skill to participants than presentations that try to convince participants about the empirical validity or internal coherence of theories based on the new language system.

ANALYSIS-SYNTHESIS-PRAXIS AS A UNIFIED SKILL

Just as language usage is purposive (we speak and write to achieve a goal) so too is the usage of theories and concepts. Context and purpose supply the regulative schemata for language use. For instance, learning salutations and greetings to visit a foreign country for a vacation is different from learning them for setting up business meetings. Analogously, learning a problem-solving language—such as agency theory or network theory or evolutionary economics theory or system dynamics theory—is shaped by the purpose for which the theory is used (for example, designing a more efficient pay-for-performance system; building a network that increases the speed of information dissemination among researchers; building a selection-promotion-retention scheme in a large hierarchy that maximizes not only the quality but also the variety of the people one selects for; or minimizing work-piece transfer delays on an assembly line).

Analysis, synthesis, and praxis form a triad in conceptual skill-transfer processes. Executives don't learn agency theory to picture their organizations in a different way, but to design better performance-management and reward systems, solve accountability problems, or mitigate information distortion in top management meetings, to name but three possible goals. The transfer of the conceptual skill from the participants' worlds (home and work) depends on the practice of the language of the new theory to structure and solve problems in contexts that are far from those in which the language was taught. Exams and exercises aimed at applying the language to problems supplied by participants may be perceived to be more successful at transferring the conceptual skill than assignments, exercises, and exams describing problems that are ready made for the language being taught. Representing, relating, and doing are all critical components of the uses of theory, and they contribute in equal measure to evidence of the skill associated with learning a new model, framework, or theory.

Appendix 1: Patterns of Thinking Executive Education Should Seek to Inculcate

A decomposition of patterns of thinking that one can hope to usefully inculcate in a development program can serve designers with a guide to useful modes and functions of thinking—as follows (see Figure 4.10).

Analytical thinking divides up ("lysis") wholes into parts that behave in identical fashion ("ana"). Some economic theories divide up a market ("whole") into a large number of buyers and sellers (traders—"the parts") who behave individually in similar or identical fashion ("price-takers," "rational," and so forth). Classical mechanics carves up wholes ("suspension system of a car") into parts ("linked masses, dashpots, and springs"). *Analysis* divides up the whole into a set of parts so that those parts bearing the same names ("springs," "traders") behave identically to one another.

Synthetic thinking (aka "*design thinking*") refers to the *combination* of two or more parts to form a whole. One can *synthesize* an investment memorandum from the information sets that different analysts and managers have provided, or an information-bearing signal from its Fourier components, or a prediction of the response of a market to a new product from the set of known or measured or inferred or predicted responses of a large number of individual would-be users of that product. If the "whole" to be synthesized is "new" then synthesis is a model for *design thinking*. Synthetic thinking proceeds according to a process of placing together parts into a whole—whether or not that whole is itself novel.

Convergent thinking (aka "*vertical thinking*") aims at producing a final result, product or output that is optimal, maximal, or in some way *better* than some alternative. Thinking through to the solution to a set of linear equations is *convergent*, as is attempting to prove a theorem in a finance theory textbook: we know a proof exists (otherwise it would not be an exercise in a textbook); the goal is to *produce* it. Structuring a paragraph in support of the header statement to a critical board report is *convergent* because the paragraph is supposed to produce an argument *for* that statement, thus making it more credible or persuasive.

Divergent thinking (aka "*lateral thinking*") leads away from a starting point to generate options, ideas, images, ways of being, ways of thinking, or tangible choosable options. Randomly listing a set of strategic options for the launch of a new product, freely associating ideas regarding possible motivations of a key character in an unfolding business story, unpacking the motivations of an analysand on the couch, allowing one's self to meander freely according to her

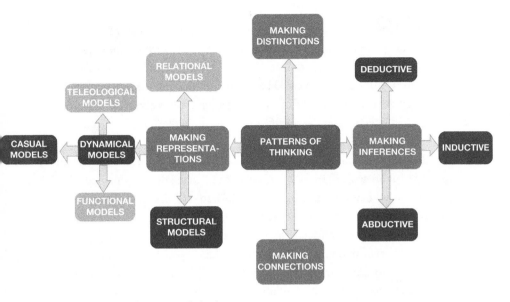

Figure 4.10. A Map of Patterns of Thinking

or his moods, sensations, and whims, and *sketching* the possible experiences of a user of a service or the interior of a new building or the emotional landscape of a management meeting are *forms of divergent thinking* in this sense.

Constructive thinking proceeds *from* an established foundation *toward* an end goal that is not predetermined—which is why it needs to be constructed. Finding—without previously knowing it exists in the first place—an equilibrium set of strategies in a market with buyers and sellers who have desires and beliefs of a particular form is constructive, as is the thinking involved in composing a musical fugue on the basis of a fixed motif based on the circle of fifths, and as is the thinking involved in designing an algorithm for computing the payoff structures of a collateralized debt obligation contract. One constructs by building something out of something else—and the difference between constructive thinking and synthetic thinking more broadly is that the parts from which constructive thinking proceeds are often given and fixed.

Deconstructive thinking challenges the foundations on which an argument, or a phenomenon, or a dialogue, or the description of an object or event— "rests." One can "deconstruct" the rhetoric of Angela Merkel by examining the propositions that would have to be true in order for her arguments to have the persuasive force suggested by the vehemence with which they are articulated, or deconstruct the policy of the U.S. Federal Reserve Bank by examining the set of propositions about human rationality and behavior that would have to be true in order for these policies to be advanced in the sincere hope of producing Pareto-superior results for the economy as a whole. One can deconstruct a U.S. Supreme Court opinion on civil liberties by showing how its substantive claims logically depend on the validity of a set of assumptions about the definition of rights and liberties and the specific forms in which they may be alienated from the humans possessing them.

Inductive thinking aims to establish the validity of a universal statement ("all swans are white") from the validity of a set of particular statements ("all of the swans we have seen to date were white"), to seek the set or the minimal set of universal statements that are compatible with a set of particular statements ("what is the most 'empirically supported' explanation for the mortgage-backed securities crisis of 2007–2008?") or to produce a set of particular statements that are most likely to "follow" from some other set of particular statements ("given the codependence of inflation with the following twenty-one variables over the past seventy-six years, what is most likely to happen to the annualized rate of inflation one, two or three years out?")

Deductive thinking aims at deriving particular statements ("this person behaves as if he were rational") from universal statements ("humans behave in ways best explained by rational choice theory" [major premise], coupled with "this person is human" [minor premise]). Deductive thinking proceeds by applying a set of operators (*modus ponens, modus tollens,* the law of the excluded middle, the identity principle) to statements or sets of statements in order to produce "new" statements that are self-evidently consistent with the statements already accepted. Proving a theorem in plane geometry, proving the optimality of an algorithm in the theory of computational complexity, and proving the existence and uniqueness of an equilibrium in a model of a market of rational traders whose preferences and beliefs obey certain conditions are all examples of deductive thinking, and they highlight *deductive thinking* as a (highly constrained) form of *synthetic* and *constructive* thinking. However, the *validity* of the *laws of logic* used to construct deductive proofs is not itself deductively provable. There are many scenarios associated with inductive thinking—such as figuring out the set of laws or mechanisms at play in a "market collapse" or a "market bubble" that are "most" supported by the evidence or the facts—which require the deployment of additional *deductive* apparatus for reaching useful conclusions.

Abductive thinking seeks to derive *the best explanation* for one or more statements of fact, which describe events or states of affairs. "There are bear tracks in the snow outside of my tent" seems to be "best explained" by the fact of there being a bear in the neighborhood that made the tracks—rather than by the fact that there is someone with a bear-claw-shaped shoe trying to make a joke at our expense—*except* if we know that there are no bears in the neighborhood at this time of the year and suspect there is someone minded to fool us into thinking there are. *Abductive* thinking cuts through the requirements of both deductive thinking (the existence of a set of universal statements that are "beyond practical doubt") and inductive thinking (the existence of a large data set on which we can compute probabilities in the form of statistical frequencies of the conjunction of various facts or statements of fact) and aims to provide a "best local approximation" to a mechanism or law from which we can infer some facts we are aiming to explain. Explaining the "Enron crisis" or the "WorldComm meltdown" by reference to mismatches between the incentives of executives and those of shareholders is "abductive" in this sense: it is not the "best-supported inductive explanation" because there has not been an exhaustive search for all possible laws and mechanisms that could explain what we know of the phenomena in question. It is also not "deductive" because we do not have a set of self-evident and logically compatible axioms from which we can proceed to derive the facts in the same way we derive theorems about the real numbers from the axioms of the real number system.

Representational thinking entails *making* representations to solve problems, to picture matters to ourselves, and to communicate about and around them with others. These can be as simple as pictures, maps, and sketches, or as furry as Fokker-Planck and Maxwell-Vlasov equations in plasma physics. As disciplines and areas of expertise have evolved ways of talking and writing about their subject matter (point masses, fields, forces, flows, D-branes, Arrow Debreu Equilibria, Nash Equilibria, Harsanyi type spaces, rationalizable strategies, network geodesics and centrality measures, social observability horizons, quantum games and strategies, neurophysiological maps of cognitive processes, orthogonal transforms, non-uniform Bezier splines, transference and counter-transference rituals, memristors, *ego* defenses, "dialectical materialism," collateralized debt obligations, credit default swaps: the list goes on) they proliferate *representations* of domains of experience—*models* of "the way things are" from the standpoint of that discipline's practitioners. Not all models are the same, and we can usefully distinguish among them as follows.

Relational models represent *relations* between objects or other entities.

Prototypical examples are a geographical map, which represents locations in a two-dimensional plane, a topographical map (three-dimensional plane), or an anatomical chart (two-dimensional or three-dimensional). A relational model is an imaging tool that is used to represent—in a manageable scale and format—the disposition (usually in space, but sometimes in space-time) of the "mapped" or modeled entities.

Structural models are relational models that contain additional information about the properties of the objects being modeled, such as their size, strength, texture, weight, and kinematic degrees of freedom. Prototypical examples are architectural drawings, engineering mock-ups, and blow-up models of atomic and molecular orbitals.

Dynamical models represent the space-time evolution of entities such as electrons, atoms, molecules, mitochondria, cells, brains, humans, organizations, markets, and societies—and beyond. They are themselves usefully distinguished in three classes:

- *Causal models* use cause-and-effect relationships and laws to derive the dynamical evolution of an entity via the set of laws or cause-and-effect relationships governing the interaction between its parts. Using such models, one derives laws of motion for muscles and joints using basic causal mechanisms relating chemical to electrical to mechanical potentials, the dynamics of human brains from laws like principles of statistical mechanics, and the behavior of markets from the statistical mechanics of brains linked by means of information transmission and reception media, which can track the effects on the states of others' brains by events in the brain of one agent.

- *Teleological models* represent the dynamical evolution of entities by reference to the goals, purposes, and objectives ("telos") of their constituent parts. Models of (real) markets as (ersatz) markets wherein self-interested and rational agents (buyers and sellers) come together to trade; or of human creatures as vehicles *for* genes that seek to increase their own evolutionary fitness; or of ideas, identities, and narratives that seek to increase their own cultural footprint by ensnaring minds are ready examples; "conspiracy theory" accounts of market failure are naive forms of teleological models.

- *Functional models* represent the dynamics of entities in terms of *functions* that these entities as a whole serve. Views of markets as functioning to maximize the joint welfare of producers and consumers, of the price system as existing in order to maximize the speed and accuracy with which information propagates in a society, of a cell as fulfilling a function within a tissue that lies within an organ system, or of ideas and theories as advancing the interests of certain classes of humans at the expense of others are all examples of functional models.

We now have a map of patterns of thinking that will be useful for designers of executive development programs who want to engage with designing a skill-based curriculum "from scratch" or from first principles. It starts from the recognition that humans are makers of representations (models and pictures) and inferences of various kinds, analyzing their sense perceptions by making distinctions and synthesizing new representations by making connections. The pedagogical designer can now break down any piece of content and experience into components that exclusively or preferentially train certain kinds of mental behavior in participants, and optimize curricular design to help participants acquire specific cognitive skills.

Appendix 2: Functions of Executive Thinking

Executives use different kinds of thinking for different purposes in different contexts, and, alongside an inventory of patterns of thinking, it is important to also map out the various *use cases*—or functions to which thinking can be applied (see Figure 4.11), such as the following.

Advocacy versus Inquiry. Executives can think *advocatively*—for the purpose of justifying an assertion or persuading. Think of a legal brief arguing a court case or a pitch to a potential investor. In this case, thinking is directional and convergent; it is aimed at achieving a specific state of mind (persuasion). People can also think *inquisitively* for the purpose of discovering information. Imagine a cross-examination or the due diligence conducted by an investor. The thinking here is nondirectional, often divergent, and may be random. It is aimed at opening one, or many, avenues for further thinking.

Understanding versus Explanation. People can understand without being able to explain, and vice-versa. For instance, we can sometimes understand another person's feelings or solve a mathematical problem without being able to explain how we did so. Similarly, we can explain why someone could be feeling the way they are without being able to feel the same emotions ourselves or explain how to solve a mathematical problem without being able to do so at the right time in the right place. Successful performance has often been used to distinguish between understanding and explanation: "If you think

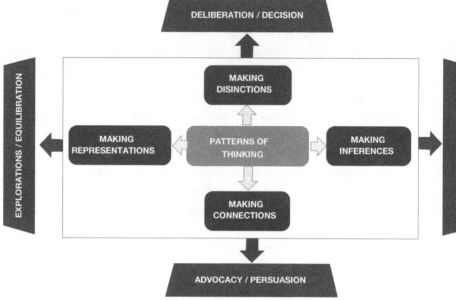

Figure 4.11. A Partial Map of the Functions of Different Patterns of Thinking

you *understand* a phenomenon, then *produce it*. Don't just describe, explain, or justify it." However, this stance understates the importance of explanation in the transfer of skills. Describing how the Black Scholes formula for pricing a call option maps on to real data is an important part of getting someone to use the formula, and describing how to make a surgical incision into an infant's armpit is a critical part of teaching how to make effective incisions. But the ability to use the formula in the right way at the right time for the right reason and the ability to operate on an infant's armpit indicate competence in derivatives pricing and pediatric surgery, respectively, which cannot be substituted by the ability to explain.

Reliability versus Validity. Thinking can be deployed to produce more reliable or more valid judgments, beliefs, propositions, and actions, but the two purposes should also be regarded as distinct. An expert can build a model that best fits the data at his or her disposal, thus maximizing the goodness of fit; she or he can also build a model that is exportable to other situations, which will maximize its reliability. The concern in the first case must be about the particular, with all the differences that make a difference to that case. In the latter, the concern will be only with the differences that make the most difference in the largest number of cases. These concerns color differently the thinking of an academic who is concerned about the universal applicability of a model or a formula, as compared to its empirical reliability, and a financier who has a large stake in a business deal, where every little detail matters. Or the difference between the industrial psychologist who may care about the relationship between moral intuition and the sense of disgust in humans at large, and the executive recruiter who must figure out in real time the moral norms and disgust reflexes of a single candidate.

Performance versus Description. Thinking can be used to describe a state of affairs—writing an account of an experiment in a scientific journal, for instance—or it can be aimed at producing a state, such as bringing about inner calm by repeating a prayer. It can also have a performative function that is distinct from its descriptive function but embedded in it. For instance, writing an account functions descriptively as an articulation of a scientific result and performatively to signal the writer's credibility, responsibility, and intellectual honesty.

Emulation versus Simulation. We regard thinking as a purely cognitive enterprise, but that is a false reduction. Thinking *like* someone is different—call it emulative—from thinking *about* how someone thinks; call that simulative. In emulative thinking, you seek to immerse yourself in another's life; to walk in his or her shoes, so to say, and understand the inner life without having an explicit cognitive model or representation of that life. In a simulation, you try to build models (logically deep, deductive, analytical, and so on), and to test them against observations of the output of another person's thinking, such as her words or actions. The distinction is relevant. It is the difference between the kind of understanding developed and used in literature and the arts (emulative) and the social sciences (simulative), or the difference between producing a screenplay for a social cataclysm (emulative) and producing a model of a social cataclysm (simulative).

Symbolic Creation versus Symbolic Manipulation. Thinking may be deployed poetically for the creation of new categories, concepts, metaphors, and associations ("the audacity of hope," "the world is too much with us," "I am not what I am," "the totalitarian ego"). It may also be deployed for the rule-based manipulation of existing categories of thought (words, concepts, models, pictures, sentences), as in the case of the derivation of a new call option pricing formula from modified forms of probability density functions of returns on assets.

On the basis of this map, it becomes possible for program designers to develop these distinctions into a pedagogical map of use cases and experiences for developing thinking skills—that will guide the ways in which they design the context and experiences comprising their programs.

5

FROM KNOW IT ALLS TO LEARN IT ALLS

Executive Development in the Era of
Self-Refining Algorithms and Ubiquitous
Measurement and Connectedness

We examine the future of executive education on a technological and cultural landscape that is imminent but different from the one we are accustomed to and show how the contextualization, socialization, and personalization of learning—avowed but distant goals of current executive education programs—are made real by the integration of a suite of currently available technologies and ways of using them that bring learners together in dense and intimate learning networks (socialization), powered by semantic and social search technologies that adapt content to individual learners' styles and preferences (personalization) and can be deployed in the setting of the learners' own organizations (contextualization)—all of which serve to optimize the learning production function for both skill acquisition and skill transfer—the two charges that the new skills economy has laid out for any educational enterprise.

The Next Disruption in
Executive Development

Let us now loosen the constraints of current market and institutional structures—some of which have gridlocked human learning for centuries—and explore possible dynamics of executive learning in particular and adult learning more generally—by asking: How can we make use of technology and human interactions to produce useful learning experience for a developing executive? Using examples whose relevance we justify through research findings as well as our own experience with designing, deploying and leading programs, we show that learning works best—it happens most efficiently and reliably—when it is *contextualized, personalized*, and *socialized*. We explore the ways in which the technologies enabling sensing, interacting, computing, searching, and storing can be leveraged by innovators and educational designers to produce learner-optimal experiences.

The science of learning may be mature, but learning technology is in its infancy. As the information technology revolution gains ground, abetted by crises that increase the prevalence and use of online and remote learning, the $5 trillion global education business is experiencing a series of changes that reshape the processes, tools, techniques, and experiences that comprise its métier. The process is driven in part by the need to rein in quickly rising costs of education, in part by the disaggregation, decoupling, and disintermediation of the entire industry, and in part by a realization—quickly becoming common knowledge—that the educational field is not delivering the skills needed by organizations and institutions.

Industrywide disruptions are not one-off events; they are akin to earthquakes in that they travel in groups—one tremor facilitating the next. In the case of digitalization, the vortex has spread from computing, telecommunications, and semiconductors to media, entertainment, publishing, travel, transportation, and now, education. It is a well-documented habit of many organizations to focus on today's disruption and not look ahead to the next day's. But those seeking development are by their nature forward-looking. Educational "products"—skills acquired and applied, and the badges, diplomas, certificates, and degrees that signal them to various degrees of accuracy and trustworthiness— are expected by buyers to have useful lives of many years, even as descriptions of specific jobs deemed "hot" by markets change over time scales of months. Executives and their organizations care about the five- to ten-year value of their learning experiences, not just about their value one to two years from now. And since five years is a short time in a landscape of institutions and organizations that are not accustomed to continuous innovation, no conscientious prospectors of the executive development industry can afford to turn their gazes from that which lies ahead of its current restructuration.

What we see when we look ahead looks more like a *destruption* than a disruption: a "destruptor" disrupts its industry by the destruction of incumbent value chains and associated activity sets or through the credible threat of imminent destruction thereof. What does this force look like in the case of executive development? Here is a scenario that looms imminent given the current ecosystem of learning tools and practices.

From Know It All to Learn It All: A Personalized Learning Assistant That Changes What We Mean by "Education"

Suppose there were a cloud-based platform that tapped into multiple relevant sensors and screens to provide real-time data on all the physical, cognitive, and emotional activities that constitute an executive's everyday "work": presentations, meetings, conversations—alongside the evolving fabric of writing emails, texts, Slack messages, memoranda, reports, and slide decks.

Suppose the platform could "see" whatever the executive saw through a sensory augmentation device, duly miniaturized to decrease its footprint so it fits neatly as an ear piece, bracelet, eye piece, or necklace. It could also make inferences about what the executive cannot see or process quickly enough when she interacts with other people and can track her gestures, emotional signs, and "tells" as well as the reactions of the executives around her—even those not in her field of vision.

Suppose the platform could "understand" what the executive were reading or writing in the sense that it could ask and answer a wide array of relevant questions about the substance and the speaker's intended use of the communication and the reference of each word and sentence. Based on its numerous sensory interfaces the platform could estimate how tired, enraged, despondent, or distracted the executive was, and after measuring the activity levels in her prefrontal cortex, via a discrete near-infrared spectroscopy cap, could, for instance, nudge her to pay closer attention to a sentence in a document or consider rewriting a piece of a critical email.

Suppose the platform could also "comprehend" what the executive is saying, as well as what other people are saying, by using speech-to-text translation systems powered by learning algorithms that recover speaker intentionality from the past usage of words and current prosody, from the way the executive intoned key words and phrases, and from the signals generated by the executive's autonomic nervous system as she spoke or wrote those words.

Suppose the platform could also "see inside" the executive's body and track physiological and neurophysiological variables such as pupil dilation, facial blood flow, and brain waves—as well as map out the executive's emotional landscape by measuring and making inferences from the tone, pitch, rhythm, and intonation of her voice and the facial action patterns of her face.

Suppose the platform could recognize the nature of the tasks in which the executive is engaged—physical, cognitive, or emotional—and the difficulties—the inferential, informational, translational, computational, motor, and visceral hurdles—she experiences in carrying them out, and, on the basis of past experience with the executive herself and many others it could supply ideas, frameworks, data, and prompts—including on-demand training modules in consultation with trusted learning partners—to help her optimize her physiological and cognitive performance on the dimensions that matter most.

Suppose the platform could constantly adapt its functioning to help the executive do better at whatever it was she was attempting to do. It would incorporate quantitative and qualitative feedback from one, or a subgroup, of the people with whom she interacts, weighting the feedback by its knowledge of each person's emotional state. That way, she would know if someone's positive feedback was prompted by an unrelated visceral high in that person or rather is a considered response.

Suppose the platform operated under the assumption that no one can learn in a space devoid of human voices and feelings and would allow the executive to share data with learning partners, coaches, and mentors, helping her learn from each of them, enabling them to learn from her, and helping them help her learn from others—and herself.

Because of its relentless adaptivity and dense coupling to the executive's own behavior and inner states, this platform would allow her to learn anything about anything—even if she started out knowing very little—in a way that would be *personalized*, *contextualized*, and *socialized*.

Suppose we had a platform that could do this all right now.

- *Question 1*: Would you then need "courses"? "classes"? "degrees"? "development modules"? "case discussions"? any of the "batch mode" learning vehicles that are both poor approximations and obstacles to continuous learning?

Suppose you, as the executive client of this platform, could share a verified, trusted "personal learning pathway"—including feedback from all others with whom you have interacted—with whomever you wished, including employers and business contacts.

- *Question 2*: Would you then need "certificates of admission and completion" to signal that you underwent certain developmental or learning experiences that have allowed you to acquire net new abilities? That you now, as a result, "have what it takes" to do a job or perform a set of tasks?

That these questions seem rhetorical is not irrelevant: personalized learning replicates—with the help of sensing, storage, and computational technology—the products, processes, and procedures of the ideally "personalized" executive development program.

But does this platform exist? Will it soon? Are we not creating a bogey man that may never come to pass to persuade of implausible claims? (This is, after all, the standard practice in the futurist genre spawned by recent advances in machine learning.) The platform we envisioned does not exist now, and may not exist because the sort of understanding that humans are capable of may require ownership of a brain and a body: "meaning" and "understanding" are not merely cognitive entities. However, we are already in possession of a fabric of experiences, connections, and content that together allow many of the futuristic-sounding features we described to start doing real work for executives and organizations: the personal learning cloud and the personal coaching cloud do not just comprise machines and digital objects. There are people behind the sensors: coaches, educators, instructors, mentors. In a post-COVID work environment, in which up to 60 percent of white collar workers report wanting to work from home more than 50 percent of the time, they can be granted access—via platforms such as Gong—to up to the minute footage of interactions and work tasks (via desktop and cloud based screen recording, video sharing, video analysis, and physiological analytics that require no more than a camera). The right combination of digital instrumentation and personalized feedback and advice and corrective blueprinting and help can, in fact, replicate many and perhaps most of the workings of the ubiquitous personal assistant we described. With a dense and accessible enough network of connected humans and sensing and computation platforms, the scaffolding required for learning the difficult-to-master skills of the executive is at hand and will spawn a new wave of disruption, which the pandemic crisis of 2020–2021 has likely brought from being five years away to being five months away.

The Next Wave of Disruption: A Precis

We have argued that and shown how *contextualization* helps learning in the face of significant barriers to skill transfer: learning on the job and for a job-related purpose often dominates learning in a classroom for a diploma in skill development results because the domain of skill application is right next to—or just *is*—that of skill acquisition. Just as knowing is for doing, so too learning is for doing—and is enhanced by the need to do something important immediately with the new skill.

Just as much of the disruption of the field of the past ten years has had to do with contextualizing learning, many of the disruptions to come within the next one to five years will have to do with *personalizing* learning. Institutionalized, certification-based education—the dominant mode in which humans have engaged in learning over the past two hundred years—is now being displaced by facilitated learning in the context of projects and jobs meant to address the "skills gap" and the "skill transfer problem" the field as whole faces, particularly for skills that are not algorithmic in nature, and are difficult or impossible to teach—but not to learn.

As developers of learning experiences and as inquirers into the ways humans learn, we understand just enough about both the way in which the labor market values the complex and difficult-to-articulate skills associated with social, relational, and emotional tasks and performances (Autor 2015; Acemoglu and Autor 2011; Deming 2017) to realize they are core differentiators for individuals and sources of value for organizations. And we know just enough about their "production function" in the context of human lifespans (for example, Heckman 2006) to know it is both complicated and different from one individual to the next. But while we recognize the urgent value of social and relational skills to executives, we are, as a field, novices at training and developing them—and perhaps even at selecting for them. While *nexi* of ability and skill such as empathic accuracy, dialogical connectedness, communicative inclusiveness and authenticity, or the executive functions of self-monitoring and self-regulation—

and the demand for these skills—plausibly account for "why there are still so many jobs in the age of machine learning" (Autor 2015), we need to come to grips with almost a century's worth of isolated, largely negative, sometimes optimistic, and widely disparate results produced by experimental attempts to modify or change behavior, ability, personality, and character (Seligman 2007; Kegan and Lahey 2009). The personalization of learning is key to the next step in the evolution of the learning industry toward greater levels of adaptiveness to context and content changes. It refers to the tailoring of the learning experience to both the external and internal environments of the learner through the proficient use of mapping, measurement, prediction, feedback, and feedforward strategies and will also include the specific abilities, moods, and neurophysiological states of the learner himself.

Adapting the learning experience to the user's own mind, brain, and body is not enough. Ten years of experiments with open learning ecosystems have taught us that effective learning is *socially embedded* and that, to be successful, learning must be *socialized*. The technologically mediated socialization of learning addresses both the feedback gap in higher education and its proficient use of mimesis to augment learning—and helps link the acquisition of algorithmic and functional skills to the development of social and relational skills. Harvard Business School's HBSOnline platform gives students incentives to answer questions from other students on the platform, helping them to hone their core skills and develop skills related to articulation, interpretation, explanation, legitimation, and justification of solutions—important parts of the nexus of high-demand social and relational skills. Large-scale platforms like edX, Coursera, LinkedIn Learning, and Udacity have found ways of increasing both learning outcomes and participation by enhancing the interactivity of their learning platforms.

Established executive development programs have always "known" that *social learning* is one of the largest sources of value they bring to participants: participants learn as much (or more) from one another as they do from their content, instructors, and learning facilitators. But knowing-*that* is very different from knowing-*how*: executive development programs have barely scratched the surface of using available technology in both classroom and remote settings to enable structuring, broadening, and deepening the ways and means by which such learning takes place. Such an approach is patently not about using algorithms to replace human work, but rather about using algorithms to amplify and sharpen its effects.

To take an example, the case discussion has for a long time been a premier vehicle for "social learning." However, the value of case discussions as skill development vehicles are greatly dependent on the expertise, presence, and often the charisma of the case discussion facilitator, and on his orientation as a learning facilitator, as opposed to a *guru* or a *star lecturer*. Even accomplished case instructors often do not focus on the development of skill sets—such as dialogical openness, connectedness, inclusiveness, actionability, and coherence—that are the hallmarks of high-performing executive teams. But in the COVID-isolation-generated era of Zoom, Webex, MS Teams, and Google Hangout meetings and group sessions, discussions can easily be recorded and transcribed; personalized, time-stamped, precise feedback can be given to each participant; and the process can be repeated so that a new way of talking, of interacting, of communing and discussing, becomes second nature to each participant. A revolution in case and discussion-based teaching is, ironically, triggered by events that seemed destined to make case discussions impractical and obsolete. This is an example of machines and the algorithms that run them helping humans become better at being human, as opposed to replacing or even "augmenting" them.

Personalizing and Contextualizing Know-How: Wolfram Alpha, Watson, Tensor Flow, and the "Working Knowledge" Landslide

The linked informational and computational resources that have been in place for the past ten years are congealing into a fabric of intelligent learning platforms based on massively distributed computation and dense communication, which are ubiquitously available and ready to be deployed, that are part of what we have called the personal learning cloud. The Google matrix (Web Search, Scholar, Patents, Applications, Code, Earth, and so on) places in the hands of the connected raw, real-time-accurate information and low-level inferences at multiple levels of resolution and analysis. It has displaced the "information transmission and imprinting" components of the learning experience and nullifies the informational advantage of all but a very small number of entities—those creating or curating the data fields, thereby acting as databases and data brokers.

In spite of being widely available, however, information is not always intelligible or useful. It is often encoded by the specialized language systems of scientists, physicians, engineers, patent agents, economists, and jurists. This creates the need for special "decoders" dedicated to making information not just accessible but intelligible to those who can use it. Enter computational platforms like Wolfram Alpha and those easily built from the IBM Watson matrix or the Google, Microsoft, and Amazon matrices. True to their name ("computational knowledge engines"), they allow users to curate, decode, and synthesize on an on-demand, on-spec basis the information encoded in ways that make it intelligible and useful for solving problems. They replicate—and thus eliminate—the function of informational *translation* that many providers of executive development programs supply—and allow users to parse for themselves relevant original research findings, cases, video modules, simulations, and data as they become available.

However, even very good algorithms for aggregating, decoding, and translating specialized information and knowledge structures will not be able to answer *specific questions* whose syntactical and semantic architecture is more complicated and ambiguous than "Define *enthalpy*" or "When was Vincent van Gogh born?" Defining—in Wikipedia style—a "collateralized debt obligation," a "credit default swap," or a Gaussian copula using synonyms, formulas, and numerical examples is far more easily accomplished than answering specific questions about the causal roles these entities likely played in the decision processes by which assets were allocated within the Royal Bank of Scotland during the month of April 2008.

Enter IBM's Watson engine for semantic query analysis, Microsoft Cognitive's suite, Narrative Science, Inc.'s *Quill*—or a customized reasoning platform based on Google Tensor Flow APIs. These allow for natural language-based interactions between an uninformed user and an expert database and knowledge base, supported by associated query, question, and challenge databases representing the stock of questions posed by other users, along with textured multilayer answers and multi-user ratings of the answers. Now we have a socially embedded and connected algorithmic agent and a distributed infrastructure for answering detailed questions in generalized domains that allow executives to get up to the state of the art in a field on their own terms, by asking the questions they need answered along with the questions others have found it useful to ask when in a situation like theirs. The learning cloud has grown to a capability that exceeds the informational aggregation, dissemination, decoding, and interpretation functions of the executive development instructor of today.

One may argue that there is still an irreducible role in executive programs for the stock of *know-how* of instructors that relates to the methods of thinking and reasoning about business problems they impart implicitly to participants or students, merely "by the way they speak"—which presumably and often, but not always, reflects "the way they think." Suppose, however, since we are talking about a deeper future, that we could enable executives the ability to competently use the machine-learning app ecosystem enabled by Google's Tensor Flow, Microsoft's Azure, and Facebook's CaffeAI *themselves* rather than through intermediaries such as chief data officers, chief information officers, chief science officers, and chief technical officers. *Directly* means just that: do your own data science, make your own inferences, design your own inquiry, make up your own mind based on methods you have yourself designed, from your own desktop—rather than depending on the wiles and whims and moods and incentives of "experts."

The current state of play, to be sure, is that there is a chasm between people who can speak to other people and people who can speak to machines (Moldoveanu 2019), that can only be bridged by a small number of ambidextrous CEOs, CTOs, CIOs and data czars who can do both. But the place and time when executives are freed to design their own inquiry for the purpose of making their own decisions may not be far away in the age of self-refining algorithms. Adaptive algorithms distinguish themselves from their nonadaptive counterparts through their ability to improve their prediction, explanation, optimization, and classification performance with repeated uses on new data sets, and indeed through a flexible and relatively loose identification of the problem statement: querying SQL databases using natural language statements, asking questions—in everyday language—that are immediately translated into structured queries that machines can decode and process, and even generating new scenarios and conceptualizations of a business situation from rich, natural language descriptions of a predicament that are automatically translated into the kind of structured languages machines heed. The greatest impact they will make to the executive development landscape is automating the use of technical and functional skills that constitute its subject matter, and making this "skill stock" available on demand.

The impact of self-refining search and optimization algorithms to executive skill development seems difficult to grasp—but it is intuitive and will have a dramatic effect on the field, even without "replacing the CXO" or other executive talent, general or specialized. Current functional and algorithmic skills are acquired and exercised through repeated demonstration using examples (case studies, content-targeted questions, problem sets, and so on) and exercises. The "see it done," "try it out," "do it now" ("see-try-do") model has been around for so long in the education business that we cannot easily see it as "just one of several models" for skill formation: we see it as "the only way to do business." While the model seems to yield results in terms of skill acquisition (for example, graduates pass the final exams in their courses because otherwise they would not be graduates), its skill transfer properties are dubious. By contrast, an adaptive algorithm embodies (currently in a few restrictive domains, shortly, perhaps, in many more) precisely the skill that adapts a problem-solving procedure to the context of its application—which is the essence of skill transfer. The machine-learning-enabled executive deploys algorithmic intelligence directly to the problems, challenges, and predicaments he or she faces—rather than needing to extrapolate from a stock of tried-and-true problems, case scenarios, and test situations. The skill transfer problem is implicitly addressed and often solved, but the traditional "exec ed" instructor is cut out of the value pie by the special combination of the executive learner, the machine, and algorithms that learn quickly from messy data and learn to learn from their own failures.

The Social Intelligence Revolution

The constant or decreasing marginal returns to purely cognitive skills (Autor 2014) that we have seen over the past ten years, coupled with increased returns to social and emotional skills (Deming 2015) suggest that the development of social, relational, emotional skills is likely the most promising area for further investment in development. Not only are these skills "most valued" by most organizations, they are also most challenging to articulate, measure, and train for.

"Nonalgorithmic" skills are those skills that cannot (currently) be replicated by the operation of algorithms, regardless of their level of adaptiveness (Moldoveanu and Martin 2008). They are often but not always emotional and relational in nature. They often have a strong epistemological and meta-cognitive component. They are often also "embodied"—dependent, for their successful exercise, on their wielder having a body that interacts with the world in just the ways a human body can. Their development often requires detailed, in-person feedback and interaction—just as coaching provides. It may seem to follow that current executive development programs that make specialized investments in nonalgorithmic skill development modules making proficient use of face-to-face interactions with highly present learning facilitators are "safe" from disruption. But that is not quite true.

Personalized and Socialized Learning via Distributed Intelligent Sensors and the Mind-Brain-Body Optimization of Learning

Alongside the "algorithmic revolution" of the past twenty years, and buttressed by advances in computational power, informational storage, and sensor technology, a second, silent, wave has been rising. It rides the growth in wearable sensors, affective computing and associated platforms, and applications that allow monitoring and real-time processing of brain-body signals of users and the inference and shaping of users' emotional and visceral states.

We sense and feel far more than we can say. We "emit' far more information than we willfully and consciously "transmit." This is the predicament for which sensors, data-rich platforms, and machines that learn from them can be of great use. From the adaptive sensor-enabled "social physics" championed by Sandy Pentland at the MIT Media Lab to the physiognomical and voice measurements provided by platforms like HireVue —a mapping, intervention, and learning paradigm that uses a distributed array of sensors and associated algorithms that make predictive inferences about social dynamics and interpersonal outcomes on the basis of a dense set of measurements of a sparse set of variables such as proximity and tone, pitch, and rhythmic patterns of voice and multi-sensor-powered affective computing platforms that allow users advance access to their own and others' emotional landscapes—the "wearable affective computing" wave is changing the way in which "relational" and "affective" skill development is pursued. How?

There are three components to the impending change in modes of learning skills that have for ages been deemed unteachable.

Measurement. Ineffable, subtle, complex states ("presence," "connectedness") and abilities or skills ("empathic accuracy," "emotional attunement," "self-regulatory response velocity," "inhibitory control") that are relevant to everyday activities and success of the executive become quantifiable and measurable using the combinations of brain-body signals they correlate with. User feedback, user feedforward, and user experience sampling allow for the "personalization" of predictive and mapping algorithms to each user, as a function of her or his context and state.

Prediction and *inference.* Wearable affective computing allows for the use of direct, real-time measurements to predict emotional states and behavioral responses, allowing users access to both higher levels of self-regulation (a major component of the X-factor skills) and finer-grained understanding of the effects of various situations and predicaments on their behavior. "Classroom" and "case-room" learning about the emotional landscape of executive work and the visceral and emotional "labor" functions it requires are replaced by a more efficacious learning platform focused on the self, guided by the self, aware of the self, and adaptive to the self of the executive and its context.

Intervention. The availability of affective remote sensing and inference platforms that measure, map, predict, and guide their users enables a new approach to affective, relational, and communicative skill development, one in which interventions and learning experiences happen continuously, on the job, in the right context, and in ways that are personalized to the state and aspirations of each individual participant.

The impact of such an infrastructure is not limited to the development of relational, communicative, and affective skill development: the ability of online learning platforms and learning management systems to access a set of variables that describe the central and autonomic nervous system responses of users allows for the real-time optimization of content (such as rhythm of presentation, tone, color schemes, cognitive load, informational complexity, and so on) to maximize traditional learning objectives even for functional and algorithmic skills. In a neurophysiologically optimized environment that adapts content to user state, functional and "quasi-algorithmic" skills like "financial statement analysis," "operations management," or "strategic industry analysis" will likely be learnable—in a fraction of the time the process requires in the current, standard settings.

Executives and their organizations come to development programs with multiple objectives that include individual skill development and organizational capability formation alongside signaling, networking, and certification. In spite of the foremost role in the learning value network that skill and capability formation have, one can take the view that strong, well-established, well-endowed, well-attended executive programs will continue to be protected from innovators who leverage algorithmic intelligence and advanced sensing to produce massive shifts in the "learning production function" along the lines we saw above. That is a poorly founded hope, on account of the effects the augmented learning cloud will have on precisely the signaling and selection effects of executive and leadership development programs. Here is why.

The Personal Know-How Network
and the Personal Coaching Cloud

Every organization seeks to answer a simple-sounding but difficult-to-unpack question when it hires a human being to do a job: Will this person be the right or best one for this job, role, function, task and team? The current informational ecosystem supplies answers in the form of "lumped-aggregated-averaged" signals of skills mastered and effort exerted. They come in the form of degrees, certificates, recommendations, ratings, and endorsements. The ability to track, measure, visualize, and integrate across real performances (meetings, reports, sales calls, presentations, and so on) represents a highly attractive proposition to most organizations. They know that the "cost of getting it wrong" is amplified by the "inability to predict on the basis of current measures"—the hallmarks of volatile, uncertain, complex, and ambiguous environments; and that the cost of getting it wrong only grows with continued employment.

What happens when you bring computational intelligence to the ubiquitously distributed data sets produced by social platforms is a sharp disambiguation of individuals' signals of skill, ability, and character that are currently lumped into "degrees," certificates," "courses completed," "programs attended," and personal ratings. The day-to-day performance and behavior of each participant becomes observable and measurable. Changes in either direction become trackable. The performance of each individual on work-relevant tasks is rendered visible. Microscopic, individualized performance tracking makes it possible for organizations to see not only whether or not an executive has the right credentials, attended the right programs, and registered the right endorsements, but also a detailed record of his performance on all the various components and subcomponents of a program, along with the views and opinions about his integrity, trustworthiness, credibility, openness, affability, and competence of those that have worked with him on all of the projects and group assignments he has been part of.

A simple rule has powered the information age:

USEFUL INFORMATION = RELEVANT DATA + PURPOSEFUL CALCULATION

Given individualized and textured data, we are within range of a set of "tracking agents" that can answer questions regarding functional and algorithmic tasks, relational and communicative tasks, and X-factor-relevant tasks. They do so by processing and learning from the tracks that an individual manager leaves in his wake of relevant tasks and assignments—the footprints he unavoidably leaves on the Web by doing the work that he does.

The network effects of this change are significant. Suppose that instead of having to hire individuals from certain cohorts of professional development organizations like business schools and consultancies, you can now hire from among different high-performing *teams* of individuals who trust implicitly in each other's competence and integrity. You no longer have to do the work of getting a group to function like a team. Organizations could then recruit *pre-formed executive teams* that work well together and could invest in developing teams rather than individual executives. They can make their make-or-buy decisions on the basis of the stock of skills and attributes these teams embody, and the problems they have successfully solved in the past. Or they can hire on the basis of a record of behaviors produced and successes achieved in work settings, rather than on the basis of learning achievements degreed and certified by diplomas. Then the signaling value to individuals and organizations of degrees and certificates decreases relative to the signaling value of detailed, transparent maps of behavioral data that can be processed to derive measures of competence and integrity. Add to this new selection ecosystem the ability to quickly pose questions and have candidates answer them orally, with little preparation time, and with the ability to measure and analyze verbal as well as nonverbal behavior (the speed of the delivery, the number of disfluencies, the average pitch and loudness variation, facial micro-expressions and their fluidity and complexity), and we may be on the verge of a radical change in the selection, as well as the development, process for the hundreds of thousands of executives in the market for talent.

Not surprisingly, the personal coaching cloud is likely to play a decisive role in the new executive development landscape. Relational and social skills are idiosyncratic, specific to individuals and their backgrounds, resistant to reduction and deconstruction, and very often glossed over by one size fits all approaches to development. Development of these skills needs to be *individualized*—which may partly be why coaching in business settings is such a quickly growing field and industry. The coaching relationship is preeminently one on one. It is me-here-now talking to you-here-now, not me-as-an-expert talking to you about my general field of expertise. It is me showing that I know my trade by the things I do, not only by the substance of the content I deliver. Retrieving from our example of the Cultivating Leadership circle of Chapter 3, it is about enlargement of the heart and soul and adaptiveness and ability to cope in a genuine fashion with a host of emotional, cognitive, and physical demands from an ever shifting environment—an enlargement of the inner vessel of the self that is the hallmark of transformative experience. More intimacy, more customization of the interaction, more precise feedback, more textured interaction—the goals are right now on the product road maps of most social communication platforms like Zoom and MS Teams—will greatly expand the realm of possible interactions between coaches and their executive clients, opening up an era in which executive development is a common developmental activity. As it perhaps always should have been: people who have developed genuine insight into the lifeworld of an executive, either by personal experience with similar predicaments or through a special acumen, exhibit a special ability to relate to others' challenges, being able to listen attentively, ask incisively, and suggest insightfully to those who are facing similar predicaments now.

As the future of higher education as a whole is set to undergo massive changes over the next decade—and current pictures for the university of 2027 (Matthews 2017) range from a fully personalized and remote learning environment with no classes, no teachers, and no official students to a technologically more sophisticated variant of what we have in place today—it is useful to develop a vision of what *executive* development can aspire to in the age of machine learning, distributed sensing, and the rapid automation of increasingly sophisticated tasks. To do so, we focus on the most important limiting steps to learning in both in-person and remote environments: the scarcity of learning-enhancing feedback and the scarcity of learners' attention and motivation. In the ideal learning scenario, learning science tells us that feedback is immediate, accurate, personal, nondispositional, incremental, contextualized, and iterative, and that learners tune in to learning experiences at the right time, for the right reason, and with the right amount of purpose and coherence. In practice, the situation differs significantly from the ideal case. The scarcity and poverty of competent feedback and the vagaries and incoherence of the attention of both learners and instructors or teaching assistants is what makes education such an arduous and often unsatisfying process that comprises classes, lectures, lecturers, quizzes, graders, and exams, together supplying the fabric of activities that constitute a "university" and a "degree program."

Feedback: Helping Humans Learn the Unteachable

The empirical science of learning offers abundant evidence of the critical link between feedback and learning outcomes. It has recently come to focus on identifying the right *kinds* of feedback for different learners, skills, and learning environments. Learning a foreign language; learning a computer language; learning to communicate cogently, empathically, and responsively; learning to suppress or sublimate behaviorally impulses that often destroy the cohesion of a team; learning to learn new skills in a specialized technical domain more rapidly—each requires specific kinds and sequences of feedback.

The neuroscience of learning has made significant advances in identifying mind-brain mechanisms that safeguard the link between feedback and learning in many environments. Timeliness, precision, intelligibility, actionability, iteration—all represent features of learning-enhancing and learning-enabling feedback across different domains of knowledge, skill, and expertise. Finally, machine learning—the use of self-refining algorithms—has made rapid advances in the last ten years *precisely* because of its use of fast mechanisms that allow algorithms to learn from their own performance via feedback that tracks their successes and failures in replicating or predicting the data sets they are trained to compress and replicate (or "understand"), thus increasing the precision and timeliness with which feedback can be given.

In spite of the momentous advances in understanding the role that feedback plays in learning, professional and higher education more generally are lagging dangerously behind what is now possible. The lecture-homework-lecture-quiz routines, in which feedback is given *en masse* lags student performance by a long time and which are not adaptive or personalized to the learners or their tasks, currently pervade most professional education. Current educational practice and the learning environment it produces live in self-sufficient isolation from consilient findings from learning science, deep learning practice, and the neuroscience of learning—together comprising "feedback science" regarding the impact of feedback on skill and competence development.

To see how feedback science can be turned into feedback practice, let us go back to a simple behavioral exchange model of learning: the learner produces some behavior—anything from a written answer to a test problem or a live presentation to a group. This is the *subject* on which feedback is given. But not all feedback is equally useful or good. Some feedback is counterproductive. Some is uninformative. Some is harmful. Much of it is useless. What kind of feedback is most useful to learning? Learning-enabling feedback is

- *Timely*: it follows *promptly in the footsteps of the learner's behavior*. Feedback given in a week about performance on a test or problem set question is far inferior to feedback the next hour or the next day. In fact, neuroscientists have found that for cognitive tasks—such as learning the grammar of a moderately complex language—*instantaneous* feedback trumps feedback that is given *even a few seconds later*.

- *Specific*: feedback that enables learning is *not general or fuzzy*. It does not evince the cluelessness of currently common grading practices in which the grader is struggling for something meaningful to say to justify a letter or number grade arrived at on account of objectives—like satisfying distribution requirements on grading curves—that have nothing to do with the reasons given for the grade. It is specific

- To behavior or output—to the *details of the learner's written answer* or verbal and nonverbal behavior, and to the components of the output that can be usefully modified in the future.

- To the *context* in which the written answer or verbal or nonverbal behavior is embedded. Good feedback points out ways in which the learner misconstrued the situation or the question.

- To timing—to the *order or sequence* in which the learner's answer or verbal or nonverbal behavior occurs. Good feedback singles out the specific points in the learner's pattern of reasoning or behavior that make the *greatest* contribution to the quality of the work. If a learner cannot differentiate continuous functions, for instance, and taking derivatives is an integral part of the chain of reasoning that leads to the right answer on an equilibrium calculation problem, then feedback that promotes learning should single out the learner's skill gap in differential calculus.

- To the learner herself—to *patterns of reasoning, calculation, or behavior* that are specific to the learner's own way of thinking or being. Good feedback is *not generic*—it is highly tuned in to the learner's patterns of thinking and behaving.

- To the *consequences of behavior or output and their interpretations*—good feedback on interpersonal, social, or relational tasks points out the consequences of the learner's behavior on others' feelings, behavior, and likely thoughts, allowing the learner to make textured inferences about the causal chain that links his behavior to their social consequences.

- *Actionable.* Good feedback provides prompts for behavioral or conceptual changes that are *intelligible, clear, and executable* by the learner. It does not merely provide an appraisal of how successful an answer or behavior was, but also a set of suggestions or injunctions for changing thought or behavior patterns that are likely to lead to a better result.

- *Credible.* Good feedback is persuasive to the learner in virtue of being

- *Legitimate*—it is connected to the learning objectives of the course or module or learning experience and to the learning objectives of the learner.

- *Justified*—it is buttressed by valid reasons, drawn from disciplinary research and/or research on optimal learning.

- *Objective or impartial*—it can be validated by others of comparable expertise to the feedback giver, and is not thus prone to personal biases that render it partial or unfairly slanted.

- *Developmental*—its intent is to help the learner improve her performance on a task or enhance her skill or competence in a domain—rather than merely to provide an ordinal or cardinal ranking of learners' effort and talent levels for the purpose of providing discriminant value to recruiters or other programs of training.

- *Iterative.* Good feedback is not a one-shot deal. It proceeds in *iterative fashion.* Just as neural networks and automata learn from multiple rounds of feedback that build on each other, learners require *sequences of feedback sessions* that help them refine their skill or capability.

- *Responsive.* Good feedback is responsive to the learner's *objections or interpretations of the feedback.* It is neither opaque nor definitive, even if and when it is legitimate and impartial.

Current approaches to executive education—and more broadly of higher education—are far from embodying the insights of feedback science. Given the foundational importance of feedback to learning and the gap between current and optimal feedback practices, we are faced with an opportunity to make the $10 billion executive development industry—and the global higher education industry—massively more effective by changing its feedback practices. What if the learning outcomes that the current lecture-quiz-test-exam course achieves in twenty-five hours of lectures and fifty hours of homework and testing can be replicated in a feedback intensive environment with just four to six hours of learner-teacher time?

There are two routes to realizing this opportunity. Each has the potential to radically change the way teaching and learning are done. One makes use of the semantic, dialogical, and conversational capabilities of AI agents and enhanced formal and natural language-processing technologies. The other relies on a new generation of teachers, educators, and instructors who make feedback the centerpiece of their curricular designs and teaching plans.

Semantic Engines and Learning Machines: Feedback on Technical Skill Development Becomes Algorithmic

Walking in the footsteps of IBM's Watson and Bluemix, and making use of deep learning ecologies of algorithms and platforms like Microsoft's Cognitive Services, adaptive feedback agents (AFAs) will take the learner's "stream of thought" attempt to solve a problem and give targeted, immediate, iterative, specific, accurate feedback on each step of the learner's process of reasoning or calculation, along with suggestions for remedial exercises and drills that develop each subskill or competency required for the successful execution of a task. Powered by the database of questions, problems, answers, and solutions from some sixty million learners (in 2018 figures) currently taking some thirteen thousand massive, open, online courses (MOOCs) and small private online courses (SPOCs) offered by seven hundred universities around the clock, AFAs will be trained to address patterns of errors, idiosyncrasies, and reasoning styles that learners exhibit. New results from feedback science can be embedded into feedback practice via updates to algorithmic platforms without the need to train up armies of teaching assistants and graders. Feedback is liberated from the fluctuations of quality, mood, resources, and acumen of human graders, for those skills that are sufficiently explicit in nature to be tracked by algorithmic agents.

The basic building block of learning in most business schools is a technical *problem*—requiring the learner to (re)produce a problem-solving method (or algorithm)—a sequence of operations that takes the evaluator from the problem statement to the solution in small and self-evident steps. An AFA takes each step in the problem-solving process (from turning a "word problem" into numbers and symbols and performing operations on these to get to the solution) and gives instantaneous feedback to the learner at each step, using intuitive prompts ("need to take derivatives here," "forgot to invert the matrix," "this is a *European* call option, use formula…") that also contain prompts to targeted tutorials ("differentiating polynomials," "inverting matrices"). A script rolling in the background films the entire sequence of operations and tutorials, so that this learning session remains available for the learner to look back on.

THE FEEDBACK-CENTRIC LEARNING FACILITATOR: HIGH-PRECISION FEEDBACK FOR RELATIONAL AND SOCIAL SKILL DEVELOPMENT

The Fourth Industrial Revolution is not only one in which many tasks previously performed by humans can be performed by algorithmic agents hooked up to server farms or running on desktops, but also one in which the nature of the highest-value tasks performed by humans have changed. They have become predominantly social, relational, and interactive. Eighty percent of the work that managers now do in organizations is performed in groups and teams. The skills most prized by business and nonbusiness organizations alike are communicative and relational in nature. They comprise as many and even more *affective skills* (empathic accuracy, expressiveness) and *executive skills* (such as problem structuration and quick task switching, impulse management, and emotional self-regulation) as they do purely *cognitive* skills. With affective computing still in a turbulent—though promising—infancy, there is a need to rapidly develop the language and base of expertise for giving feedback on *interpersonal, relational,* and *communicative "genres" of work,* such as board presentations, sales pitches, negotiations, deliberations, processes of collaborative inquiry and debate, that will enable and foster real learning of skills that are (still) quintessentially human and currently very "hot" in the labor market. "Communication skill" is now used as a "catch-all," low-resolution label, which makes the development of all of the skills that go into "communicating" very far from the elaborate evaluation rubrics that have been developed over a century of practice in teaching and grading calculus, microeconomics, structured language programming, or thermal system design quizzes. But progress on creating the practices that will promote the rapid acquisition and transfer of such "hot skills" requires that we think carefully about the semantic and syntactic (for example, coherence and completeness) and dialogical and interactive (for example, responsiveness, attentiveness, informativeness, attunement, presence, empathic understanding) of the learner's behavior in a social context—and that our feedback practices advance to a much higher level of precision: it is the use of a particular word in a particular way, the flight of the shadow of distaste on a visage, the mismatch between the speaking rate of a speaker and that of the slowest-talking member of audience that should—and now can—be singled out by perspicacious coaches with access to raw footage and to algorithms that track behavioral effects.

Once turned into practice, the science of human feedback transforms the way we think about the skills that we value most but feel most pessimistic about being able to learn or teach: the social, emotional, and relational skills that most businesses prize most. You say "charisma," "collaborativeness," and "relationality" cannot be taught? You may be right. But if by that you mean it cannot be learned, you are likely wrong. Much of what is unteachable can be leaned through feedback that is precise, adaptive, targeted, iterative, actionable, and developmental.

The coach trained in feedback science focuses on the basic unit of social work of the learner—2D footage, or VR or 360 degree footage of a presentation, meeting, gathering, or work session in which the learner interacts *for real* with others. Each communicative act (in increments of no more than ten to fifteen seconds) of the learner is mapped into all of the ways in which it conveys information (such as her *message*: use of imagery and image, coherence, completeness, responsiveness; her *voice*: tone, pitch, dynamic range—and the emotions they convey, as well as their fit with her message; her *body movements*: amplitude, periodicity, expressiveness, dominance, submissiveness—and their fit with her message; her *facial actions and microexpressions*: basic emotions, expressiveness, congruence, positivity, negativity, attention), and the effect of each "micro-behavior" of the learner on each of the members of her focal group is fed back to her, along with actionable suggestions for incremental, adaptive changes.

Using Personalized Sensing to Improve Learners' Attention Allocation and Optimize Online Skill Acquisition

Ten years of intense practice and research on online learning have clearly shown that e-learning is not just "regular learning, electronically delivered." It is often less. But it can also be more, as described in this section.

The classroom environment is not electronically replicable to a degree of fidelity that makes the learning experience of the classroom and the e-learning program perfect substitutes for one another. Assuming that the "content"—what is being said and the specific visual and auditory form in which it is said—is identical in the two settings, the classroom environment constrains the learner's attention and shapes his or her microbehavioral responses via several factors:

- The immediate presence of the instructor—with whom the learner feels connected in a "quasi-dialogue" that takes place verbally and nonverbally

- The immediate presence of other learners, whose mutual expectations and joint attention focused on the instructor or blackboard or screen further constrain the degree to which the learner can produce behavior that disrupts the experience of the class

- The shared and mutually reinforced norms and normatively grounded expectations of "classroom behavior" by participant and instructor

- The inconspicuous *absence* of stimuli that induce behavioral or cognitive wandering, which may be found in abundance in other environments (for example, at home)

Now consider an online environment. The behavioral and perceptual constraints and inducers supplied by the classroom experience are missing. Moreover, they are supplemented by an environment seemingly designed to produce maximum distraction and dilution of focus—the learner's home. The "learning stimulus" that comes off the platform must compensate for the absence of the constraints of the physical classroom. Current e-learning experiences are clearly not able to fully compensate for these constraints. Informal reports of the average participant's average "attention span reductions" of the orders of 5x to 10x in a remote learning environment are unsurprising. If online learning vehicles are to be at least as successful as in-person environments at producing or facilitating learning, then what we call "teaching" needs to be redesigned from scratch. "Chunking" online content into shorter activity units is only a small part of the redesign, as is the instrumentation of visuals so that the learner's hungry but quickly bored eyes always have something interesting to look at, like a hand drawing, a block diagram, or writing on a screen, rather than a static slide. If the body-brain-and-mind context of the learning experience supplies the critical set of differences between in-person and remote learning environments, then designing and engineering the e-learning experience for skill development requires we first reconceptualize the entire psychophysiological variable space in which learning happens. What does this variable space look like?

The emergence of sensing and measurement technologies for inference of emotional states via physiological measurements (Cacioppo et al. 2000; Healey et al. 2010; Setz 2012) offers an opportunity for the optimization of "learning experiences." Physiological and neurophysiological sensing afford an expanded state space of intrapersonal variables relevant to learning through their impact on attention span and focus, perceptual acuity, working memory, and so on. They can be used to design both the content and the *form* of an online experience in ways that maximize skill development. Key to using neurophysiological measurements to optimize the design of pedagogical vehicles is a set of models of the effects of learners' emotional and visceral states on their learning processes and outcomes, and of the correlation and of the learning stimuli of the e-learning platform with the salient set of emotional states.

Emotional states and emotional landscapes (sets of interrelated emotional states) are not easy to map and classify. But difficulty does not entail impossibility. Even a naive and coarse-grained approach goes a long way to helping us organize the variable space. More than three hundred emotions can be classified in terms of their valence (positive like joy? or, negative, like rage?) and the level of arousal they are associated with (active like disgust? or passive, like sadness?) by pooling together large numbers of responses of human subjects asked to rate and rank their own emotions in a structured fashion (Seitz, Lord, and Taylor 2007). Within this more structured state space of emotions, we can ask, to what extent are emotions in the four quadrants of this classification system (active-positive; active-negative; passive-positive; passive-negative) conducive to different learning outcomes? Even a set of weakly informed prior expectations (learning is maximized when the learner's emotional states are in the "north-east-east" quadrant [mildly active and positive]) can help provide useful heuristics for content design.

Sharper distinctions yield new insight. We can model the emotional landscapes of feedback and evaluation processes with respect to their immediacy (how soon after the work is produced?), accuracy (how specific to errors and mishaps?), materiality (is the feedback used developmentally or as a selection tool?), and opacity (how easy to link the feedback to the material taught?) and ask,

- To what extent are more or less precise/immediate/opaque forms of user feedback related to heightened fear, stress, and anxiety?

- To what extent do these emotional states impede or enhance learning?

We can use the emerging causal map to design feedback instruments that optimize the average learner's response by tuning his or her levels of precision and timeliness, and by adjusting the forms of feedback used.

Recent development of "affective-visceral remote sensing" techniques for mapping physiological measurements to emotional states (Setz 2012) allows us to ask these questions at the level of individual learners. The relationship between individual stress level and learning outcome will vary between individuals. So will the "optimal stress level" the learner needs to feel to do well on a test. The "affective style" of an individual learner (Davidson 2003)—his propensity to feel certain emotions when exposed to certain stimuli and to behave in particular ways when feeling a certain emotion—can also function as a reliable moderator of optimal learning outcomes of different learners in different contexts (more or less personal, more or less formal, more or less intense, more or less evaluative) and afford an additional degree of freedom in the adaptive design of learning vehicles.

We are at a stage of simultaneous technological developments in multiple disciplines that, once integrated, allows for the development of affective-visceral sensing enabling discrimination among different groups of emotions and in some cases of different emotional states.

- Cardiac function sensor measurements (heart rate, cardiac output, stroke volume) (Cacioppo et al. 2000) allow us to distinguish between emotional pairs such as (fear, anger), as well as between emotional pairs such as (anger, disgust), (fear, anger), (fear, disgust), (happiness, surprise), (happiness, disgust), and (sadness, disgust).

- Heart rate variability measurements, moreover, allow us to distinguish between emotions that involve the different components of the autonomous nervous system (sympathetic, parasympathetic), and therefore to distinguish between strong (stress-related responses) and weak (depressive-withdrawing responses) emotional states (Seitz 2012).

- Facial muscle movement sensors (Cacioppo et al. 2000) allow us to track the relative positivity (as a function of the activation of the *zygomaticus major* and the *orbicularis oculi* muscles) or negativity (via the activation of the *corrugator supercili* muscle). Measurements of facial muscle activation can be carried out by noninvasive means, using Facial Action Coding System–enabled video camera recorders (Donato et al. 1999; Ekman 2007).

- Vascular blood flow measures (such as finger pulse volume, total peripheral resistance, and face temperature) can be used to distinguish between emotion pairs that differ in both intensity and valence (anger, sadness; sadness, happiness) (Setz 2012).

- Electrodermal activity measures such as skin conductance level and the number of nonspecific skin conductance responses can be used to distinguish between different levels of psychophysiological stress, and between emotional response pairs (disgust, happiness).

- Speech parameter measures (Setz 2012) can be used to discern levels of intensity of the emotional state of the speaker by focusing on the speed (relative to baseline), pitch, and prosody of the voiced signal in order to distinguish, for instance, between "anger complex" emotions (irritation, sarcasm, rage) and "joy-complex" emotions (happiness, glee).

- Noninvasive, unconfined, low spatial resolution measures of brain activity—like electroencephalographic (EEG) signals of cortical and hemispheric activation levels in the superficially accessible parts of the brain—provide reliable estimates of both levels of intensity (alpha and beta wave amplitude ratios) and emotional negativity (hemispherical inactivation, translating in higher alpha wave amplitude).

- Noninvasive, confined, high spatial resolution measures of brain activity—like brain-oxygen-level-dependent (BOLD) signal levels from different parts of the brain—can provide measurements of activity levels in brain areas (prefrontal cortex and subcomponents, limbic system, motor cortex) whose activity has been reliably implicated in different perceptual, sensory-visceral, motor, and cognitive activities that compose what we refer to as *learning* (Logothetis 2008).

- Eye-movement measures can be used both to discern between different emotional states of the user (as blinking rate is correlated with the valence of the experience and shiftiness is correlated with loss of attention) and as identifiers of the stimuli that produce microlevel variations in physiological responses (via eye tracking movement monitors, which can now be made to work on Zoom and Microsoft Teams videos).

Because *in vivo* deployment of affective remote sensing technologies sometimes leads to measurement noise and "missing data," the key to the use of neurophysiological remote sensing to reliably identify and map emotional states of e-learners is the concatenation of measurements taken by a suite of measurement devices that produces multiple outputs for every user state. Sensor "fusion" algorithms (for example, Setz 2012) can distinguish between different groups of emotions at various valences and degrees of arousal. This enables the construction of simple classifiers for learners' emotional states based on multidimensional aggregates of emotional state data.

To turn the affective remote sensing capability into a genuine "learning experience design instrument," we need to also be able to map the space of stimuli making up the "learning vehicle"—a video lecture, an interactive presentation, or a quiz, test, or exam. The range of possible "moves" that its designer can make can be described in terms of a set of variables that intuitively and comprehensively capture the degrees of freedom at our disposal.

- *Visual complexity* relates to the informational content of teaching vehicles— such as slide decks and mock-ups—that are used to convey information. It can be measured at the pixel or voxel level (how many color schemes? How many combinations?), or at the level of different visual objects the user is likely to use in order to parse or make sense of the visual stimulus.

- *Semantic complexity* of the content—of both visual and auditory stimuli—relates to the degree to which the vocabulary used by the teacher is transparently accessible to the learner (without the need for a translational device, like a dictionary or Wikipedia).

- *Syntactic complexity* relates to the logical depth of the informational representation used by the instructor in various forms. It can be a measure of the inferential depth of arguments, of the computational complexity of formal proofs, or of the Kolmogorov complexity of certain visual objects used to illustrate a procedure (such as proof construction on a graph).

- *Rhythm* relates both to the speed at which visual cues change (as in flipping through slides and frames) and the *syncopation* patterns of alternating visual cues (that is, the variance of changes in *tempo*).

- *Speech-expressiveness measures* (such as prosody ("tone"), speed, and pitch) relate to the space-time-frequency characteristics of voiced and unvoiced speech of the presenter in the medium.

- *Color schemes and color combination patterns* relate to the patterns of colors used to encode visual stimuli used for teaching purposes.

- *Modality* relates to the ways in which information of different kinds (symbolic, narrative, schematic, graphical) is presented to the user, and includes both the specific mode in which the information is presented, and the sequence and combination of modes in which it is presented (in other words, multimodality).

- *Interactivity level* relates to the frequency, relevance, informativeness, auditability and material implications (high stakes versus low stakes) of the user's own participation in the learning experience, whether through answering or asking questions or inputting answers to a quiz, or making remote presentations to co-users.

These represent a set of *design or policy variables* for the online learning experience, whose specific values may be optimized to produce *learning-optimal* emotional landscapes, and adaptively changed as a function of user emotional states—as reconstructed from a brain-body sensing suite. To fully specify the problem of using neurophysiological measures to optimize learning experiences, we have to also specify a set of *outcome or performance measures* for personalized, electronic skill development. These include the following:

- *Performance on tests, quizzes, and assignments* that are directly related to the content of the learning experience, and which directly measure skill transfer in the specific domain of the course being taught.

- *Performance on cognitive function tests*—many of which have already been automated and are available for dissemination in an online environment (for example, Lumosity's gamified battery of prefrontal function tests)—which include working memory tests, multimodal recall tests (can you recall the name associated with a visual stimulus), tests of the logical depth of inferential chains that the participant can follow, reproduce, or produce, and tests of the computational complexity of inferential procedures the participant can engage in (such as, "finding an equilibrium in a competitive game").

- *Performance on perceptual function tests*—which relate to the set of higher-level (object recognition) and lower-level (stimulus registration) perceptual skills that the participant may be expected to acquire in virtue of achieving a certain level of performance.

Automating the testing process, together with the inclusion of new measures for the evaluation of skill transfer outside of the "training set" enables us to use the e-learning environment to design experiences that optimize not only imparting a specific skill to a participant in a particular domain ("financial statement analysis"), but also the transfer of higher-level cognitive skills (convex optimization, iterative dominance reasoning, proof construction) to domains (software design specifications, user experience design, contract design) that are far from that in which the skill was originally developed. Thus the expanded set of performance measures for the learning vehicle design allows online learning designers to make progress on the *skill transfer problem* that is central to the executive development field.

The combination of a state space model (instantaneous measurements of brain-body states that correlate with emotional and visceral states), a design variable model (the set of moves and maneuvers that online designers can make to change the learning experience), and a set of performance measures in a single platform for the optimization of skill transfer via e-learning allows us to do the following:

- Design optimal sequences of voice-video-data stimuli sequences for maximizing presence and participation, as evidenced by the physiological and neurophysiological response of the learner

- Design optimal uses of graphics and optimal topologies of graphical interfaces for the maximization of participation and presence

- Design optimal sequences of participatory and individual tasks and exercises for the maximization of learner presence and participation and the maximization of skill transfer

- Design new tools and technologies for immersion of the e-learner into the know-how and know-what of the domain of skill transfer sought via the design and engineering of stimuli that trigger high-intensity affective responses

- Design optimal acoustic backgrounds for the maximization of learner participation and presence and the maximization of skill transfer to the learner on the basis of feedback from physiological remote sensing of the learner

- Design optimal visualization and visual-auditory content superposition techniques and interfaces for the enhancement of learner states and propensities associated with learning or with learning more quickly—such as working memory size and accessing speed and working; visual-spatial reasoning; deductive, inductive, and abductive reasoning abilities; specific methods of inquiry and modes; and specific methods and blueprints for argumentation

Consider how the optimization of an e-learning skill acquisition for facilitating the learning of competitive game theory might proceed within the variable-space and measurement-space we have introduced. "Solving" a game entails finding—and playing, in an interactive situation—one of a set of undominated strategies, or strategies that maximize the payoff for the user given other users' strategies. A brain-body-state-based optimization procedure for a game-theory-learning module might look as follows:

- We design and optimize an audiovisual interface for introducing basic concepts (game trees, payoffs and beliefs, iterative dominance reasoning, and the calculation of reaction and best response functions) for maximal retention and on-demand recall.

- We use the set of brain-body measurements (such as eye movements to different parts of the screen; skin conductivity as a function of prompt and locus of attention; facial expression; facial temperature distribution and breathing and heart rate, indicating annoyance and anxiety levels; cortical activation levels) of test participants to adapt and optimize the syntactic complexity (how logically complex?), the semantic complexity (how many new words and novel phrases per frame?), the visual complexity (how difficult to encode the image in terms of familiar subimages?), the tempo and syncopation (how often and how predictably do visual stimuli change?), and the color scheme (which colors, what sequences, what dispositions on the screen, how predictably are certain colors associated with certain semantically distinct pieces of information [payoffs, strategies, agents]?) to minimize a composite set of emotional states that are aversive to learning and skill transfer (anxiety, boredom, ennui, anger).

- We measure the degree of near skill transfer (whether or not the participant can parse an everyday situation into a strategic form game; how reliably the participant can define the different, logically independent components of a competitive game; how reliably and how quickly a participant can reproduce definitions of terms of art such as *rationality of players, common knowledge, Nash or correlated equilibrium*) as a function of different emotional states and different audiovisual stimulus combinations.

We can also focus on measuring the transfer of procedural knowledge of game theoretic reasoning—including belief formation, interactive reasoning, and strategy selection—that we can achieve using an online learning vehicle, by varying the following:

- The type of games participants are induced to play: familiar games (tic tac toe, end-games in chess, Go, Prisoner's Dilemma, WolfPack) versus unfamiliar games (matching pennies, stag-hare hunt, bargaining); competitive games versus cooperative games; mixed-strategy equilibrium games versus pure-strategy equilibrium games; games of perfect information versus games of imperfect information)

- The informational and computational complexity (two-player, two-strategy games versus five-player, four-strategy games) of the games that participants play

- The frequency of the test games (every few minutes versus every session; one game at a time versus several games at a time)

- The incentive-intensity of the test game (whether or not performance on the test counts for the final grade; whether or not the participant can gain or lose—face or money—as a result of poor performance as a player in a competitive game)

Access to both the set of design variables (screen layout, GUI dynamics) and a set of *thought probes* (quick-fire, pop-up questions about the current beliefs of the participant about the structure of the game and about the beliefs other participants have about the structure of the game and about the beliefs about the structure of the game each of them has)—as well as to measurements that correlate with instantaneous perceptual-cognitive-affective states (via brain-body measurements)—allow us to infer the degree and the depth to which participants think about the incentive and belief structure of the game (for instance, the number of moves they think *ahead* in the game, or the number of moves they think ahead, conditional upon the number of moves they think other players think ahead)—as a function of both the design of the interface (visual, semantic, syntactic complexity, rhythm, color, audiovisual integration) and the instantaneous emotional state of the participant (anger, irritation, boredom).

We can then do the following:

- Optimize the interface for the optimal transfer of the proximal skill (mastery in playing strategies based on equilibrium considerations) in *these* particular games, or in games of *these* particular types

- Identify sources of error and suboptimal reasoning related to the emotional states of the participant that are independent of the design of the interface (for example, anger arising from moral indignation leading to suboptimal strategy selection in an ultimatum game)

- Measure the degree to which the transfer of a higher-level, interactive social reasoning skill that is applicable outside of the domain of the course has been achieved (in some cases, using fMRI BOLD signal measurements generated by the brains of participants engaged in a strategic game [played for real, monetary payoffs] before and after the completion of the course or module).

"Side-Benefits": Multitasking, Supertasking, and the Enhancement of Executive Function in e-Learners

So far, our discussion has focused on the problem of redesigning electronic learning vehicles to correct for the lacunae in learning environment in the electronic medium vis-a-vis the classroom experience. However, the possibilities for disambiguating the measurement of skill and quantifying componential enhancement in skill development via affective and perceptual remote sensing of the user experience opens up the possibility of using e-learning vehicles to produce improvements in specific skills that are not adequately addressed in the classroom environment.

These are often the skills a new generation of problem solvers and decision makers most need in a hypertextual and hyperconnected work environment. Consider in particular on the nexus of skills associated with media multitasking (Ophir, Nass, and Wagner 2009), which is (usually) associated with an executive function such as suppression of unwanted interference and adaptive, goal-dependent resource allocation to various subtasks that need to be sequentially energized and deenergized. The finding that media multitasking decreases task performance levels at the individual level should concern designers of online learning environments—which are likely to provide precisely the kind of learner experiences that simulate multitasking.

However, recent findings suggest that there are significant interpersonal differences in multitasking ability (Watson and Strayer 2010): some individuals seem to do *better* on individual tasks in the presence of the cognitive-perceptual-affective interference provided by a multitasking environment. Jaeggi and colleagues (2007) corroborate the prevalence of significant intersubject differences in ability to perform at a high level in a multitasking environment, and adduce evidence of significant differences at the level of brain activation patterns in successful versus unsuccessful multitasking. It seems plausible, consequently, that performance in online courses that make significant use of multitasking skills can function as a *selection filter* for super-taskers. Can they also function as engines for the development of super-tasking skills?

Consider the X-skills decomposition we introduced in the first chapter and focus on the *executive functions* of the brain—currently thought to be correlated with heightened activity levels in various parts of the frontal lobes (Smith and Jonides 1999; Stuss 2011). The literature offers up various taxonomies for these functions, but those emerging from clinicians having to solve practical problems of addressing neuropsychological deficits in their patients are by far the most helpful to engineers of learning vehicles trying to solve practical problems and include the following (Stuss 2011):

- Task energization (speeding up and slowing down the performance of various tasks)

- Monitoring of states of self, task, and environment (keeping track of stimulus and response content as well as one's visceral feelings in real time)

- Task setting (adjustment of scheduling one's mental activities and setting of appropriate subtasks)

- Behavioral emotional self-regulation (suppression of propensity to act on aversive preferences or counterproductive temptations)

- Emotional self-regulation (suppression of the propensity to evince or even experience a certain feeling in response to a stimulus or recollection)

- The meta-cognitive and meta-perceptual integration of multimodal stimuli (visual-auditory, olfactory-visual, for instance)

They can also be categorized in a more cognitively-oriented approach (Smith and Jonides 1999) as

- *Focusing* on specific parts of a stimulus, to the exclusion of noise or irrelevant detail

- *Scheduling* cognitive, perceptual, and behavioral processes with regard to their value contribution to the performance of different tasks

- *Planning or designing a sequence* of subtasks aimed at attaining some goal

- *Updating and adjusting* the contents of working memory to adapt to environmental changes

- *Encoding or recoding* various representations of stimuli in working memory for maximum efficiency in task performance

The digital learning environment is well suited to the design of interventions and experiences that help participants develop executive functions through targeted practice. This turns the *problem* that media multitasking poses for individual task performance into an *opportunity* for (1) selecting media *super-taskers* on the basis of performance on specially designed testing instruments that stress executive control functions, and (2) *developing* multitasking abilities through the design and deployment of interventions aimed at improving executive functions in participants. The key to doing so stems from realizing that all executive functions have to do with the production of complex action sequences *in time* and under time or average speed constraints. Incorporating "speed-sensitive" versions of quizzes, problems, and other learning tasks will likely help instructional designers that want to turn the "short attention span" problem into the "executive function enhancement" opportunity.

The "Disruption Matrix": An Entrepreneur's Compass for Innovating in the Learning Industry

Earlier, we provided design compasses for chief learning officers and executive program providers in the current landscape. Radical disruption, however, generates new landscapes and calls for a different sort of compass—aimed at the *entrepreneurs* of the EdTech space fixing their attention on the executive development market. The compass, in the form of a three-fold filter, is a nested sequence of questions that innovators and entrepreneurs should ask themselves, and which follow from our analysis of the social and technical landscape that lies just over the visible horizon of executive education. Each question induces a filter on opportunities and feature sets (see Figure 5.1).

The filters do not relate to "table stakes questions" any startup or incumbent business should attempt to answer (such as about competitive and regulatory forces; the market power of suppliers, customers, and employees; and technological lock-ins and trajectories that can shift competitive ground). They relate to the ways in which the new product, service, and associated business are attuned to the dynamics of the executive development industry and can withstand the industrywide changes it itself creates, as described in the following.

Filter 1. Does the newborn product or service deliver greater personalization and/ or socialization and/or contextualization of the learning experience? If only one or two, then at what cost to the other(s)?

Example: E-to-Me, Inc. provides an algorithm-based tutor for any senior manager or board member who needs to learn a business discipline currently con-

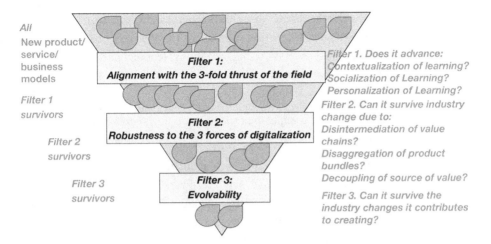

Figure 5.1. An Innovator's Compass for the Executive Development Market

sidered to be "quantitative" (accounting, finance, operations research) very quickly (on time scales of hours to weeks—on account of having to use this knowledge in a time-sensitive situation and of superior pedagogical designs that adaptively optimize learning stimuli to learner behaviors, states, and traits). It uses the executive's current predicament and unstructured materials (documents, spreadsheets, and slide decks he or she needs to parse and understand) as starting points for the "learning experience." Learners can ask questions about definitions and uses of words, phrases, formulas, and data formats, in "everyday" language or in the language system that is most convenient to them. They do not need to speak a word of jargon, nor do they need to phrase their questions in grammatical, connected, cohesive, complete sentences and paragraphs. They can inquire about best practices of activities to which various words and phrases refer. The algorithmic intelligence unit gives answers tailored to the sophistication of the user's queries and questions. It matches the answers to the user's time constraint (and perhaps even her or his working memory constraint, which the system can, over time, measure).

It gets high grades on contextualization (it starts from the learner's predicament, not some academic's rubrics and PowerPoint slides) and personalization (it matches answers and prompts to its estimates of the user's abilities and states and remembers the user's state-dependent actions). Its founders need to think carefully about the ways in which the social network of learners is created and maintained—specifically, the ways in which learners communicate, coordinate, and collaborate with other users, whose knowledge of and expertise in the same subject may be similar or different amongst them. This may require the designers to introduce a different set of "social operations" (conflict or disagreement resolution; disambiguation) than those required by a machine that coaches individuals working in isolation.

Filter 2. Can the newborn product or service survive the dynamic of disintermediation, disaggregation, and decoupling that is currently reshaping the industry?

Example: Eliza Jones, Inc. is a fledgling virtual business school "for executives whose motto is 'Don't waste my time'." It is built on the premise that all business expertise is dialogical and communicative in nature. There is no such thing as a concept or method without the conversation it is part of. This attitude has profound implications for its product design. Its founders believe that teaching people "finance theory," "economics," "accounting," "marketing," and such is not just useless but a big mistake, because it obfuscates the details of practice and context and gets them to perpetuate the mistakes of the past. It also makes them immune to change and maladaptive to subtle changes in the social nuances and technical details of context.

Rather, Eliza Jones's products teach "the grammar and semantics of finance" in short courses with names such as "How to talk to your commercial loan officer"; "How to get your analyst to give you the information you need about tech deals"; and "How to persuade your local hedge fund to have a look at your mid-size cash-positive business." Because it believes all business disciplines (and others too) are simply "ways of talking," it treats business education like a set of language courses, complete with vocabulary, grammar, pronunciation ("How to punctuate your sentence like an investment banker", "How to get the prosody of a consumer goods product pitch just right for WalMart buyers", "How to write and email like a senior consultant"), and listening and comprehension exercises, using levels, "lingots," and Blockchain-verifiable digital badges to allow users to signal their degree of expertise in a discipline to others on social networking platforms. It uses AI-powered "conversational agents" that can stretch a user's ability to speak a "new business language" under the pressure of time (and of other people watching the unfolding "game"). To source the kernels for its learning algorithms, Eliza Jones uses advisors and consultants drawn from what are currently the most highly regarded business schools and economics, philosophy, semiotics, psychology, computer science, and neuroscience departments in the world, and rewards them with equity-like claims on its product lines in the form of royalties-on-net-margins that extend seventeen years out (mimicking the lifetime of a patent in the United States).

Eliza Jones does well against the "disruptive trio" of disintermediation, disaggregation, and decoupling. It is difficult to disintermediate its product, as it only uses faculty members as designers and developers for products that are ultimately its own and limits their carve-outs to slivers linked to the product they help design. It is also difficult to disaggregate its product, as any realistic unbundling of language learning is bound to feel unnatural: reading, writing, oral expression, and aural comprehension—along with dialogicality and discursivity—come "as a package" in the teaching and learning of a language.

Finally, there is no obvious way to decouple the different sources of value that it brings to its users (networking, different aspects of linguistic—and therefore functional—skill) and preserve the value associated with each component: people on the platform get together ("networking value") in order to learn a discipline *as a language*; the written, aural, and oral components of this competence are part of an inseparable nexus or whole ("skill acquisition value"); and the signaling value of the platform is based *only* on the fact that it is successful at producing the kind of skills it is designed to produce (and not because "it is Columbia University," for instance).

Filter 3. Can the newborn product or service survive the dynamics it is itself creating in the industry?

Example: McKharvard, a new B Corp, is a new elite training and development enterprise that is seeking to consolidate the $10 billion MBA/EMBA/Executive Education market "under one roof," using the distributed real estate infrastructure of the world's leading strategy consulting firm and the brand name and teaching prowess of the world's best-known business school. Its goal is no less than to provide "defining experiences"—at different levels of selection, certification, and development—for all two-hundred-thousand-plus current takers of GMAT tests and one hundred thousand executives around the world seeking specialized, dedicated training that helps them develop the "hot skills" leading organizations behave as if they think their executives should have. Its business model is to target test takers and talented undergraduates directly, with programs custom designed to their specific career interests and individual abilities, and at prices that undercut (sometimes by a lot) the prices of competing MBA, EMBA, and executive education programs.

There is some reason to believe that McKharvard could and should consolidate the market quickly, as there are very few combinations of universities and corporations (IMD-BCG? Stanford-Accenture? Wharton-Goldman Sachs?) that can replicate its status, reach, and prowess, and none that can move as quickly as the HBS-McKinsey duo. Does the breakthrough enterprise change the industry in a way that challenges its own business model?

Well, the demand for selection and training into the market for organizational leadership and corporate control remains the same as before, except that instead of being serviced by three hundred business schools and the odd consultancy acting separately and providing natural segmentation and stratification in terms of price and quality, it is now serviced by a single large organization, potentially at many different levels of intensity (10-day to 360-day programs and everything in between, at various price, selectivity, and certification levels). It is true that most *business schools* will be left with massive unfunded liabilities (the salaries and benefits of faculty members they can no longer cover) and that many universities that depend on *their* business schools to subsidize their otherwise non-net-income-generating activity sets will end up either bankrupt or wards of their states or countries. But, McKharvard does not produce changes at the level of the industry that challenge *its own* ability to survive.

By contrast, consider Filtronics, Inc.—which provides individual-level predictive analytics for organizations seeking executives at all levels. Using combinations of genetic, neurophysiological (fMRI), cognitive, and behavioral tests and measures, it provides individuals and corporations with "much better than chance" estimates on any individuals' potential to lead, manage, execute, create, ideate, and deliver. Its founders believe that education, understood as a developmental activity, is a hoax, and that the only real function of an educational system is to select for individuals that have the skills their future employers value.

Buoyed by recent findings of the predictive power of fMRI scans (Gabrieli 2016) and using the latest affective and cognitive "remote sensing" technology, Filtronics offers large organizations a proven battery of tests that reliably filter out "B-players." In spite of the obvious appeal of Filtronics's approach to would-be employers (and perhaps the early-stage success of the company, provided the technology works and its founders do not squabble), there is something self-undermining about its approach. *Giltronics*, Inc. for instance, can take the same approach to the market for recent college graduates and provide filters for "fresh off the bench" graduates. Their tests will be different from those of Filtronics in some respects and similar in others. But since recent graduates will within three or four years turn into aspiring executives whose tests are the inputs to the Filtronics filter, the outputs of the latter will be dependent on those of the Giltronics prefilter. And soon, Kidtronics, Inc. will successfully speculate research that shows early stages of child development are critical to the formation of precisely the high-value skills that employers of individual contributors, managers, and executives alike value most (Heckman 2006) and will create its own search and filtering engine that takes as inputs tests performed on twelve-year-olds. Or eight-year-olds. There is something fundamentally self-undermining about the ubiquitous filtering approach to education, in that Filtronics's success fuels a cycle of testing-based filtering that undermines the reliability and predictive validity of its own measures.

One closing thought, borne out of a state that resembles contemplation more than it does inquiry, calculation or deliberation: the future of executive development is open—to innovation, redesign, and re-configuration—in ways it has not been in the past. Because of the relentlessly pragmatic and results-oriented nature of executive life, the field is a very useful proving ground—and hopefully a playground—for innovations that can and likely will change the future of higher education more broadly. Very few of the novel structures and dynamics of learning experiences, of certification, and of interactions among learners and between learners and learning facilitators, are not also relevant to the higher ed field as a whole. Thus, while the future of executive development is open—because there are no psycho-physical or socio-physical laws that will determine its course, and the structures that have constrained the emergence of truly novel approaches have been eroded to the point of near-insignificance—it is also the case that innovation in this space will also open the future of many other areas of the educational field.

REFERENCES

Acemoglu, D., and D. Autor. 2011. "Skills, tasks and technologies: Implications for employment and earnings." In *Handbook of Labor Economics*, ed. O. Ashenfelter and D. Card, chap. 12. New York: Elsevier.

Alexander, R., P. Broadfoot, and D. Phillips, eds. 1999. *Learning from Comparing: New Directions in Comparative Education Research: Volume 1: Contexts, Classrooms and Outcomes*. Oxford, UK: Symposium Books.

Anderson, J. R., and G. H. Bower. 1973. *Human Associative Memory*. Washington, DC: Winston and Son.

Anderson, J., and G-J van Wijk. 2010. "Customized executive learning: A business model for the twenty-first century." *Journal of Management Development* 29 (6): 545–555.

Arrow, K. E. 1974. *The Limits of Organization*. New York: Norton.

Autor, D. 2015. "Why are there still so many jobs? The history and future of workplace automation." *Journal of Economic Perspectives* 29 (3): 3–30.

Baldwin, T. T., and J. K. Ford. 1988. "Transfer of training: A review and directions for future research." *Personnel Psychology* 41 (1): 63–105.

Barnard, C. 1938. *The Functions of the Executive*. Cambridge, MA: Harvard University Press.

Barnett, S. M.. and S. J. Ceci. 2002. "When and how do we apply what we Learn? A taxonomy of far transfer." *Psychological Bulletin* 128 (4): 612–637.

Bassok, M., and K. J. Holyoak. 1989. "Interdomain transfer between isomorphic topics in algebra and physics." *Journal of Experimental Psychology: Learning, Memory, and Cognition* 15 (1): 153.

Bechara, A., and A. R. Damasio. 2005. "The somatic marker hypothesis: A neural theory of economic decision." *Games and Economic Behavior* 52 (2): 336–372.

Bersin and Associates. 2013–20."Executive Development and Corporate Training."

Billing, D. 2007. "Teaching for transfer of core/key skills in higher education: Cognitive skills." *Higher Education* 53 (4): 483–516.

Bolton, P., and M. Dewatripont. 1994. "The firm as a communication network." *Quarterly Journal of Economics*: 809–839.

Cacioppo, J. T., G. G. Berntson, J. T. Larsen, K. M. Poehlman, and T. A. Ito. 2000. "The psychophysiology of emotion." In *Handbook of Emotions*, 2d ed. New York: Guilford Press.

Canals, J. 2011. "In search of a greater impact: New corporate and societal challenges for business schools." In *The Future of Leadership Development*, ed. J. Canals, 3–30. London: Palgrave Macmillan.

Christensen, C. R, D. Garvin, and A. Sweet. 1991. *Education for Judgment: The Art of Leading Discussions*. Boston: Harvard Business School Press.

Churchman, C. W. 1967. "Guest editorial: Wicked problems." *Management Science* 14 (4): B141–B142.

Conger, J. A., and K. Xin. 2000. "Executive education in the 21st century." *Journal of Management Education* 24 (February). Via Factiva (accessed August 5, 2014).

Crotty, P. T., and A. J. Soule. 1997. "Executive education: Yesterday and today, with a look at tomorrow." *Journal of Management Development* 16 (1): 4–21.

Cunha, F., J. J. Heckman, L. Lochner, and D. V. Masterov. 2006. "Interpreting the evidence on life cycle skill formation." *Handbook of the Economics of Education* 1:697–812.

Datar, S., and D. Garvin. 2010. *Rethinking the MBA: Business Education at a Crossroads*. Boston: Harvard Business School Press.

Davidson, R. J. 2003. "Affective neuroscience and psychophysiology: Toward a synthesis." *Psychophysiology* 40:655–665.

Deming, D. J. 2017. "The growing importance of social skills in the labor market." *Quarterly Journal of Economics* 132 (4): 1593–1640.

Detterman, D. K. 1993. "The case for the prosecution: Transfer as an epiphenomenon." In *Transfer on Trial: Intelligence, Cognition, and Instruction*, ed. D. K. Detterman and R. J. Sternberg. New York: Ablex.

Docebo. 2014. "E-learning market trends & forecast 2014–2016 report." https://www.docebo.com/landing/contactform/elearning-market-trends-and-forecast-2014-2016-docebo-report.pdf (accessed February 2017).

———. 2017. "eLearning market trends & forecast 2017–2021." https://www.docebo.com/resource/elearning-market-trends-and-forecastreport-2017-2021 (accessed February 2017).

Donato, G., M. S. Bartlett, J. C. Hager, P. Ekman, and T. J. Sejnowski. 1999. "Classifying facial actions." *IEEE Transactions on Pattern Analysis and Machine Intelligence* 21 (10): 974–989.

Dunbar, K. 2001. "The analogical paradox: Why analogy is so easy in naturalistic settings yet so difficult in the psychological laboratory." In *The Analogical Mind: Perspectives from Cognitive Science*, ed. D. Gentner, K. J. Holyoak, and B. N. Kokinov, 313–334. Cambridge, MA: Bradford Books.

Eccles, R.G., and N. Nohria. 1992. *Networks and Organizations: Structure, Form, and Action.* Boston: Harvard Business School Press.

edX. 2015–2020. Impact Reports. www.edx.org.

Ekman, P. 2007. "The directed facial action task: Emotional responses without appraisal." In *Handbook of Emotion Elicitation and Assessment,* ch. 3. New York: Oxford University Press.

Fama, E. F., and M. C. Jensen. 1983. "Separation of ownership and control." *Journal of Law and Economics* 26 (2): 301–325.

Fernández-Aráoz, C., B. Groysberg, and N. Nohria. 2011. "How to hang on to your high potentials." *Harvard Business Review* 89 (10): 76–83.

Gabrieli, J. D. E. 2016. "The promise of educational neuroscience: Comment on Bowers." *Psychological Review* 123 (5): 613–619.

Garicano, L. 2000. "Hierarchies and the organization of knowledge in production." *Journal of Political Economy* 108 (5): 874–904.

Garvin, D. A. 2007. "Teaching executives and teaching MBAs: Reflections on the case method." *Academy of Management Learning & Education* 6 (3): 364–374.

Gentner, D., J. Loewenstein, and L. Thompson. 2003. "Learning and transfer: A general role for analogical encoding." *Journal of Educational Psychology* 95 (2): 393–408.

Gentry, W. A., R. H. Eckert, V. P. Munusamy, S. A. Stawiski, and J. L. Martin. 2013. "The needs of participants in leadership development programs: A qualitative and quantitative cross-country investigation." *Journal of Leadership & Organizational Studies,* 21 (4).

Goleman, D. 1995. *Emotional Intelligence: Why It Can Matter More Than IQ.* New York: Bantam Books.

Gray, W. D., and J. M. Orasanu. 1987. "Transfer of Cognitive Skills." *Transfer of Learning: Contemporary Research and Applications:* 183–215.

Haykin, S. 2014. *Neural Networks and Learning Machines,* 3d ed. New York: Pearson.

Healey, J., L. Nachman, S. Subramanian, J. Shahabdeen, and M. Morris. 2010. "Out of the lab and into the fray: Towards modeling emotion in everyday life." In *Pervasive 2010: Lecture Notes in Computer Science,* ed. P. Floreen, A. Kruger, and M. Spasojevic. New York: Springer.

Heckman, J. J. 2006. "Skill formation and the economics of investing in disadvantaged children." *Science* 312 (5782): 1900–1902.

Hong, L., and S. E. Page. 2001. "Problem solving by heterogeneous agents." *Journal of Economic Theory* 97 (1): 123–163.

Ioannidis, J. P. A. 2005. "Why most published research findings are false." *PLoS Medicine* 2 (8): e124.

Jaeggi, S. M., M. Buschkuehl, J. Jonides, and W. J. Persige. 2007. "Improving fluid intelligence with training on working memory." *Proceedings of the National Academy of Sciences* 105 (19): 6829–6833.

Jensen, M. C., and W. H. Meckling. 1992. "Specific and general knowledge and organizational structure." In *Contract Economics*, ed. L. Werin and H. Wijkander. Oxford, UK: Blackwell.

Johnson, B. C., J. M. Manyika, and L. A. Yee. 2005. "The next revolution in interactions." *McKinsey Quarterly* 4: 20–33.

Kegan, J., and L. Lahey. 2009. *Immunity to Change: How to Overcome It and Unlock the Potential in Yourself and Your Organization*. Boston: Harvard Business Press.

Kelley, T., and M. Whatson. 2013. "Making long-term memories in minutes: A spaced learning pattern from memory research in education." *Frontiers of Human Neuroscience* 7: 589.

Kreps, D. 1990. "Organizational culture." In *Perspectives on Positive Political Economy*, ed. K. Alt and D. Shepsle. Cambridge, UK: Cambridge University Press.

Kroner, G. 2014. "Does your LMS do this?" http://edutechnica.com/2014/01/07/a-model-for-lms-evolution/ (accessed September 2015).

Kuhn, T. S. 1962. *The Structure of Scientific Revolutions*. Cambridge, MA: MIT Press.

Lake, B. M., T. D. Ullman, J. B. Tenenbaum, and S. J. Gershman. 2017. "Building machines that learn and think like people." *Behavioral and Brain Sciences* 40 (E253).

Leibenstein, H. 1976. *Beyond Economic Man*. Cambridge, MA: Harvard University Press.

Lloyd, F. R., and D. Newkirk. 2011. "University-based executive education markets and trends." Unicon White Paper (August 15). http://uniconexed.org/2011/research/UNICON-whitepaper-markets-trends-Lloyd-Newkirk-08-2011.pdf (accessed July 9, 2014).

Logothetis, N. 2008. "What we can and cannot do with fMRI." *Nature* 453 (June): 869–878.

Luchins, A. S. 1942. "Mechanization in problem solving: The effect of Einstellung." *Psychological Monographs* 54 (6): i–95.

Matthews, D. 2017 "The shape of things to come in higher education." *Times Higher Education*.

McKay, D. J. 1993. *Information Theory, Inference and Learning Algorithms*. Cambridge, UK: Cambridge University Press.

Meister, J. C. 2001. "The brave new world of corporate education." *Chronicle of Higher Education* (February 9): B10–B11.

Milgrom, P., and J. Roberts. 1990. "The economics of modern manufacturing: Technology, strategy, and organization." *American Economic Review*: 511–528.

Mischel, W. 1974. "Processes in delay of gratification." *Advances in Experimental Social Psychology* 7: 249–292.

Mischel, W., Y. Shoda, and M. I. Rodriguez. 1989. "Delay of gratification in children." *Science* 244 (4907): 933–938.

Moldoveanu, M. C. 2002. "Language, games and language games." *Journal of Socio-Economics* 31 (3): 233–251.

———. 2009. "Why and how do theory groups get ahead in organization studies? Groundwork for a model of discursive moves." *Strategic Organization* 7 (3): 235–276.

————. 2011. *Inside Man: The Discipline of Modeling Human Ways of Being*. Stanford, CA: Stanford University Press.

————. 2014. "The integrative self-development laboratory." White Paper. Rotman School of Management, University of Toronto.

————. 2015. "Unpacking the 'big data' skill set: It's not just—or even mostly—about the data." *European Business Review* (January-February).

————. 2019. Intelligent artificiality: Why AI does not live up to its hype—and how to make it more useful than it currently is. *European Business Review* 31(7).

Moldoveanu, M. C., and J.A.C. Baum. 2014. *Epinets: The Epistemic Structure and Dynamics of Social Networks*. Stanford, CA: Stanford University Press.

Moldoveanu, M. C., and M. Djikic. 2017. "Feedback: The biggest broken loop in higher education—and how to fix it." *Rotman Management Magazine* (Spring).

Moldoveanu, M. C., and O. Leclerc. 2015. *The Design of Insight: How to Solve Any Business Problem*. Stanford, CA: Stanford University Press.

Moldoveanu, M. C., and R. L. Martin. 2008. *The Future of the MBA: Designing the Thinker of the Future*. Oxford, UK: Oxford University Press.

————. 2010. *Diaminds: Decoding the Mental Habits of Successful Thinkers*. Toronto: University of Toronto Press.

Moldoveanu, M., and N. Nohria. 2002. *Master Passions: Emotion, Narrative, and the Development of Culture*. Cambridge, MA: MIT Press.

Ophir, E., C. Nass, and A. D. Wagner. 2009. "Cognitive control in media multitaskers." *Proceedings of the National Academy of Sciences* 106 (37): 15583–15587.

Palmisano, S. J., ed. 2013. "Capitalizing on complexity: Insights from the Global Chief Executive Officer Survey." *IBM Insights Report*.

Reed, S. K., A. Dempster, and M. Ettinger. 1985. "Usefulness of analogous solutions for solving algebra word problems." *Journal of Experimental Psychology: Learning, Memory, and Cognition* 11 (1): 106–125.

Reeves, M. and M. C. Moldoveanu. 2011. "Organizational algorithmics: An algorithmic atlas of business problems." Boston Consulting Group internal report.

Ringel, M., A. Taylor, and H. Zablit. 2015. "The most innovative companies: Four factors that differentiate leaders." Boston Consulting Group (December).

Salovey, P., and J. D. Mayer. 1990. "Emotional intelligence." *Imagination, Cognition, and Personality* 9: 185–211. Available at http://www.unh.edu/emotional_intelligence/EIAssets/EmotionalIntelligenceProper/EI1990%20Emotional%20Intelligence.pdf (accessed June 2016).

Schrage, M. 2014. "Big data's dangerous new era of discrimination." *Harvard Business Review* blog network (January 29, 8:00 a.m.), http://blogs. hbr. org/2014/01/big-datas-dangerous-new-era-of-discrimination.

Seitz, S., C. Lord, and C. Taylor. 2007. "Beyond pleasure: Emotion activity affects the relationship between attitudes and behavior." *Personality and Social Psychology Bulletin* 33 (7): 933–947.

Setz, C. 2012. "Multimodal emotion and stress recognition." PhD diss., ETH Zurich.

Seligman, M. 2007. *What You Can Change—and What You Can't: The Complete Guide to Self-Improvement.* New York: Random House.

Silvestri, R. F. 2013. "Building leaders through planned executive development." *Leader to Leader* 68 (Spring): 19–26.

Simmel, G. 1923. *Soziologie,* Vol. 2. Berlin: Duncker and Humblot.

Simon, H. A. 1973. "The structure of ill structured problems." *Artificial Intelligence* 4 (3–4): 181–201.

Smith, E. E., and J. Jonides. 1999. "Storage and executive processes in the frontal lobes." *Science* (1999): 1657–1661.

Snook, S. A., R. Khurana, and N. Nohria. 2011. *The Handbook for Teaching Leadership: Knowing, Doing, and Being.* San Francisco: Sage.

Spence, M. 1973. "Job market signaling." *Quarterly Journal of Economics*: 355–374.

———. 1974. *Market Signalling.* Cambridge, MA: Harvard University Press.

Sterman, J. 2000. *Business Dynamics: Systems Thinking and Modeling for a Complex World.* Boston: Irwin/McGraw-Hill.

Sternberg, R. J., and P. A. Frensch. 1993. "Mechanisms of transfer." In *Transfer on Trial: Intelligence, Cognition, and Instruction,* ed. D. K. Detterman and R. J. Sternberg. New York: Ablex.

Stuss, D. T. 2011. "Functions of the frontal lobes: Relation to executive functions." *Journal of the International Neuropsychological Society* 17 (5): 759–765.

Terwiesch, C., and K. T. Ulrich. 2014. "Will video kill the classroom star? The threat and opportunity of massively open online courses for full time MBA programs." Working Paper, Mack Center for Innovation, University of Pennsylvania Wharton School of Management.

Thorndike, E. L., and R. S. Woodworth. 1901. "The influence of improvement in one mental function upon the efficiency of other functions. II. The estimation of magnitudes." *Psychological Review* 8 (4): 384.

Tulving, E. 1966. "Subjective organization and effects of repetition in multi-trial free-recall learning." *Journal of Verbal Learning and Verbal Behavior* 5 (2): 193–197.

Tulving, E., and D. M. Thomson. 1973. "Encoding specificity and retrieval processes in episodic memory." *Psychological Review* 80 (5): 352.

Watson, J. M., and D. L. Strayer. 2010. "Supertaskers: Profiles in extraordinary multitasking ability." *Psychonomic Bulletin and Review* 17 (4): 479–485.

Wittgenstein, L. 1953. *Philosophical Investigations.* New York: Macmillan.

World Economic Forum. 2013. *The Future of Financial Services.*

Yalom, V. J., and S. Vinogradov. 1993. "Interpersonal group psychotherapy." *Comprehensive Group Psychotherapy*: 185–195.

INDEX

CPSIA information can be obtained
at www.ICGtesting.com
Printed in the USA
LVHW110302021021
699282LV00006B/19/J